The Gendered and Colonial Lives
of Gurkhas in Private Security

Series Editors: Victoria M. Basham and Sarah Bulmer

The Critical Military Studies series welcomes original thinking on the ways in which military power works within different societies and geopolitical arenas

Militaries are central to the production and dissemination of force globally but the enduring legacies of military intervention are increasingly apparent at the societal and personal bodily levels as well, demonstrating that violence and war-making function on multiple scales. At the same time, the notion that violence is an appropriate response to wider social and political problems transcends militaries: from private security, to seemingly 'non-military' settings such as fitness training and schooling, the legitimisation and normalisation of authoritarianism and military power occurs in various sites. This series seeks original, high-quality manuscripts and edited volumes that engage with such questions of how militaries, militarism and militarisation assemble and disassemble worlds touched and shaped by violence in these multiple ways. It will showcase innovative and interdisciplinary work that engages critically with the operation and effects of military power and provokes original questions for researchers and students alike.

Available Titles:

Resisting Militarism: Direct Action and the Politics of Subversion
Chris Rossdale

Making War on Bodies: Militarisation, Aesthetics and Embodiment in International Politics
Catherine Baker

Disordered Violence: How Gender, Race and Heteronormativity Structure Terrorism
Caron Gentry

Sex and the Nazi Soldier: Violent, Commercial and Consensual Contacts during the War in the Soviet Union, 1941–1945
Regina Mühlhäuser (translated by Jessica Spengler)

The Military–Peace Complex: Gender and Materiality in Afghanistan
Hannah Partis-Jennings

Politics of Impunity: Torture, the Armed Forces and the Failure of Transitional Justice in Brazil
Henrique Tavares Furtado

Conscientious Objection in Turkey: A Socio-legal Analysis of the Right to Refuse Military Service
Demet Çaltekin

Poetic Prosthetics: Trauma and Language in Contemporary Veteran Writing
Ron Ben-Tovim

The Gendered and Colonial Lives of Gurkhas in Private Security: From Military to Market
Amanda Chisholm

Forthcoming:

Beyond the Wire: The Cultural Politics of Veteran Narratives
Nick Caddick

War and Militarisation: The British, Canadian and Dutch Invasion of Southern Afghanistan
Paul Dixon

Inhabiting No-Man's-Land: Army Wives, Gender and Militarisation
Alexandra Hyde

Mobilising China's One-Child Generation: Education, Nationalism and Youth Militarisation in the PRC
Orna Naftali

Martialling Peace: How the Peacekeeper Myth Legitimises Warfare
Nicole Wegner

The Gendered and Colonial Lives of Gurkhas in Private Security

From Military to Market

AMANDA CHISHOLM

EDINBURGH
University Press

For Debbie and Charlie (mom and dad): without your unconditional love, support and faith in me, this project would not have been possible.

Edinburgh University Press is one of the leading university presses in the UK. We publish academic books and journals in our selected subject areas across the humanities and social sciences, combining cutting-edge scholarship with high editorial and production values to produce academic works of lasting importance. For more information visit our website: edinburghuniversitypress.com

© Amanda Chisholm, 2023, 2024

Edinburgh University Press Ltd
The Tun – Holyrood Road
12(2f) Jackson's Entry
Edinburgh EH8 8PJ

First published in hardback by Edinburgh University Press 2023

Typeset in 10.5/13 ITC Giovanni Std by
Cheshire Typesetting Ltd, Cuddington, Cheshire

A CIP record for this book is available from the British Library

ISBN 978-1-3995-0115-6 (hardback)
ISBN 978-1-3995-0116-3 (paperback)
ISBN 978-1-3995-0117-0 (webready PDF)
ISBN 978-1-3995-0118-7 (epub)

CONTENTS

FIGURES

Listening to a Gurkha Wife

As I began reading Amanda Chisholm's revealing book about the complex lives of the Nepali men who have become Gurkha security personnel and about the thinking women who are married to them, I thought of my father's World War II photo albums. I paused in my reading and pulled out the albums, their bindings now crumbling, their dry onionskin page dividers crackling.

I turned the pages. The small black and white photographs were still intact. And there were Gurkha men looking back at me. They looked – or rather my father chose to take photos of them when they looked as my father wanted to remember them – stoic, determined, focused on their physical wartime tasks. The Gurkha men were short, compact, equipped with rifles, wearing their distinctive one-brim-up felt hats. They were carrying out tasks behind enemy lines in northern Burma. The year was 1943. In one photo, Gurkha men were standing at attention to greet a pith-helmeted senior British officer who had just flown in to fine-tune strategy. In another, Gurkhas were leading mules loaded with war-making supplies across an open field. In a third, Gurkha men were straining hard against ropes to drag an unmotored glider plane into position. Gliders were the innovative means by which the combined British, Australian and American unconventional units were secretly sending supplies 'over the hump' to allies in China.

As a young girl, the daughter of a World War II veteran, I absorbed my father's admiring descriptions of the Gurkha men with whom he served. He told me of their loyalty and unflinching toughness. They were also, for him, honourable men. The Gurkhas became central figures in my father's masculinised narrative of his war.

Figure F.1 Gurkha soldier standing at attention, on a deployment with the British army in a joint operation with US and Australian troops, northern Burma, 1943. Photograph by Dr Cortez F. Enloe, 1943. Rights: Cynthia H. Enloe.

Figure F.2 Gurkha soldiers deployed with the British army in a joint operation with US and Australian troops, northern Burma, unconventional glider operation, 1943. Photograph by Dr Cortez F. Enloe, 1943. Rights: Cynthia H. Enloe.

What Amanda Chisholm shows us here in these pages is that that admiration has become both a multigenerational asset and a burden for thousands of men from Nepal. It is a source of pride, yes. It is a militarised, racialised, masculinised 'brand' that is globally marketable, yes. But it is also a personal weight for a man to shoulder. Reading the chapters that follow, we come to understand that each individual, fallible Nepali man who gains entry into the Gurkhas must try to live up to the impossible expectations others have of a Gurkha.

Security analysis, it turns out, is an investigation of gendered expectations.

Amanda Chisholm shows us that the expectation-wielding others are themselves gendered and myriad: the Gurkhas' white male security company managers; the masculinised government and corporate clients who hire those Gurkhas, supplying private security companies; the Gurkhas' male comrades; their own mothers and fathers, who have such high hopes for their sons-turned-Gurkhas; the women to whom the Gurkha men are married, women who had virtually no say in whom their husbands would be. Then, too, we learn here, there are these

Nepali men's own internalised expectations to measure up to, no matter how tired they are, how fearful they feel, how much they miss their families time zones away back home.

To investigate security seriously – as a political concept, as a lived reality, as an aspiration and as a globalised commercial product – it is clear that we have to follow Amanda Chisholm as she takes us from a wartime compound in Kabul, to a hotel in Qatar, to rural villages in Nepal.

It was Seira Tamang who awoke me from my father's postwar Gurkha fantasy. Seira Tamang is today an influential Nepali feminist researcher and activist (be sure to check her writings here in the References). When Seira and I first met, though, she was an undergraduate student in a seminar on Hannah Arendt. It was a passage in one of Arendt's dense essays that prompted her to talk about her father, a Nepali man who had become a Gurkha. But Seira did not stop with her father. She began describing and writing about the lives of her mother and her aunts, wives of Gurkhas. Suddenly, I could see that my father's wartime camera lens had been too narrowly focused. It was Seira who first taught me to be curious about the Nepali women married to Gurkha men.

Amanda Chisholm continues to widen the lens and to deepen our curiosity. She exposes the racialised, postcolonialised, multilayered workings of both the masculinities and the femininities that shape private and state militarised security.

Moreover, as you will soon appreciate, she conducts her gender-smart security analysis with candour. Amanda Chisholm is honest in her surprise. She is candid in her discomfort. She is generous in her self-reflection. This is what doing a political ethnography takes.

As you plunge into the chapters that follow, listen carefully to Jitendra and to Sherba. Lean in to listen to Songita and Neha.

After reading this book, a guard at the door of an embassy will never again look the same. Neither will a blazer-wearing security official in a hotel lobby. Nor will a lecture about "global security."

Cynthia Enloe
April 2022

ACKNOWLEDGEMENTS

Writing this book has been a labour of love. It has taken over a decade to curate and weave together the various stories and experiences of the people I was fortunate enough to meet and to learn a great deal from. I would firstly like to acknowledge the Gurkha communities in Afghanistan and Nepal, who warmly and enthusiastically opened their homes, and shared their histories and their hopes for their futures with me. I have so much gratitude to Sameer, Indra, Mohan, Tristan, Ian, Padam, Bikram, Sherba, Rabindra and Jitendra, as well as Neha, Hira, Sunika and Neta, who all demonstrated enormous kindness in helping me navigate my travels through Afghanistan, Qatar and Nepal, along with helping me think through the complexities of global security regimes from the vantage point of workforces and families from Nepal.

I want to give special thanks to both Basanta Bhatta Chettri and Swastika Kasaju, without whose help in navigating cultural cues and broader logistics of researching in Nepal, as well as thinking through various encounters in my fieldwork, the analysis would not have been as rich and nuanced. I am forever grateful to Basanta for living a kind of motorcycle diaries fieldwork adventure with me throughout rural Nepal in the summer of 2016, and to Angela Pietrobon, who helped me curate my words and prose, in order to write the complexities of the stories featured throughout the book.

My thanks go to the King's College London School of Security Studies writing sprints group, for giving me the collective space and community; to Winnie and Winston; and for the summer of 2021 spent with my parents on the family farm in Canada, all of which proved foundational for the actual writing of this book – specifically during intense periods of isolation and crisis during COVID lockdowns. I am also grateful to my feminist global community, who intellectually nourished me and supported me (often with multiple glasses of wine and/or Zoom dance parties) throughout this writing of this book, and to Cynthia Enloe, Seira Tamang, Neha Chowdhury, Julia Welland, Tom Gregory, Susan Martin, Megan MacKenzie, Marsha Henry, Cristina Masters, Maya Eichler, Saskia Stachowitsch, Lisa Tilley, Kiran Phull, Mark Condos, Hanna Ketola, Claudia Aradau, Debbie Lisle and Juanita Elias, who read multiple chapter drafts and were always there to talk through ideas that underpin this book. Finally, I would like to thank Victoria Basham, Sarah Bulmer, Ersev Ersoy and Sarah Foyle, for believing my ideas were worthy of a book, and who supported me from proposal to publication.

Bringing Gurkhas to Market: Race, Gender and Global Economies of Security Workforces

In September 2012, I was asked to speak at a conference on private military and security companies (PMSCs) in London, UK. I presented my research on Gurkhas, a group of men from Nepal with a 200-year colonial military history with the British, who were working as security contractors in Afghanistan. Using the Gurkhas' own words, originating from my interview transcripts, I described these men's struggle to find work to support their families, their desires for more economic opportunities and their frustrations over the ways PMSCs treated them differently from their white Western colleagues. During the 'Question and Answer' section of my presentation, a director of a large security company stood up and, in response to claims attesting to the poor treatment of Gurkhas, pronounced 'but that's the market'. For him and a large portion of the audience, this statement was akin to a common-sense declaration, which spoke of the naturalness of the labour and recruitment practices that constitute the overall working conditions of Gurkhas by the private security industry. (Fieldwork entry, 2012, Royal United Service Institute, London)

I wrote the above journal entry a decade ago and I am still drawn back to my feelings of frustration. I experienced this feeling of out-of-placeness due to the seemingly shared sentiment amongst the audience of the unfortunate but inevitable market logic. For me, this logic obscured the concrete violence, the colonial histories and the affectively lived lives of Gurkhas, and other men from Global South countries, who participate in the security industry as racialised contractors.

This book locates its analysis in the context of the lives and experiences of Gurkhas and their families: a militarised community from Nepal with over 200 years of military service with the British that now participates in global security markets as racialised contractors and families. The book understands the global security market as one rooted within concrete social relations that structure experiences and conditions the possibilities for those who come to participate in it as security contractors. Gurkhas are valued as contractors through racial and gendered logics that consider them naturally amenable to performing (cheap) military labour. Their families, and particularly their wives, are understood as the grateful benefactors of these security-related migration arrangements – which have uplifted the women from abject poverty and empowered them as economic and political subjects. To quote Sunika, a Gurkha wife: 'They think you are crazy if you are anything but happy.'

The research shows that both Gurkhas and their families are much more than these broader tropes and that their experiences are far from inevitable. In illustrating the multiple experiences of Gurkhas, Gurkha wives, security managers and security clients, I illuminate how militarism, affect, political economies and colonial histories organise the global workforces of private military and security companies, or PMSCs. Drawing upon fourteen years of research and three years of ethnographic fieldwork with security communities throughout Nepal and in Afghanistan, the book's motivating questions are: how is security created through PMSC operations, what role does affect play in shaping this security, and how is this security experienced by the men and women who engage in this marketplace?

The Gurkha experiences discussed in this book are representative of those of a growing group of men from the Global South taking up work for PMSCs as security contractors and supportive staff. Described by the industry as third country nationals, or TCNs, these contractors are often found in menial labour positions of static guarding or convoy protection. They are exposed to incredible risk and yet gain the least, financially and politically. Their experiences and a broader geopolitical critique of security labour chains are almost completely absent from overall discussions on the growing privatisation of war and security.[1] In fact, ten years after the aforementioned conference on PMSCs, the common-sense 'that's the market' declaration persists, rendering research into this area seemingly banal.

While the experiences of Gurkhas and their families are largely absent from our understandings of global security, the same cannot be said for academic commentary on PMSCs. Over the past two decades, PMSCs have become a heavily debated topic across a number of disciplines, specifically in focusing on how (particular liberal) states privatise security in the waging of war and the underlying structures that enable this, such as the neoliberalisation of state security (Leander 2005, 2013; Leander and van Munster, 2007; Krahmann 2008, 2017; Eichler 2015; Avant and de Nevers 2011) and the end of US military conscription, paving the way for marketising military labour (Eichler 2014). This scholarship on private security has challenged the long-held normative assumption that the state has a monopoly on violence and examined the significant role PMSCs play in producing knowledge and expertise about everyday practices of security (Leander 2013; Krahmann and Leander 2019). Other research that views these companies as fixed (if not problematic) global actors has investigated how the companies can be categorised and better regulated (see, for example, the UN Human Rights Special Procedures working group on the use of mercenaries 2018 report; Singer 2003; Avant 2005; Kinsey 2006; Leander 2012; Macleod and Dewinter-Schmitt 2019; Loader and White 2015).

Scholarship in the area is both theoretically and empirically rich, spanning a multitude of disciplines and subfields including international relations (IR), criminology, law and ethics, security studies, sociology and critical military studies. Throughout these various fields of study, it becomes clear that PMSCs are now central in the selling of armed and unarmed protection, risk management and consultancy, training, cyber security and big data, and logistic support (Abrahamsen and Leander 2016; Eichler 2015; Berndtsson and Kinsey 2016). The US-led wars in Afghanistan and Iraq have resulted in an increased demand for PMSC services, to the point that many Western states can no longer conceive of waging war without using them (Krahmann 2008; Leander and van Munster, 2007). Beyond the diversity in the security services offered by these companies, the sheer scale of their operations is also noteworthy. Group 4 Security (G4S Ltd), a large global security company, employs over 585,000 people and operates in ninety countries. As such, how PMSCs are changing normative positions on how warfare is conducted, which people are called to perform this work, and how these workforces are organised have all become areas of concern.

With few exceptions, what is missing from the literature is the acknowledgement that these companies intensely rely upon gendered and racialised market logics in determining who they contract to do security work. Importantly, this racialised and gendered nature of global security markets is not, as the opening vignette might suggest, inevitable. Quite the opposite: the organisation of labour is deeply political.

Feminist global political economy (GPE) research on global labour (Peterson 2008; Elias 2005; McDowell 2009; LeBaron 2010; Henry 2015; Enloe 2013), more broadly, and the well-established feminist research on private security (Chisholm 2014a, 2015a; Barker 2015; Mynster Christensen 2015; Ware 2012), more specifically, have shown the ways in which gendered hiring patterns and broader gender and race logics naturalise divisions of labour. The formal pathway into private security, often through former combat military service, has denied women's entry into the market as security contractors (Eichler 2014, 2015). However, as women are increasingly allowed to serve in combat roles, this may change. While women may not yet serve in any great numbers as security contractors, they are still working within the industry. For example, women take on a large portion of the human resources, administration and intelligence desk work (Eichler 2014, 2015). Looking for the women has shown the gendered divisions of labour within PMSCs, as well as the concrete labour that spouses do to support contemporary warfare (Hedström 2017; Basham and Catignani 2018; Chisholm and Eichler 2018). It has also demonstrated how private security households sit at the nexus of global militarism and neoliberal capitalism, two key operating processes underpinning contemporary warfare (Peterson 2008; Chisholm and Eichler 2018), and how these households are 'brought in to participate as gendered sites, to sustain the broader western military outsourcing of security work to PMSCs' (Chisholm and Eichler 2018, 565). In fact, as I discuss in more detail in Chapter 4, the role of the household and the social reproduction of security constitute an overlooked, yet foundational space that enables global security regimes to organise their workforces and operations as they currently do (see also the work of Basham and Catignani 2018; Cree 2020; and Hedström 2017).

Beyond looking for women, feminist scholarship on PMSCs has also shown how a masculine and militarised logic around what security is and how we achieve it is sustained. Joachim and Schneiker explain PMSCs as 'masculine multipliers' that help state militaries 'claim acceptable forms of masculinities' such as peacekeeper roles whilst outsourcing more contentious roles to private companies (2015, 114). Higate (2015) highlights the hypermasculine performances of (particularly white) Western men who work in global security and the potential risks such performances have for keeping people safe. My own work (Chisholm 2014b, 2015a) has demonstrated how logics of racism and race enforce masculine hierarchies between white Western contractors and men from the Global South. As such, this research has also shown how gender, as a logic and structure, organises men in particular hierarchical ways and enforces a remasculinisation of security (Stachowitsch 2015).

Considering masculinities in conjunction with race and colonial relations also shows how the industry does not produce all men as equal. Western contractors maintain an ideal archetype of what a contractor should be, and subsequently are assumed already to have the necessary professional skill sets to do their job and do it well. Alternatively, Gurkhas are understood as having a raw martial talent that requires the mentoring and managing of their Western counterparts (Chisholm 2014a). The natural versus professional binaries, as feminist political economists remind us, devalue labour (Elson and Pearson 1981; Safa 1981; Enloe 2014; Peterson 2004, 2005, 2008; Agathangelou 2004; McDowell 2009; Whitney 2017; Chisholm and Stachowitsch 2016). Feminisation is a process through which 'women's work' is immediately devalued through its association with naturally acquired skill sets. Appealing to women's supposed biologically suitable nature to do this work obscures any sort of professionalism or training involved in preparing for it (Hochschild 1985; Boris and Salazar Parreñas 2010). Consequently, it is not seen as valuable in the global marketplace, since women are seen as naturally doing this work, regardless of circumstances.

In a similar way, race is mobilised as a marker to devalue Gurkha labour.[2] This devaluation is connected to the smooth functioning of capital markets, which, as Peterson argues, rests upon hierarchies of workforces and gendered valuations that continue to use feminisation and racialisation as important markers to devalue labour; this is key to driving labour prices down, and, importantly, this socialising often begins in the home (2005, 81). Gurkhas, when compared to white Western contractors, are understood to be less qualified, more naturalised and more amenable to work that is flexible, precarious and poorly paid (Chisholm 2014a).

These naturalising gendered processes are also embodied. These embodiments are 'structured by complex global hierarchies and polarised labour markets' (Wolkowitz 2006, 5), so that the feminisation and racialisation of work and workers, and how these are felt on the body, will be different. These hierarchies are sustained through colonial and patriarchal structures and are often refashioned to appear 'up to date', but at their core they privilege particular white forms of masculinity over other racialised masculinities and all femininities (Enloe 2014, 21–2). McDowell (2009, 146–7) examines patriarchy in the everyday through the social and spatial relations of masculinised forms of security work. She illuminates embodiments of race, class and gender in aesthetics and in how the body moves as it comes into contact with others, deciding who to let in and to keep out. These security guarding practices are all productive in creating the 'body capital' of the security door guard. The security work I focus on throughout this book aligns with McDowell's (2009) analysis of the embodied nature of security work through a service economy – one that brings into immediate contact the service provider and the consumer. In my research, this includes the physical and personal security involving VIP protection, convoy protection and static guarding in environments deemed hostile. At the time of this study, in Afghanistan, this type of security work for clients included the static guarding of the United Nations compounds and guest houses, foreign government embassies, commercial compounds, banks and other infrastructure sites, as well as the homes of more affluent private residents. This guarding was predominantly performed by Gurkhas, other security contractors labelled TCNs and local Afghans. The level of security training varied amongst these men. Other security work involved creating standard operating procedures, managing static guarding duties, writing intelligence reports, regular monitoring and keeping clients safe with detailed security plans on travel and broader mobility across the city of Kabul and within the country. The latter type of security work was generally inside the same compounds that the clients lived and was performed by either Eastern Europeans or a multitude of those of Western nationality, including British, Canadian, US, Australian, South African and New Zealand men with former military or police experience.

In both types of security, contractors and clients often shared the same social spaces during work and leisure hours. It is a service-based economy, where security is delivered through a series of performances involving intelligence briefings, perimeter checks, physical security and regular training that ensures the client knows how to respond, should 'contact' be made. The way the worker interacts and performs the work in real time, and how the quality of this work is interpreted by the client, are foundational to how security contractors are valued. Here, the service work is embodied. The service provider, and how they dress and perform their work, are core parts of the service.[3] Indeed, as Chapter 5 discusses, the security client comes to expect and value different security labour from different contractors. Western security clients often assume that Western men will offer security through intelligence briefings and situational awareness, whereas Gurkhas are valued through their pastoral care – making others feel safe and secure by asking how they are doing and feeling, and by taking a general interest in them as people, beyond someone to protect.

Overall, feminist political economy scholarship on global labour[4] highlights the gendered and racialised politics that underpins this (de) skilling of work in its various locations, rather than assuming it is natural, normal or inevitable. Drawing upon diverse industries, including care work, textiles, factories, agribusiness and security, feminist political economy scholars have shown the various ways market practices have brought into existence women's and men's gendered, classed and racialised bodies in order to position them within structural hierarchies, examining how individuals shape these gendered and racial power structures. They share a commitment to engaging with particular histories by way of denaturalising race and gender, and by demonstrating the differences in gendered and racial subjectivities in particular market practices. Both radicalisation and feminisation alert us to the politics that sustains hierarchies in security workforces and move us quickly away from thinking that Gurkhas' position as TCN labourers is somehow natural or inevitable.

Investigating the security industry as a feminist question of labour opens analytical and empirical pathways into understanding the continually decentring and privatising of warfare. Particularly, a feminist political economy analysis illuminates PMSCs' effects on local populations who are called to work in or support war making, as well as the security clients who are the recipients of this security labour. It also helps to show how security labour gets valued through marketing practices and everyday security encounters between clients and contractors (for more details see Chapters 3 and 5). Exploring PMSCs as a feminist question of labour also alerts us to what kinds of work are being performed, who does this work and how it gets valued and recognised. It makes us pay attention to affective relations and the ways in which they sustain the status quo, as well as the broader care work being done by security contractors and households that keep the industry going. This book applies a feminist political economic analysis, firstly, to illuminate the household as a key economic site in private security and to uncover the unpaid labour that takes place in and around the household, including the informal and subsistence work that is done. Secondly, this analysis shows the significance of emotional, affective and immaterial labour. Finally, it demonstrates the costs and 'depletion' (Rai, Hoskyns and Thomas 2013) that stem from the undervaluing of both the household and these types of unpaid labour.

Where Are the Women? Locating the Household in Global Security

Feminist political economists show how the household is not a side benefactor of the security industry, but an integral economic space that fundamentally supports the industry. They have illuminated the (gendered) reproductive labour done in the household, known as social reproduction, to recentre the concrete activities, largely occurring within the home, that go into reproducing and sustaining global economies (Luxton 2018). V. Spike Peterson (2005, 2008) describes reproductive labour as including all life-sustaining activities, as well as teaching – through language, emotion and discourse – the next generations important beliefs about naturalised gendered and racial divisions of labour, which 'ensure that . . . gendered divisions of labour/power/authority are the only apparent options' (2005, 82). Such labour is most often a responsibility placed upon women (Blumberg 1978; Waring 1989). This labour facilitates global markets through, for example, sustaining communities (Hoskyns and Rai 2007), reproducing the next generation of global workers (Bakker and Gill 2003), doing financial planning and managing the remittances that come through migrant work (Safri and Graham 2010), and managing financial debt (Montgomerie and Tepe-Belfrage 2017).

What arises from this feminist scholarship is a recognition that the household remains a key economic site that shapes and is shaped by global market forces. Feminist research has shown how reproductive labour within the household has changed with the market shifts in contemporary state–market relations (LeBaron 2010; Ehrenreich and Hochschild 2003; Peterson 2008; Hoskyns and Rai 2007). These include the reduction of welfare provisions and rising austerity measures within Western states (Bruff and Wohl 2016) and the increasing informalisation of household labour (Peterson 2008), as well as the increasingly neoliberal economic politics in Asia (Elias and Gunawardana 2013); the Nepal form specifically (Acharya 2008) has led to the increase in women working outside the home and altered how the household operates as a gendered site. While households become more global as markets increase their own reach, they are not the same. Due to the ways in which households are structurally situated within broader organising logics and practices of patriarchy, imperialism and capitalism matter in terms of what labour is being done and the social burdens that are placed upon household members (Ruwanpura 2007; Rai, Hoskyns, and Thomas 2013; Hedström and Olivius 2020; Safri and Graham 2010).

Taking the household seriously as an economic actor shows how the private security industry is able to extract labour from these sites (most often from women) without formally acknowledging this work. It can also alert us to the ways households are often coerced into supporting market relations, the social exclusion and adverse incorporation (Hickey and du Toit 2007; Phillips 2011) involved in extracting this reproductive labour, and the gendered harm involved in work of this nature. In the case of foreign employment, remaining household members have to pick up the slack and continue to do all the household and community work despite having fewer hands to help.[5] Considering the household as a key economic space in global security renders visible the work done in the household to keep life going and to provide care work so that other men and women can pursue work in formal security markets. It also highlights the globalised, gendered nature of this work and why it continues to fall largely on women (Basham and Catignani 2018; Chisholm and Eichler 2018; Enloe 2000; Hedström 2017; Hyde 2013).[6] Feminists exploring the household within broader global military settings, including households in the Kachin province, Myanmar, the UK, Nepal, the US and Canada, have empirically documented the concrete ways in which global militarism and military operations fundamentally rest upon the work of the household.

The household is also a site where affective and intellectual investments are made in support of global militarism (Rashid 2020) and foreign security markets (Chisholm and Ketola 2020). The desire for military and security service as a pathway to an honourable and good life motivates Gurkhas and their households alike. The financial certainty the industry can potentially bring acts as a prime motivator, showing why families and Gurkhas sign up for foreign security work after the men's military careers. Yet, as Chapter 4 explicitly discusses, militarism and identifying as martial communities are not the sole defining features of how Gurkhas and Gurkha wives imagine themselves, their hopes for a better future and their solidarities with one another. Indeed, security markets may try to categorise and define these men and women in particular market-driven ways, where their value comes through their martial histories, but such assumptions can never fully account for how they come to enter the industry and their broader motivations for staying in these markets.

Experiencing War: A Feminist's Fieldwork Reflections on PMSCs

I centre my analysis on the feeling and affective bodies that take part in the everyday, banal activities of doing security work and supporting the global security industry. This research has involved spending time with and talking to the Gurkha men who stand guard, conduct perimeter checks and do convoy protection. It has also involved speaking to the clients who negotiate how to manage their own personal security with continual security briefings and drills performed by security contractors. Finally, it has included a deep consideration of the Gurkha spouses back home, and how they each care for and manage their household, sustain and reproduce life, and hold their family together – teaching their children to know and love their father, who migrates for extended periods of time to work in security. This book is about these people, how their bodies come into contact with one another, how they are valued and how they affect others and are affected. It looks at how security bodies feel their way through the security industry. I am indebted to the critical feminist and postcolonial work on gender and war that locates bodies, the corporeal and affect as central to understanding militarism, war and peace.[7]

This book is based on over a decade of ethnographic based research in Afghanistan, Nepal and the UK. The research has involved conducting over 180 interviews, often speaking multiple times with the same community members, as well as taking substantial ethnographic and autoethnographic research notes. Notes and interviews have been rigorously analysed and revisited over the past fourteen years.[8] I began my fieldwork in Kabul, Afghanistan, in 2008. Having recently finished my graduate work in Canada, I went to Afghanistan to find out more about who these men working in the security industry were. At the time, research was emerging about PMSCs, but was focused largely on a macro scale and positioned around certain normative claims about the industry: either that it made good business sense for states to use private security forces, or that it was politically dubious and extremely problematic for rule of law, transparency and accountability to draw upon market-based security actors. In both cases, the archetype of who the security contractor was remained key. He (almost always imagined as he) was understood as either a professionalised security actor or a rogue mercenary. In either case, it seemed to me at the time that these depictions of who security contractors were tended to be heavily reductionist. I was fortunate enough to be able to get in touch with some of my former military contacts to obtain an official invitation and have a visa extended to me so that I could travel to Kabul to find out more.

When I first arrived in Kabul, I volunteered for a small research institute and lived in the same compound that the institute's office was located. I was quickly introduced to the broader security community in

Kabul and invited to various social events hosted by different security companies in their respective compounds. Within a month I managed to be invited to stay and do some voluntary research work for one particular company in exchange for free room and board. This security company specialised in providing Gurkhas, highly skilled ex-military men from Nepal, for larger security companies and the United Nations. At the time I had no idea who Gurkhas were and what supposedly made them uniquely suitable for security work. Meeting Gurkhas and learning more about their broader narratives and histories would send me on a completely different pathway to understanding the security industry to what I had initially intended. In fact, meeting my first Gurkhas back at the guest house owned by IDG, a Gurkha security recruitment company, in 2008 fundamentally shaped the direction of my research.

My time in Afghanistan included working on proposal writing and country security briefs for new staff. I also continued to socialise frequently with broader security communities outside the compounds, spending time in the evenings at La Cantina (a local bar and restaurant) or going to Friday brunches at the Serena Hotel (one of the few five-star hotels in the city). During this stay in Kabul, I established tight-knit relationships with a variety of people who either worked as security contractors or were protected by them. Over time, I gained knowledge of the everyday engagements and lived experiences that were a part of commercial security in Afghanistan. I began to understand this community, and to empathise with them, even if I did not always agree with them.

My fieldwork also took me to Nepal on five separate visits, first in 2009 and then again in 2015, 2016, 2017 and 2018. During these visits I spent time with Gurkhas and their families, immersing myself in their home lives and in the broader political and economic/social structures that help facilitate the men's recruitment into global security. I developed friendships that still exist today. I am forever grateful for their generosity in feeding me, caring for my wellbeing, inviting me into their communities, and explaining to me their own perspectives and understandings of themselves and their roles within the broader security industry.

This fieldwork also profoundly impacted my personal life. In Afghanistan, I spent an extensive amount of time with security contractors from the UK. I married (and subsequently divorced) one of them, and as a result moved to Hereford – a small UK town in the Midlands known for its SAS (Special Air Service) camp and private security companies managed by former SAS soldiers. This marriage fostered a deeper and very personal connection to the men who serve around the world as highly professionalised security contractors, and their spouses who stay home. Spending time within this community also made me curious about all the reproductive labour within the security industry that fundamentally supports the men's transitions from military to private security, and also about how it is fundamental to the flexibility in work patterns that the security industry demands (see Chisholm and Eichler 2018, as well as Chapter 4).

Over the last decade, I have been positioned in multiple intersubjective entanglements that have immediately impacted how I am perceived, but also how I interpret various field encounters. I lived in Kabul, Afghanistan, as a protected white female client of Canadian nationality, working with a security company that provided Gurkha security contractors to the UN and other international clients. I have also been a researcher, in this role being invited into people's homes and sharing meals with Gurkhas and their families throughout Nepal on multiple occasions. In each of these encounters with different communities that make up the global security workforce, I have related differently. My own positions as a researcher, a spouse, a surrogate daughter, a friend, and an expert have changed over time, depending upon which groups within the broader private security community I am associating with.

The culmination of my fieldwork that underpins this book has involved personal and intellectual journeys filled with surprise, excitement, shame and guilt. My research remains empirically rich and often defies the very theoretical categories of state/market and private/public that have been used to make sense of the security industry. It draws upon the complex web of networks and stakeholders involved in global security who facilitate this market in diverse ways. It renders visible the gendered and racialised practices that shape Gurkhas as racialised contractors – whose personal martial race histories continue to define them, providing them with access to this global market as preferred TCNs, and at the same time conditioning how they experience the industry. This research, for me, has shown that it is impossible to understand the motivations involved in the work or why social inequalities endure within the industry without accounting for how the colonial histories that have shaped Gurkha communities persist in the contemporary structural aspects of how one comes to work in security, as well as how these imperial histories continue to be affectively lived in the present.

Living with and working alongside a multitude of security contractors has also enabled me to see the men and women who work in and support the industry in complicated ways. Through numerous and detailed conversations with the Nepali wives, I was alerted to similarities and contestations in how security households (my previous household included) are created by, sustained by and supportive of this global industry. Whereas the women in my community in Hereford saw their supportive role as managing the household and assuming the responsibilities of child rearing and elderly care work – so as to not burden their spouse with these banal activities – Gurkhas and their spouses were both heavily involved in these duties. Chapter 4, on the global security household, brings to the fore the security families facilitated by security markets in varying ways. Through my own experience and that of those I have interviewed, the chapter illuminates the role that security clients play in how 'the market' values and divides security labour. It is through these various encounters that I am able to show more of the embodied nature of social distinctions between myself and those I research. But I am also able to be more attuned to how these distinctions come to matter more broadly amongst those I have interviewed – how various encounters between clients, contractors, recruiters and households are made meaningful in often unpredictable ways, where similarity and difference are constructed in the moment.

'Staying with the Trouble'

Fieldwork is always a social enterprise. We, as researchers, create our stories through the stories we are told. We then abstract from those stories detailed in our interviews and observations what we find most relevant (Basham 2013, 9). Our own personal stories of how we come to be researchers who are curious about the topics we choose also matter. These stories shape research design as we think through questions we find it compelling to pursue, the overall ethics of how we will conduct our research, and the connections we will pursue and sustain and the ones we will let go of. Therefore, declaring one's position(s) in research and in relation to the research process is much more complicated than a statement on positionality. It requires us to think through the ways these positionalities and histories fundamentally inform our research. Here, Marsha Henry's (2003) article, 'Where Are You Really From?', and Megan Daigle's (2015) book, *From Cuba with Love: Sex and Money in the Twenty-First Century*, are informative. Daigle, in a thoughtful and engaged manner, illuminates the colonial and gendered structures of power that continually impact us as researchers and in how we relate to our fieldwork community. Similarly, Henry, from the standpoint of a first-generation Canadian of the Pakistani diaspora, reminds us that representing ourselves as researchers and being represented by others is a 'continual process located in complicated social and historical contexts' (2003, 232).

To account for the experiences, encounters and connections with the seemingly diverse group of people who all come to be involved in supporting the global security industry, as well as my own shifting positionalities and encounters with these communities in producing my own research, I draw upon Sylvester's 'art-making logic of collage' (2012, 3). Art-making logic of collage brings together common wisdoms and novel ways of thinking about the privatisation of war. It 'tacks onto a board' these many perspectives of what the security industry is and how security work is imagined – for me to analyse, and for the reader to ponder. Importantly, the interconnections illuminated throughout this book need to be theorised rather than assumed to be natural, normal or inevitable. I do not assume that I can extract a truth of militarism or colonial histories through my encounters during fieldwork (Pedwell 2012, 176). Rather, I write about the layers of meaning, of feelings and of tensions that materialised in the fieldwork I conducted 'over there' in Afghanistan and Nepal, as well as the reflections and emotional and intellectual curiosities that I continue to carry with me every time I reflect on my research.

Like Henry's (2003) call to be mindful of shifting positionalities and representations that impact how we produce knowledge, Donna Haraway (2016) asks us to 'stay with the trouble'. Here, she maps out a world making that involves continual partial and contingent relations between humans, non-humans and technologies. Haraway's commitment to 'stay with the trouble' is a commitment to reveal contestations, fractured logics and identities that materialised in fieldwork. Staying with the trouble means learning to divest from smoothed-over imagined futures and to be 'truly present'. We unlearn holding on to universalising concepts of race, class and colonial histories, and instead pay attention to how they condition our encounters[9] with the world, but do not overdetermine our positions to one another. Rather, it is these relational engagements that illuminate how we are more than our histories. It is through staying with the trouble – that is, paying attention to the thick description of the present – that we find how our present is made up of 'unfinished configurations of places, times, matters and meanings' (Haraway 2016, 1) that give rise to how we understand and relate. Staying with the trouble is a key epistemological reminder from Haraway not to overwrite fractured stories. But it is also a reminder to reflect upon how those we encounter in the field and our own histories immediately shape what is constituted as important and worthy of reflection, of comment. For Haraway:

> It matters what matters we use to think other matters with; it matters what stories we tell to tell other stories with, it matters what knots knot knots, what thoughts think thoughts, what descriptions describe descriptions. (2016, 12)

I take these methodological and epistemological cues from Henry, Daigle, Sylvester and Haraway seriously as I work through and present my own accounts, theorising and reflections on my last fourteen years of researching Gurkhas in private security. I write about the various security actors who shape and are shaped by the global security industry through what Lugones (2010) identifies as the 'fractured locus'. Lugones's location of knowledge making of the self and other at and through a fractured locus reorientates us away from 'thinking of the global, capitalist, colonial system as in every way successful in its destruction of peoples, knowledges, relations, and economies' (2010, 748). Alternatively, the concept opens space to think about how capitalism and militarism are processes 'continually resisted, and being resisted today' (2010, 748). Identities are continuing to be (re)made through multiple relations to capitalism, militarism, imperialism and gender. Within this spatiality of fractured locus, the creativity to live and be something more than capital subjects emerges. Indeed, the works of Henry, Daigle, Sylvester, Haraway and Lugones make me account for my own shifting positionalities and past partial histories, and that of those I have researched, and how they have come to matter in producing knowledge about private security.

I Am Not Joanna Lumley

In 2008, I sat down in the dining room in the security compound where I was living in Kabul. Two Gurkha men came into the room, and we exchanged polite pleasantries. They were my first formal interviews. I invited them to sit across the table from me and as I got out my recorder and my pen and paper, I started explaining my research and my interests in researching them and other Gurkhas. One of the men looked at me smiling and said: 'Oh, so you're like Joanna Lumley.'

My body immediately tensed at this seemingly friendly declaration, and I smiled awkwardly, shifting in my seat.

'Oh no, I'm not like her,' I replied. I then laughed nervously, and they joined in. I am not sure if any of us knew really what we were laughing at. I changed the subject and began asking my first questions as I turned the tape recorder on. (Fieldwork entry, 2008, Kabul)

Some fourteen years later I still reflect upon this encounter. What were my affective investments in disavowing Joanna in this moment? Who was she to me and why was I so quick to deny the men's association of me with her? Joanna Lumley received notoriety for her character Patsy on the British sitcom 'Absolutely Fabulous'.[10] She is also a daughter of a British Gurkha officer, and in 2008 gained media attention within the UK for her advocacy in fighting for British Gurkhas' rights to be UK citizens. To me, Joanna Lumley embodied the archetype of a civil white female colonial subject. Saturated with privilege and through various media portrayals, whether intended or not, Lumley assumed the central referent point in Gurkhas' fight for citizenship – she was their saviour. Did these men mean to hint at these colonial positions to which I was attuned and sensitive when they drew this comparison? Or was this meant as a seemingly banal (and maybe complimentary) association. We are both white and we both inherited (albeit different) colonial histories that placed us in privileged positions.

This vignette demonstrates that research is not about a 'dispassionate observation' and reflection of the field, but rather our research works to 'embody the concreteness of intersubjective entanglements' (Kurowska 2020, 5) we have while studying 'the field'.[11] Looking back, I remember desperately not wanting to be *that expat*: the one who walks into another country oblivious of their own privilege and leaves a trail of symbolic or other violence in their path. Of course, since this first encounter with Gurkhas detailed above, I have reflected more on my privilege, and have learned more about positionalities and about how we can never disavow the colonial histories that we inherit – mine included.

Today, I am more forgiving of my initial visceral response to being compared to what I saw as a colonial benefactor – the daughter of a colonial British officer. Whereas in 2008 I thought that, if I tried hard enough and learned enough, I could overcome my inherent privilege, I know now that I will always carry this history with me. I am reminded of Donna Haraway's writing, which encourages us to relearn how to imagine and write about politics with partial connections, whereby we continue to acknowledge these histories we inherit (2016, 13). Her work is situated within a long and vibrant contemporary history of anti-racism and queer feminism that has shown how identities, however shifting, matter in how we think about and practice research, and how disavowing them does not make us better researchers. Writing ourselves into our research is about a commitment to illustrating that, within the knowledge production process, what we can legitimately say about an issue, a community, or a political project and the ethics of how we then represent them are bound up in the shifting identities of us as research-ers and of those we research. It is this point that I try to hold on to. My own fieldwork is materialised and rendered meaningful through the various engagements I have had with a multitude of diverse actors, each having come to the security industry from different histories that have partially situated them (and myself) in relation to each other, but in ways not idiomatic. Rather, it is in the relations, which carry their own partial histories and affects, that parts of my own histories, my gender, and my experiences have mattered.

Being reflective and thinking about positionalities in the field is not just a methodological issue; it is a theoretical one as well. Those we research often 'defy being cast in the role of "theorised others"' (Krippendorff 2000, cited in Kurowska 2020, 436). Kurowska recalls how 'the observed' spoke back in her own research, through a wink by the border security agent that unsettled her own position as the observing researcher. In mine, it came through being compared to Joanna Lumley. In these moments, as researchers we are put on the spot to narrate and analyse more relationally (Kurowska 2020, 436). We are forced to look at our privilege and our positionality in relation to structures of power in that moment. This demands that we take seriously and theorise power and how power relations function in our research process. Power relations are imbued with identity politics and are central to this book. Being alert to questions of my own priv-ilege and positionalities as a researcher also points me to questions around how structures of racism, capitalism, colonialism and patri-archy inform the life conditions and positionalities of Gurkhas and their spouses, of security company managers, and of the security clients being protected. How do these structures impact how these different security actors understand the security industry, and what constitutes good and honourable security work? How might these structures shift over time and in different situations? How do these structures entangle with the personal histories of these various security actors in how they make sense of what security is, how they experience it and how they support the broader security industry? This book engages with these questions.

Structure of the Book

This book is positioned within the existing rich body of feminist political economy scholarship. It is motivated by two interrelated questions: what work is required by PMSCs, and what is the nature of this work? To begin to answer these questions, each chapter is grounded in the everyday lives of particular security actors within the global security industry to illustrate entanglements of militarism, colonial histories and affect. These actors include security contractors, security company managers and directors, security clients, and wives of security contractors. Overall, the book shows the contested and often ambiguous relationship between these concepts. It uses the everyday as an analytical entry point to show how militarism affectively materialises and is made meaningful and differentiated depending on the site and the specific people involved.

Chapter 1, 'Colonial Encounters, Militarism and Affect in Global Security', lays out the conceptual and theoretical foundations for the book. It shows how affect and militarism are foundational concepts in understanding how PMSCs recruit, market and manage Gurkha workforces and sustain buy-in by Gurkha families. The analysis is grounded in everyday encounters to map out how the key concepts of affect, colonial economies and histories, and militaries weave together. Drawing upon cultural and political economy feminists, the chapter illuminates how affect binds communities together and is foundational to how experiences are interpreted, as well as how affect becomes marketised.

What binds Gurkhas to their participation in these current global security configurations that rest upon their continual exploitation? How do affects of love and colonial structures shape and naturalise these current racial divisions of labour in private security? Chapter 2, 'Bringing Martial Race to Market: Imperial Encounters, Militarism and the Making of Gurkhas', explores how the colonial gendered histories that have shaped Gurkhas and the British military 'stick' to both of these communities affectively and structurally. Drawing largely upon postcolonial military scholarship and feminist affect literatures, this chapter highlights how their respective military histories inform their contemporary security experiences and structure the divisions of labour. Next, Chapter 3, 'Locating Love in the Gurkha Security Package, explores how these histories and the affect of love bind both Gurkhas and British Gurkha officers in an exclusive 'Gurkha security package' family. It draws upon works by Megan Mackenzie (2015) and Aaron Belkin (2012), who both explore aspects of love in fostering brotherly bonds. This chapter further develops this work by examining how colonial histories condition love in military bonding. It draws upon the metaphor of family to show how the British officer assumes a head of household position and the Gurkha the role of his dutiful son. The British contractor is already assumed to have the knowledge and professional skill sets, while the Gurkha needs the validation of his (white) colonial officer to make him a 'complete' security contractor. The analysis moves to examine how these colonial histories play out in contemporary security markets, detailing how Gurkhas are branded as knowable, trustworthy and valued contractors through their relationship with their British national officers. It includes excerpts from detailed and often multiple conversations with Gurkhas and British national, former Gurkha officers who are now managers and owners of Gurkha security companies.

Chapter 4, 'The Happy Gurkha Housewife: Reproductive and Affective Labour in Global Security Households', moves on to explore how affects of happiness, hope and love also sustain the household as a key unacknowledged economic site that continues to support the global security industry. It demonstrates the material and affective work that households do to support the security industry. The ease with which these men come to participate in global security owes much to the militarised communities they come from. Gurkha households and the broader community remain the 'standing army' that 'picks up the slack' while the men migrate (often for years) for work. Indeed, these households feature heavily in the creating and sustaining of the resilient Gurkha workforce that PMSCs desire and demand (Chisholm and Stachowitsch 2016). This chapter explores what kinds of work are performed in the household that enable the global security industry to recruit and mobilise Gurkhas. It empirically documents the ways in which wives (re)produce security work and militarism as an honourable and a safe/secure lifepath, how they hold their international families together, and the (depleted) care work they provide. Drawing on the work of Sara Ahmed (2004, 2010, 2014), the chapter also explores the role of happiness as a future-orientated affective relation, how it underpins the way they make sense of their own position as wife/supporter of their husband's security work, and how this happiness sits alongside more ambivalent emotions of anxiety and insecurity, as well as the frustration of being a Gurkha wife to a foreign worker. Overall, this chapter concretely accounts for all the material and immaterial labour Gurkha wives do to support their husbands and the broader security industry. It also shows how the affect of happiness and 'the happy Gurkha wife' profoundly conditions how these women make sense of their own experiences and life choices.

Chapter 5, 'Race, Gender and the Political Economy of Feeling Secure', is concerned with how security is produced and valued through everyday encounters between the client and the security contractor. Security, particularly in Afghanistan, is often done in intimate and communal spaces where the contractors and clients spend both work and leisure time. This raises complex dynamics, particularly between female clients and male contractors. This chapter brings into focus, from the perspective of those being protected, how security work is perceived, what kinds of security work are valued and the role the client plays in naturalising divisions of security labour. Drawing upon feminist GPE scholarship on domestic industry, in particular work in intimate settings, this chapter highlights the vulnerabilities and spatial politics of security that arise through doing security in the everyday.

The Conclusion, 'Slow Death and Failure in the Life Building of Gurkha Communities', ends the book with an overall assessment of militarism and compares these practices with other sites and sightings of militarism in the global market. It specifically looks at failure as affectively lived, and how those who have failed to become Gurkhas continue to experience similar pulls into militarism and military pathways as Gurkhas and their families. Sameer was one such man. I met him in Doha, Qatar, where he was working as a security guard after failing at becoming a Gurkha. I had never before engaged with anyone who had failed in their quest to become a Gurkha, and yet Sameer's story of failure is much more common than stories of success.

> My heart sank as [Sameer] told me of his failure and how he still tried to navigate a life that would be honourable and respectable for him and his family. In that moment I was struck by the tension I felt in the room and the curiousness that I, as someone who had been researching Gurkhas for almost a decade by then, had never actually engaged with anyone who had failed at becoming one.

What does it mean to think through the prism of failure about how security is made and how this kind of security continues to carry profound emotional and affective investments? The Conclusion draws specifically upon feminist cultural theorists' work, particularly that of Judith Halberstam, Lauren Berlant and Sara Ahmed, to explore how affect 'sticks' to particular communities and informs their life pathways. The chapter also makes use of the concept of failure to highlight that, despite the breakdown of families and the toxic emotions of regret and shame embodied by contractors and their families, both groups are still motivated to participate in this industry. The chapter thus grapples with a question of agency. Given the challenges, pain and often impossibility of everyday life for these communities, located on the periphery of global security markets, how can we think through what pulls them into this life pattern? It seeks to show how the motivation to take up arms and participate in the industry needs to be understood beyond a self-actualising and conscious decision making – through unreflected life pathways that are imbued with affect. The chapter then concludes the book by suggesting further empirical and conceptual avenues for future development – namely, how the coloniality of this global security industry also conditions the workforces of other Global South and Eastern European communities.

Conclusion

Throughout this book, I remain curious of how the structures and logics of militarism and capitalism are gendered and how they shape contemporary security market relations. The book's starting point is with colonial encounters, with the aim of uncovering how global imperial histories continue to shape global security market practices. As such, it explores how militarism takes shape and is made meaningful in these markets from a non-Western positioning. The book builds upon the existing critical security/military studies that understand both militarism and security not as concepts with an ontological truth, but rather by way of how they come to have meaning through the language, practices and experiences we associate with them.

This research accounts for what kinds of security work are actually being done and the nature of this work. This includes the material everyday rituals and routines, but also the emotional and affective care work. I remain interested in how affect gets marketised and how emotional labour in the household is taken up in support of the global security industry. By bringing the intellectual traditions of feminist security studies and feminist GPE into conversation, the book presents a much more nuanced and sophisticated exploration of how global security markets continue to shape (and be shaped by) racialised and gendered structures and experiences. As war making is becoming increasingly privatised, this book explores how globalising practices of affect, militarism and capitalism shape and are shaped by everyday concrete market relations amongst diverse security bodies, and how care work, social reproduction and the household become key sites and practices for this new privatised waging of war.[12]

Figure I.1 Amanda Chisholm conducting a focus group with Gurkhas returning from Afghanistan, Kathmandu, Nepal, August 2017. Photo credit to Robic Upadhayay.

It is the ambiguity located in everyday security practices that tells us something important about how we think of these 'security assemblages' (Abrahamsen and Williams 2009). Ethnography developed in this research helps us think through the politics from below (Lyon-Callo and Hyatt 2003), how security might 'touch us' (Sylvester 2012), and how the everyday remains a fundamental site and space where security is (re)produced in racialised and gendered ways.

Within the everyday lives of the security contractors, the clients, and those wives who support the industry are also stories of resistance – through adaptation, rejection, adoption and simply ignoring what the market expects. These resistances may be subtle or overt, but they continue to be a part of what it means to live and work within this global industry. The everyday, then, remains a key analytical entry point to understanding how security markets function, how value is determined/resisted/adapted, and how people find communities as well as a sense of self that is shaped by markets and militarism, but not overdetermined by them. The goal of this book is to highlight the contestations, the fractures and the ambiguities – the simultaneously felt joy and shame, love and pain – that continue to shape how these communities and individuals live and negotiate the broader processes of capitalism and militarism within global security. It is these conceptual

Figure I.2 Amanda Chisholm talking with a Gurkha wife, a Gurkha son and Gurkha, in Pokhara, Nepal, November 2018. Photo credit to Robic Upadhayay.

entanglements and their significance in shaping the broader security industry to which we now turn.

Notes

1. V. Spike Peterson's (2008) '"New Wars" and Gendered Economies' is a notable exception here. This piece provides a feminist political economy mapping of the changing nature of global gendered labour drawn into support wars that are increasingly marked by decentralisation and marketplace economies. My own work and that of Barker (2015) and Mynster Christenson (2015) have also explored gendered and racialised practices that underpin global security markets.

2. Nevins and Peluso's 2008 edited volume *Taking South East Asia to Market* documents the ways in which race, colonial histories and global capital all entangle to shape workforces, the way they are mobilised and the market value they hold. Other exemplary texts that demonstrate how race and racialisation act together as a marker and process to render certain Global South labour cheap are Shiloh Whitney's (2017) 'Byproductive Labour', Robert Miles's (1982) *Racism and Migrant Labour* and Rochelle Ball's (2004) 'Divergent Development, Racialised Rights'.

3. My intellectual thinking on the embodied nature of gendered work is indebted to the work of Agathangelou (2004) in *The Global Political Economy of Sex,*

which details how the value placed on labour through market transactions is embodied and racialised. In her work on the global sex and care industries, Agathangelou documents how the whiter one's skin is and the more one is culturally affiliated with the West, the more value is placed on one as a worker. Wolkowitz's *Bodies at Work* showcases the changing nature of work within the service industry, which is transforming 'how we think about the role of the human body in economic life and employment relations' (2006, 1). Boris and Salazar Parreñas's *Intimate Labors* explores a variety of activities that make up intimate labour, including 'bodily and household upkeep' and the bodily and emotional closeness involved in sex and care work (2010, 2). Finally, Gutiérrez-Rodríguez's (2010) *Migration, Domestic Work and Affect: A Decolonial Approach on Value and the Feminization of Labor* shows how affective labour is done in all domestic and care work in the production of wellbeing and liveability. In each case, these scholars show how value becomes embodied and performative through the service industries of sex work, care work, call centres, hair styling and security bouncing.

4. Feminist political economy scholarship on care work is diverse and empirically rich. See, for example, the following titles: Stasiulis and Bakan's (1997) 'Negotiating Citizenship' explores how Haitian and Philippine nannies and domestic workers negotiate Canada's live-in care immigration system; Ehrenreich and Hochschild's (2003) *Global Women: Nannies, Maids and Sex Workers in the New Economy* explores the multitude of service work globally and the structured and embodied nature of this work; Benoit and Hallgrimsdottir's (2011) *Valuing Care Work: Comparative Perspectives* examines economic organisations as well as intimate settings to show how personal service work is shaped by broader welfare state developments; and Gutiérrez-Rodríguez's (2010) *Migration, Domestic Work and Affect: A Decolonial Approach on Value and Feminization of Labour* provides a detailed look at how affect and emotions underpin value in domestic and care work globally.

5. Rai, Hoskyns and Thomas (2013) have developed depletion theory to think through how the changing nature of work that takes family members physically away from their households impacts social reproduction.

6. The scholarship that shows how reproductive labour and households are central to the functioning of global markets is diverse and features in a multitude of subfields, including economics, development studies, international relations and political science. Luxton (2018) offers a good overview of this literature.

7. I am grateful for Väyrynen's (2019) work on everyday and mundane peace, which locates the ontology of peace in living relational bodies, departing from understandings of peace that are abstract and understood as 'void' of war or more orientalist views of 'the local', which only show communities as being resistant or resilient to Western interventions. For Väyrynen, 'Peace is something that becomes expressed and takes place through acts and points of everyday contact between variously situated and variously vulnerable bodies' (2019, 156).

8. I am indebted to the intellectual generosity and theoretical framing of the following people – many of whom read my working draft papers and chapters, often multiple times, throughout this writing process. These include: Saskia Stachowitsch, Maya Eichler, Julia Welland, Thomas Gregory, Susan Martin, Marsha Henry, Kyle Grayson, Cristina Masters, Lisa Tilley, Meghan MacKenzie, Debbie Lisle and Juanita Elias.

9. I draw upon postcolonial theorising and a use of encounter here that 'focus on the embodied nature of social distinctions and the unpredictable ways in which similarity and difference are negotiated in the moment' (Wilson 2017, 455).

10. 'Absolutely Fabulous', or 'Ab Fab', ran from 1992 to 1995 and 2001 to 2004 on the BBC; see IMDb, 'Absolutely Fabulous', available at: <https://www.imdb.com/title/tt0105929/>; Wikipedia, 'Absolutely Fabulous', available at: https://en.wikipedia.org/wiki/Absolutely_Fabulous>.

11. It also shows us how these positionalities shift, sometimes instantly. See, for example, Ann Phoenix's (1994) 'Practicing Feminist Research: The Intersections of Gender and "Race" in the Research Process' for a discussion of how inter-sections of class, race and gender are often situated within the research process and not contained as ontological truths in the researcher; Louise Ryan's (2015) '"Inside" and "Outside" of What or Where? Researching Migration Through Multi-Positionalities', where she highlights how the researcher does not hold a solely inside or outside relationship with those she researches; and Andrea Nightingale's (2011) 'Bounding Difference', which explores the ways in which the embodied performance of gender, caste and other aspects of social differ-ence collapse the distinction between the material and the symbolic.

12. This is an emerging field of study within feminist security studies and feminist global political economy that explores how war and postwar economies struc-ture everyday gendered work and the household. See, for example, Hedström's (2017) work on the militarised household and the militarised social reproduc-tion of Katchin households. See also True's (2020) work on social reproduction, care work and depletion as gender harm in post-conflict communities.

CHAPTER 1

Colonial Encounters, Militarism and Affect in Global Security

Vignette One

I was sitting across a coffee table from Jitendra in Kabul, having a cup of tea in the security compound where he worked and lived in the district of Wazir Akbar Khan. Jitendra was a former Singaporean Police Gurkha officer who currently worked in Afghanistan as a line manager for a team of Gurkhas. Since retiring from the Singaporean Police, Jitendra had worked as a security contractor, first in Iraq and now in Afghanistan.

Jitendra told me about a close encounter he had in a convoy protection detail while working in Iraq a few years ago. During this convoy, his vehicle broke down and he had to wait for military support, having no idea when they'd arrive.

Jitendra: I was in the middle of a remote and very open area that was known for attacks on convoys.
Amanda: Were you afraid?
Jitendra: Of course, I was afraid. But I also knew I was a Gurkha and Gurkhas do not run. I had to be strong. It's in my blood. (Kabul, Afghanistan, 2010)

Vignette Two

Rabindra sat there quietly as his wife Sunika explained how she forced him to become a Gurkha. I felt surprised as she told me this. An atmosphere of tension filled the room. This tension sat at odds with the general excitement that only moments earlier had filled the room as people buzzed in and out of the living room, preparing for Sunika and Rabindra's daughter's wedding to be held the next day.

In the over ten years of researching Gurkhas, I'd never encountered this experience before. Perhaps it was because I had failed to ask. I never had asked Gurkha men what it was like to be fathers, husbands, sons. I, like all the other military commentaries about these men, had focussed on their military service.

Sunika: Rabindra never wanted to be a Gurkha, he missed seeing his children grow up, he missed me.

We all sat there, in quiet pause. (Fieldnotes, Dharan, Nepal, 2017)

Introduction

I approach my research by understanding global security as a 'sociopolitical' set of regimes that 'begins and ends with bodies' (Värynen and Puumala 2015). Security bodies, such as those introduced in the two separate fieldnote vignettes, offer a glimpse into how affect and emotions matter in the ways each person connects to and makes sense of what it means to be a Gurkha working in global security. The vignettes show how security bodies are always affective bodies.[1] These bodies are constituted through past histories that flow into the present and emotional connections to futures not yet lived. They are social. Centring analysis on the affective body, including the Gurkha security contractor, Gurkha spouses, security clients and security managers, then offers a different understanding of global security and global politics that tells us much more about the ambiguities, rhythms and routines of global security that existing theories, devoid of theorising bodies, currently offer.[2] The chapter proceeds by showing how concepts of affect, militarism, political economies and colonial histories entangle in the making of the global private security industry and in shaping the experiences of militarised communities who participate in global security but originate outside the West.

Affect and Global Security

Affect shapes our experiences of war. It involves the moods, sensations and 'energies [that] transmit through bodily encounters' (Åhäll 2018, 40). These include the joys, pleasures, compulsions, shame, guilt and disgust that people feel in relation to war. It also involves the emotional capacities for love and forgiveness as communities and individuals go through a process of healing post war and post violent encounters (Penttinen 2013).

Affects move us: sometimes toward war, feeling it to be necessary and even honourable, and sometimes away from war. Paying attention to affect means paying attention to how our bodies feel their ways through the world (Ahmed 2004; Väyrynen 2019). Indeed, how we feel about the world tells us a great deal about how the world actually works (Haraway 2016) and how war touches us (Sylvester 2012: MacLeish 2013). We can experience an out-of-placeness (Hemmings 2005), which can offer us important cues into power relations and our own situatedness within these relations that underpin the practice of war.[3]

Affect intimately connects to emotions. IR scholarship tends to treat affect as something that occurs pre emotions and pre conscious.[4] This might include body sensations, sweating and an increased heart rate; alternatively, emotions include fully conscious feelings of sadness, fear, anxiety, joy and pleasure, for example. While I mention this distinction here, I am not interested in conceptually separating emotions and affect. Both are so deeply entangled in how they materialise and are observed in my research. Like other feminist scholars before me,[5] I explore what emotions and affect do politically in the context of global private security. I am curious about how they attach to logics and practices of militarism, how they stick to colonial subjects such as the Gurkhas, and how they condition the lifepaths of the various security actors, as well as how these actors relate to one another. I question how affect and emotions work to bind particular security communities together and to form boundaries that seemingly naturalise divisions of labour, obscuring the labour of some and valorising the labour of others. To do this, I directly engage with Ahmed's (2004), Halberstam's (2011) and Berlant's (2011) theorising of affect and look at how affect relates to the broader curiosities of war and militarism located within feminist security studies (Baker 2020; Åhäll 2018; Gregory 2019) and feminist political economy (Hochschild 1985; Whitney 2017).

Affect and emotions frame how we make sense of our own positionalities in war, and also those we encounter within war. Thomas Gregory's (2019) pioneering work on affect and security draws upon over 154 declassified incident reports from US checkpoint operations in Iraq to demonstrate how feelings and affect both played a fundamental role in how US soldiers understood hostility and imminent threat as embodied in the racialised Iraqi citizen. Most compelling in Gregory's work is his discussion of how affect informs feelings of hostility and how these feelings were fundamental in US soldiers' decisions to use lethal force or not. The instincts US soldiers rely upon to enable split-second decisions on whether to engage with lethal force are not neutral; they are shaped by past encounters with civilians and racial perceptions of local populations. Those Iraqi civilians who became saturated with the affect of fear could not easily escape this affective fixing. Indeed, as Gregory highlights, by virtue of being Iraqi, their bodies were rendered killable. Gregory's work shows that feelings and affect are concepts that literally underpin decisions of life and death.

Gregory's work connects to a broader literature on affect and emotions in global politics. This literature is rich and diverse. It includes Hutchison's (2017) work on trauma as a collective affect that binds communities together. MacLeish's ground-breaking ethnographic work on a military community in Fort Hood, a US base, offers a rich and compelling case study of how war affectively 'excites bodies, cultivates capacities, gives value to things, provokes subjective interpretations of surprising behaviours and forms connections' (2013, 14). Åhäll (2016), Welland (2018) and Dyvik (2016) have all drawn upon affect to examine the joys and pleasures of war, while Basham (2015) has illuminated how the affect of boredom makes up a significant part of war making, and Penttinen (2013) has highlighted the capacity for joy, love and forgiveness in war. Rashid (2020) and Ben-Asher and Bokek-Cohen (2020) detail the affective labour done by members of military households in reproducing the honourable sacrifice of their family members who have died, contributing to the broader support of war making and statecraft for the Pakistani and Israeli states. Baker's (2020) edited volume, alongside González, Gusterson and Houtman's (2019) edited collection, gives further scope and depth to how militarism takes on multiple manifestations and emotional investments as it moves through the world and through different bodies and histories. Conceptually, bringing emotions and affect into the study of war and global security offers a 'type of scholarly and political sensibility [that] could conceptualize the influences' of both, even when it does not seem immediately apparent (Bleiker and Hutchison 2008, 128).

The aforementioned scholarship, spanning diverse subfields of IR and cultural studies, highlights how affect and emotions are both social and political. They give depth to our human existence through relations with others and ourselves (Hemmings 2005, 552). They can be weaponised to support state war making (Crane-Seeber 2016), and to reinforce Western liberalism and liberal military intervention (Razack 2007; Caso 2020; Welland 2017), as much as they can be the driver for forgiveness (Penttinen 2013). They are felt at both a personal and a community level. Affect and emotions circulate – they stick, they set boundaries between 'us' and 'them', and they make communities as much as they can tear apart solidarities. We share those moments of tension, of excitement and of anger as emotions circulate[6] – even though we might relate to them differently (Ahmed 2004). Both offer a descriptor for a 'feeling of existence' (Anderson 2016, 735).[7] For instance, affect and emotion helped me think through my own experiences as a researcher encountering a tense atmosphere, as shown in the opening vignettes with Rabindra and Sunika.

I am interested in understanding how affect underpins the processes through which subjects become invested in the social norms and structures of militarism (Baker 2020).[8] Specifically, I want to explore how affect underpins investments in militarism and the broader global security industry. Affect allows us to see how the different security actors detailed throughout this book come to invest in particular life patterns, histories and structures that orientate them within the security industry (as spouses supporting the industry, as racialised contractors, as professional contractors, as security clients). Affect, as it circulates, also becomes felt in a way that normalises the different forms of labour done in the security industry (who we trust to protect us, for example), which labour is valued and how these different forms of security labour are divided.

Affective Attachments and Circulations

Affect does not reside in individuals, but in how it materialises as it attaches to particular subjects.[9] For example, Åhäll (2018) shows how gendered affects of caring, and gentle and passive dispositions attach to the subject woman. These affective attachments shape how we connect with the subject woman and her relationship to war. Åhäll (2018) draws upon this affective subject woman to demonstrate that females who fight in wars are always held to a different (gendered) standard: they are judged more harshly or seen as more deviant when they act violently. This is because those female individuals who participate in violence act out of sync with how we affectively relate to the idea of woman. Like the subject woman, the Gurkha subject is also saturated with affects – those being bravery, playfulness and cheerfulness (discussed in greater detail in the next chapter). These affects also inform how these men and their actions are mediated and evaluated.

These affects and their relations to the Gurkha subject move as the subject travels through global security circuits and different people become orientated to who Gurkhas are. For example, my own affective attachments to Gurkhas as security providers will be different from those of someone who has never encountered them or been protected by them. These associated affects and feelings orientate us either toward subjects we perceive as good or away from the subjects and objects we understand to be bad. Ahmed offers an example of the stranger that is helpful here. The stranger is saturated in affects of danger and fearsomeness. Perceptions of the stranger (Ahmed 2004), the soldier (MacLeish 2013), the woman (Åhäll 2016), and in my research, the Gurkha are based upon often instantaneous judgements of who these people are (honourable, fearsome, loathsome), mediated through broader cultural cues and histories. Again, affect is not located in these subjects. It is produced through an evaluation of how we read and feel particular subjects when we encounter them (Ahmed 2004, 6). Returning to Jitendra's story, his commitment to stand his ground despite feeling fear is a result of his affective relations to the Gurkha subject – a subject that is saturated with colonial tropes of not running from fear. 'In my blood' refers to his own personal and long history around Gurkhas – men who do not flee in the face of fear, and those who run toward violence. It is his reflection of his own Gurkha history, and not wanting to let down this history, that orientates Jitendra's experience to dangerous

Figure 1.1 Image of a framed Gurkha soldier alongside Gurkha regimental framed photo, in Jhapa, Nepal, August 2017. Such commemorations of Gurkhas in the living room area of Gurkha homes are common features. Photo credit to Robic Upadhayay.

situations as one who recognises danger and feels fear, but does not turn away from them.

As much as affect circulates, it also comes to stick to certain bodies – bodies like Jitendra's. By stick, I mean to explore how histories often come to shape the Gurkha in the present. These histories frame how we affectively connect, how we feel when we encounter these men and how they feel about themselves (Ahmed 2004; Hemmings 2005). Gurkhas' bodies are made meaningful through their specific martial histories. Contradictory colonial tropes of playfulness and fierceness and loyal and simple produce an 'almost but not quite' martial colonial subject who is forever bound to their colonial white professional subject, and these tropes are immediately connected to the Gurkha body. 'Gurkha' as a colonial affective subject circulates and comes into contact with other security contractors and clients in security markets in how they are marketed and how they become to be valuable (Chapter 3). Affect materialises in how men such as Jitendra understand their own experiences and subsequently behave in war. It circulates outwardly to the social in how others observe and judge this behaviour. This judgement is, as mentioned, always mediated through a broader culture and history that shapes who these subjects are.

Figure 1.2 Military medals awarded to a retired British Gurkha, in Pokhara, Nepal, November 2018. Photo credit to Robic Upadhayay.

Sticky Histories

It's in our blood, but the British make us professional. (Gurkha focus group, Kabul, Afghanistan, 2008)

The identity of Gurkha comes out of the colonial encounter between the British and Nepal (Enloe 1982). Through a multitude of military anthropological writings describing these men as fierce Nepali hillmen,[10] detailing how they were vastly outmeasured in military equipment and training when compared to the East India Company but continued to show strength, the admiration for these hillmen's commitment to war began. 'Better to die than be a coward' is the British Gurkha motto. It adorned the various Gurkha community centres I visited throughout Nepal, and it was repeated to me in my encounters with Gurkhas and British Gurkha officers. The motto symbolises the men's histories and relation to war, and their relationships as soldiers who have an unfettered commitment to waging war and resilience in violent encounters.

The Gurkha subject is also one that is affectively circulated through these martial race imperial histories that come before the subject and circulate in contemporary global security markets. Gurkhas carry with them a martial race history rooted in a particular military colonial project that sought to naturalise martial talents on to Nepali rural communities. These (gendered) talents of military brutality, aggression and loyalty to the British crown and their identity of being simple/literal men produced Gurkhas' value and worth as entangled with the British military (white) officers. Gendered stories of their military valour continue to feature in popular books about Gurkhas, often authored by former white British Gurkha officers, and were repeated in numerous conversations I had over the years with both Gurkhas and British Gurkha officers, discussed in more detail in Chapter 2.

One story in particular that is often repeated involves a Gurkha's close encounter with a German soldier. In this exchange, the Gurkha takes a swipe at the physically larger German with his famous kukri.[11] The German says, 'Ha, missed!', to which the Gurkha replies, 'Shake your head' (Gould 1999, 1). A British Gurkha officer told me in conversation how he was asking the Gurkhas he was in command of during a military mission to jump out of a plane as part of a military operation the next day. The Gurkhas responded immediately with 'Yes, sir,' but had worry in their faces that the commander did not understand. When he queried them as to why, one of the Gurkhas asked: 'Sir can we have parachutes?' Of course, these military jokes are embellishments, but they are also illustrative of the contradictory colonial tropes of Gurkhas' martial prowess juxtaposed with an endearing childlike naïvety. These military stories, often told as jokes, reinforce the notion of a naturalised childlike innocence and yet a brutal warrior. The Gurkha is one to be feared as well as taken care of. Gurkhas carry these histories with them as they enter security markets. These histories stick to their bodies in such a way that makes them, as a security director once told me, 'easy sells' in global security, and at the same time they condition how the men's security work is valued (explored further in Chapter 2). Such pronouncements of Gurkha histories, flooding into the present and shaping future trajectories, align with what Väyrynen and Puumala (2015) call the 'past continuous', where both the past and present intertwine in shaping Gurkha security bodies, how they are valued and how they affectively experience security.

The broader colonial and racial politics that underpin how these men come to participate in and experience the industry is not unique to PMSCs. Race, in global markets, acts in structural and agential ways (Tilley and Shilliam 2018). It is not an ideology or merely identity politics. Rather, race (like gender) 'must be apprehended as a mode of classifying, ordering, creating and destroying people, labour power, land, environment and capital' (Tilley and Shilliam 2018, 537). Race continues to play a role in normalising and naturalising hierarchies of labour power, economic geographies, land ownership and economic dispossession as much as it obscures them through appeals to the idea of the free and unfettered market, and the deserving and undeserving. In order to gain a more sophisticated view of how security markets function, colonial histories and practices of race need to be central to the analysis.

In current security markets, both Gurkhas and the Gurkha officers who market their skill sets draw upon particular aspects of Gurkha colonial histories to offer the security market a description of who Gurkhas are and the market value of their labour. Their over 200 years of military service with the British, memorialised in numerous celebratory books on their military feats, produces a somewhat timeless colonial trope about who these men are. This colonial history marks Gurkha bodies as valuable because of their association with white Westerners. The Gurkha is fierce but also literal, is loyal to the British and has an unfettered desire for and commitment to military service. He is to be trusted, but is also in need of leadership. The martial race histories continue to stick to these men's bodies, saturating 'Gurkha' with affects of fierceness, loyalty and playfulness, and affectively binding them and their worth to their white British national counterparts. These affects circulate in how Gurkha is marketed to other security clients and companies – bringing in their long tradition of military service with the British as a key aspect of their value.

These colonial histories 'plac[e] bodies in spatial relations along racially defined lines' (Ahmed 2000, 85–6, as cited in Hemmings 2005, 562). These lines enable a devaluing of particular bodies that does not seem possible for white/Western bodies – at least not in the same way. We assume white Westerners are professional, while Gurkhas have to prove their professionalism (see Chapters 3 and 5). It is the movement of affect between gendered, colonial and racial histories and logics that allows others to attribute emotional value to particular bodies (as in Fanon's (1967) analysis of the negro as an animal, as bad, mean and ugly, for example). The Gurkha, then, is made the martial raced warrior – aggressive and simple. In these cases, it is the gendered and colonial histories that 'stick' and that do not need to be declared (Ahmed 2004, 127). Such value gets taken up by global markets in how Gurkhas are not only provided with access to security markets, but also naturalised in labour divisions within the industry. These sticky emotions and saturated affect work to immobilise and reduce Gurkhas' bodies – but also, as I will discuss, other bodies such as female and white bodies, relegating them to specific spaces and labour roles in global markets.

The stickiness informs not only how others affectively relate to Gurkhas on a social level, but also how the men relate on an individual and more personal level. Both Jitendra's and Rabindra's affective relations to Gurkha were shaped by past histories of contact, told through oral histories passed down by generations, as well as through regimental histories told by former military colleagues. How the subject Gurkha is impressed upon us may depend on histories that remain alive insofar as they have already left their impression (Ahmed 2004, 8). Jitendra's impression of the notion of Gurkha and his affective connection not to 'let down' his own Gurkha heritage of fierceness and bravery profoundly shaped how he responded, despite feeling fear. But the emotions of both fear and bravery were not inwardly owned by Jitendra. They are emotions connected to a wider community of men affectively bound to the identity of Gurkha, which conditions them to perform bravery amid violent encounters in a willing and eager way. The Gurkha subject is illuminating in how emotions materialise both inward (inside Jitendra and Rabindra) and outside (social binding of the community and heritage of the Gurkha). In other words, emotions and affect are always both individually and collectively felt (Ahmed 2004, 9).

Affective Relations to Militarism

Militarism is a central feature of the broader social and political arrangements in the preparation for, and conduct of, organised political violence (Rossdale 2021, 45). Like patriarchy, militarism is a core concept critical scholars draw upon to locate why war persists as it does, who is called upon to participate and invest in war logics, what is at stake for different security bodies, and what we might do ethically to move away from this kind of violence. Yet, as Rossdale indicates, there is no single understanding or type of militarism. Rather, how scholars draw upon its politics and implications for our understanding of organised violence continues to be context-specific and "determined by particular formations of power at operation in any particular environment" (Rossdale 2021, 45).

For some scholars, militarism is the common sense, the 'that which gets taken for granted' that naturalises, normalises and even makes war pleasurable for some (Enloe 1993; 2000). For others, militarism is understood as the driving (gendered) logic that underpins the planning and preparation for war waging. Indeed, feminist scholars, more than any other subfield, have shown us that security and militarism are always inherently entangled and reinforcing (Wibben 2018). These feminists argue that one becomes militarised when one begins to see the world as inherently violent, as a world that requires strong and offensive militaries (Enloe 2000). Militarism is often supported through other structures of patriarchy (Enloe 1993) and imperialism (Barkawi 2017) that give the gendered and racialised divisions of labour that underpin war the appearance of timelessness and naturalness. As such, militarism takes on a masculine feature (Enloe 1993) because masculinity continues to be the formal structure that links war and militarism (Hutchings 2008). Feminists who articulate the practices and processes of militarism as such illuminate its aim in the production of security through territorial control, domination and hierarchy. How this is achieved depends upon historic and contextual factors.

For others still, militarism is also ambiguous in how it is felt and supported in the everyday. It can be marked through apathy – when we stop caring or being outraged when our states engage in violent attacks overseas and continue to spend high amounts on military weaponry (Basham 2018). Feminist scholars have also explored how militarism is entangled with gendered performances within security markets and how militarised masculinities are refashioned to expand securitising practices further in humanitarian spaces, but also programmed to exclude women from participating as security experts/knowers (Stachowitsch 2015; Eichler 2014). Other scholars still explore militarism and war making as they get caught up in the intimate and embodied spaces – in how, for example, the gendered and racialised bodies of the infantry soldier (MacLeish 2013) and the disabled veteran (Baker 2020; Myrttinenn 2020) are produced through war. For these scholars, militarism is deeply embedded in war making and state building that does not immediately translate into a clear distinction between militarised and non-militarised spatiality (Howell 2018).

Emerging feminist research on militarism also indicates the role of emotion and affect in its travels and what it does politically – further complicating how and where we see militarism materialise.[12] For these scholars, militarism becomes 'sticky' (Ahmed 2014; Åhäll 2016) through our various affective encounters – observed, for example, in the ways martial raced colonial soldiers have been understood as brave and yet also infantilised (Barkawi 2017; Caplan 1995). This was certainly the case with the many Gurkha security contractors I met and spent time with. Their imperial military heritage continued to be a marker for how the industry valued them, but also for how they internalised their own self-worth and role as security contractors.

The growing literature on militarism and affect speaks to the ways in which the body is central to understanding militarism.[13] Importantly, as Jitendra's testimony illustrates, capacities to 'affect and be affected' are not reducible to individual bodies, but rather are always already conditioned by the 'histories that come before subjects' (Ahmed 2014). Jitendra drew upon the generations of men before him who conducted their security work with valour and stoicism. In moments of fear, he did not want to let those histories down. Here, the imperial encounter(s) between the British and Gurkhas cannot be separated from how the communities I spent time with in both Nepal and the UK understand their own contemporary positions within the global security industry.

The various scholarly works focusing on feminist accounts, whilst illuminating and important in their own right, do not adequately capture the complexities and nuances of militarism shown in my fieldwork and explored throughout this book. They do not address how a particular common sense emerges and is sustained in contexts where it is rendered clear that militarism is an impossible path to achieving that which one desires, or where the very attachment to militarism has become toxic. As I discuss specifically in Chapter 2, what is distinct about the Gurkha and British security communities is their location at the intersection of global capitalism and militarism. Both logics function in tandem as mechanisms that perpetuate each community's buy-in around economic and security arrangements that position one at the centre and the other at the periphery. The Gurkha community participates in these global markets to improve their own economic prospects – to have a chance at the good life. They look specifically upon security work and militarism as a pathway to this good life, viewing it through the lens of their two centuries of military service – honoured through oral accounts of military valour and passed on through generations, rendering any other pathway almost nonsensical. To make sense of their participation, militarism must be seen as both a geopolitical and economic logic, just as much as it needs to be examined as affectively felt.

To unpack affective investments in militarism – how militarism 'claims its subjects' (Rashid 2020), I conceptualise affect as 'things that happen' – in impulses, sensations and 'social worlds of all kinds that catch people up in something that feels like something' (Stewart 2007, 2). Importantly, these are not capacities that are reducible to individual bodies but rather capacities that are always already conditioned by the histories that precede them. Ahmed's notion of 'circulation' allows us to move away from situating affect merely in the immediacy of bodily reactions (2014, 212), and instead to think about the ways in which investments in militarism, including the felt and sensed dimensions of these investments, have specific histories.

I am also interested in how economic and colonial structures underpin certain affects. I specifically draw upon Lauren Berlant's (2011) concept of cruel optimism to show how militarism located in these non-Western Gurkha communities is both affectively felt and structurally experienced. Detailed more in Chapter 5, cruel optimism illuminates how communities located on the periphery of these security markets, who often risk the most and gain the least, continue to invest affectively in these economic patterns. For Berlant (2011), optimism manifests in an attachment to an object of desire and a desire to maintain that attachment. For Gurkhas, optimistic attachments are found in militarism and attached to the idea of the Gurkha (a subject saturated with militarism) as a way to achieve the good life (Chisholm and Ketola 2020). These attachments are about sustaining life's continuity and world making. As Chapters 3 and 4 detail, such attachments connect to a future-orientated happiness that is often intergenerational. As one individual succinctly said: 'I become a Gurkha and sacrifice so much personally so that my children and children's children, not yet born, can have more opportunities.' Such optimism become cruel when the very pursuit proves toxic, and impossible.

I take a cue from feminist political economy scholars who remind us that capitalism and market relations are always mediated through gendered and racialised logics. Geeta Chowdhry and Sheila Nair's (2004) edited volume, *Power, Postcolonialism and International Relations: Reading Race, Gender and Class*, and Beverly Skeggs's (2004) *Class, Self, Culture* are great examples of works that explore the ways in which global politics and economies are shaping and being shaped by gender, race and class practices in global contexts. Bringing this scholarship into conversation with the substantive body of work on military labour (Ware 2012; Barkawi 2017; Rashid 2020) shows how militarism goes global, by way of how military circuits of labour are produced and sustained – through militarism as a logic that normalises the global support of and participation in global security, and also the uneven economic geographies that sustain access to (cheap) marital raced/militarised security contractors. Certainly, it is the shared colonial histories between the Gurkhas and their British Gurkha officers (discussed in the following chapter) that not only make Gurkhas intelligible as martial security contractors, but affectively bind them to the British and to these particular colonial narratives on who they are and where their value as contractors originates. This, of course, is not to place a preference on saturated histories of individual actions and performances as a way of explaining why people orientate themselves to global security in particular ways. Indeed, war histories that shape affective bodies are also filled with stories of individuals and communities acting against cultural, gendered and racial norms (Väyrynen and Puumala 2015) – bodies, while they are conditioned by particular international and national colonial and gendered histories, are not completely determined by them. Being mindful of how affect emerges from and is rendered meaningful through the everyday banality of those who are involved in global security becomes an analytical starting point to navigate the messiness experienced by these security bodies and how they feel their way through the world.

Affective Economies and Global Security

While both emotion and affect are certainly foundational in shaping bodies in and through war, I am also concerned with the commodification of affect and how it circulates within security markets. In other words, what is the affect that is producing the labour involved in the business of making people feel secure? This includes the labour done to produce affects of safety and security. Globally, there is an increasing economisation of affect and emotions in post-Fordist global political economies that makes exploring how and under what conditions these labour practices get taken up a timely project.[14] Emotional labour requires the inducement or suppression of particular feelings, of self – managing one's own feelings in such a way as to sustain an outward appearance that produces a desired state of mind in others (Hochschild 1985, 7).[15] It involves the manipulation of one's emotions (Boris and Salazar Parreñas 2010, 6). In security work, this kind of emotional labour might be providing clients with the reassurance of their security through regular and ritualised performances of security, through perimeter checks and daily intel briefings, as well as getting them involved in security drills. It also might include the pastoral care work done by checking in with the clients to make sure they feel safe and well. This kind of emotional labour is necessarily productive of an affect for others, and fostering a specific atmosphere involves not only creating certain 'postures and gestures' in the way one performs, but also managing one's own 'inward' emotions; this is how to come across as genuine and convincing (Hochschild 1985).

Such labour is done in a context of interactive service economies, where face-to-face encounters and embodiments are key aspects of the work being done (McDowell 2009).[16] It is both the worker's body and the service provided that are included in this form of labour. There is also an intimacy to this labour. The security contractor is placed in immediate and often intimate contact with the client (detailed further in Chapter 5). Contractors and clients get to know each other through observing the daily personal and ritualised habits of one another – from what each eats for breakfast and lunch, to physical fitness routines, to what each does during their leisure time.

Everyone in the security industry does some form of affective labour in the broader production of making people feel safe. This includes the Western security managers who take on a mentoring role in managing their Global South and local security workforces – including learning about personal matters their team faces in order to address them and make their team resilient. It also includes how Gurkhas make clients feel safe through investing in getting to know their clients' personal lives, including how many children they may have and what foods they like, and also by carrying a smile. It even includes the emotional work (female) clients do to manage (un)wanted advances by Western security contractors during the off hours, when they frequent the same social bars and restaurants around the city. This labour gets divided and (de)valued along hierarchies of race and gender. In my research, this kind of labour appeared in how British Gurkha officers 'managed' Gurkhas in a fatherly and pastoral way in order to get the best out of them, discussed in detail in Chapter 3. It also materialised in how the Gurkhas and other men labelled third country nationals, providing emotional labour to clients to make them feel safe and secure (see Chapter 5). While everyone does affective work as part of their work life,[17] what I am particularly interested in is exploring the affective dimensions of security labour alongside the categories of race and gender on a global scale. How are security labour activities divided along hierarchies of race and gender? Who does the dirty work, that work that is devalued and thankless? What labour is valued and recognized and what labour is rendered invisible?

Feminist scholars have been at the forefront of exploring both affective and emotional labour, conceptualising both in close proximity, with one often foregrounded as the primary term of analysis, depending on the analytical aim. These two forms of labour, in their embodied specificity within the global security industry, show that this kind of security labour is about producing affects for others to consume (making clients feel safe); doing reproductive work that sustains and makes security labour power resilient (keeping home life going); and metabolising unwanted affects and affective 'byproducts' of security work (Whitney 2017) (swallowing verbal abuse from Western clients and contractors letting off steam). By byproducts, Whitney means to include how producing affect for others invariably has constitutive effects for the subjectivity of the worker. In other words, looking at such byproducts can account for how and in what manner affect stays inside working bodies.

Emotional labour is embedded in the feminist socialist work of the 1980s onwards and tends to explore the feminising nature of 'women's work' and account for the broader global care work industries. It often refers to a post-Marxist critique on immaterial labour, including 'the toil of using ideation, imagination and performative speech and gesture to cultivate a specific state of mind or emotional quality in oneself and in the target consumer' (Whitney 2017, 20). Affective labour, alternatively, is generally referred to as 'the production and exchange of vital energy serving as a form of biocapital' (Whitney 2017, 656). Affective labour, a concept rooted in political economy scholarship, has a longer intellectual tradition within feminist research (Hochschild 1985; Weeks 2011). The concept has been used to understand the relationship between labour and capital from Fordist to post-Fordist society better – particularly how more global work involves affect in producing a positive and liveable environment for the client/consumer (Gutiérrez-Rodríguez 2010). Weeks's (2011) research is informative here. Her book

The Problem with Work showcases the affective dimensions of work, and in her case, the politics of postwork imaginaries that demand nurturing capacities to feel hope and/or mourning for (dys)topic work futures. Consequently, Weeks shows how affect becomes vital to understanding why certain political imaginaries fail whilst others succeed.

Feminist political economists continue to draw upon both forms of labour to demonstrate how work is often immaterial, gendered and raced, and how women and people of colour tend to take on more emotional work than (white) men do. The work of Hochschild (1985) on flight attendants producing a positive environment through a cheery disposition and that of Gutiérrez-Rodríguez (2010) on nannies and domestic workers producing a liveable and calming home for their clients both demonstrate this point. They, like other political economy feminists, tend to employ a Marxist-based gender analysis to showcase how affects circulate, and how those doing the affective work become exploited through the structural inequalities that rest upon Global South/North demarcations and raced/gendered divisions of labour (Anderson 2000; Salazar Parreñas 2008). Yet, as Brown (2016) reminds us, these relations and the affective labour contained within them are not owned by individual subjects such as 'the nanny', 'the child' or the 'client'. Brown focuses on the diverse everyday lives of global nannies and how they negotiate their own shifting subjectivities to produce a different vocabulary for how we talk about affective labour. Drawing upon Ahmed's understanding of affect, her work does not assume a common 'nanny' subject. Rather, she treats emotions such as 'love, care, guilt and abandonment as unstable commodities that are not possessed by a biological mother but rather as continually shaping subjects and their interactions with others' (2016, 211). By doing so, Brown 'historicizes and politicizes the effortful labor of care workers by linking embodied lives to a history of emotional associations with similarly raced and gendered bodies' (2016, 212). As such, certain bodies – in Brown's case, Global South nannies, and in mine, Gurkhas – have affective histories that enable a sticking of certain affects to them, with the understanding that these histories do not overdetermine their capabilities as individual selves. Overall, feminists who draw upon affective and emotional labour are concerned with what work is actually done, the nature of this work, and the ways in which feelings are negotiated and experienced through these working bodies (Brown 2016).

Feminist political economy work on affective and emotional labour is rooted much more in the political projects of recognising value in women's work, connecting reproductive work in the home to 'productive' economic spaces, and mapping out how the workplace is gendered and what kinds of labour are required and expected from women as opposed to men. Hochschild's (1985) work is exemplary in this case as it demonstrates how work gets assigned as women's work, and how feminisation as a political and economic practice devalues labour and the gendered harm done to women, as well as other socially marginalised communities. I follow a similar pathway by drawing upon both forms of labour to render visible the (in)visible security work and to show how forms of security work become racialised and gendered.

Throughout the over 180 interviews I conducted with various security contractors, managers and spouses, what became abundantly clear was the amount of affective labour that is done at all levels. This labour materialises in informal mentoring support of junior and racialised colleagues through training and professional networking. It is also observed in caring and pastoral work, largely done by the racialised contractors toward their (often white Western) clients. Moreover, it is demonstrated in the emotional work that spouses do to keep the physically absent husbands/fathers connected to their families back home. Affective labour can also be seen in the ways in which the men's work is honoured and valorised by spouses, in all the reproductive work done at home while these (mostly) men are away. While little research has been done to explore how the security industry is shaped by affect, feminist political economy scholar Hochschild (1985) has highlighted how this immaterial labour gets taken up in market relations. In *The Managed Heart*, for example, she asks what happens when the employer 'exercises a degree of control over the emotional activities of employees' and she also explores how capitalism begins to appropriate 'private' feelings for commercial gain (1985, 147).

When it comes to the security industry, looking into 'bringing affect to market' means beginning to render visible how security markets attempt to control (and commodify) how feelings are managed. Affect, emotion and feelings are deeply intertwined in the roles we understand immaterial labour to play in private security. Yet, as the following chapters will demonstrate, they are not the same; nor do they materialise in the same way in global security. When pointed at PMSCs, the lens of affective labour enables a rethink on how social hierarchies materialise between white Western security contractors and Global South contractors, particularly how Gurkhas' labour is often (de)valued and how more emotional work is demanded of them. Centring analysis on affect enables a further breakdown of conceptual divides between productive and reproductive work, why certain bodies do different work and how value in this work is articulated (discussed in more detail in Chapters 3, 4 and 5). My own research has also intimately connected the social reproductive work done in security households to how militaries and security companies wage war and conduct operations globally. This research has paid attention to the ways in which the household as an economic and security actor and site continues to be obscured from broader theorising about global economies of war and security. In all of these cases, the reproductive work done in these households becomes devalued through its association with women's work, yet remains indispensable in how global security is practised.

Doing the Affective Dirty Work

When a worker is obligated to absorb whatever customers choose to project without returning anything except a cheerful smile, then the task of feeling management becomes the task of containing others' waste affect in herself. (Whitney 2017, 648)

The final aspect of affective economies this chapter seeks to cover is that of 'affective waste' (Whitney 2017). Taken up in more detail in Chapter 5, the concept of affective waste illuminates the fact that emotional work is not one-directional – from worker to client/consumer. Affect also circulates back around, from the client/consumer to the worker. Whitney's 2017 research on affect as byproductive highlights how a part of producing affect for others to consume is also about absorbing other people's negative feelings.

As discussed, in my research, affect's waste, and those tasked to manage it, are revealed in how Gurkhas make an atmosphere conducive for security and making people feel safe, Here, I am reminded of a verbal exchange I witnessed between an affluent Afghan man and an ex-Indian army Gurkha officer while staying in a security company compound. The Afghan man began yelling at the Gurkha. The verbal abuse raised such a commotion that people came out of their offices to witness the exchange. While the Afghan man ranted and raised his hands toward the Gurkha's face to gesture in anger, the Gurkha quietly stood, arms by his side, not blinking or giving any emotional reaction. This abusive encounter was not a unique case, but rather the type of interaction that I witnessed numerous times as Gurkhas and Afghan security guards were talked down to by Western and non-Western expats alike. Such an exchange or circulation of affect exists to 'produce experiences of affective impermeability for privileged subjects at the cost of burdening marginalized others' (Whitney 2017, 649). As Whitney (2017) notes, the swallowing of this abuse stays in the bodies of those who are tasked with absorbing and metabolising unwanted affect. In this case, while the letting off of steam might regenerate the Afghan elite, the absorbing of this negative affect by the Gurkhas often leads to depletion. By accounting for affective waste, we address not only how affective economies might produce and redistribute life, making some feel safe and secure, but also the exploitative nature of these economies that leaves others depleted.

Taking into account Whitney's concept of affect as byproduct enables us to see the exploitation of certain security bodies and the regular wearing out of them. It raises questions around who is allowed to be the one who can yell and make a scene as a way of blowing off steam. Who are the ones who have to absorb these negative emotions, who have to stuff them down and not respond? And finally, why is it that the global poor, both men and women, are assigned to take on this type of dirty work? Again, returning to the feminist political economy work on feminisation and racialisation of global labour helps us conceptually think through the gendered and raced politics of global work.

Gutiérrez-Rodríguez's (2010) research on global nannies illuminates how the offloading of domestic work is felt as liberating and freeing to the (often white) female employers. At the same time, this work is loaded on to brown and black women, who, during interviews, stated their feelings of worthlessness and invisibility as they went about physically removing waste and dirt from the home. This waste removal was affectively experienced in how they felt about themselves and the (de)value of the work they performed. Yet, even in the more 'skilled' (often white) profession of airline attendant, as documented by Hochschild (1985), these (mostly) women absorb the negative affect of passengers while producing (successfully or otherwise) an affective atmosphere of cheerfulness and safety for the passengers. Whitney's articulation of affective labour as byproduct enables us to compare both these labour sites and bodies to show that, while both are metabolising negative affect, the racialisation of domestic work and the broader outsourcing to brown and black women's bodies also enable the deskilling, invisibility and further devaluing of this kind of labour (2017, 651). Whitney importantly connects this kind of division of labour to a broader global racialising of labour as part of an outsourcing of undesirable and dirty work to women and men from the Global South (2017, 652). Indeed, Western white women can uplift/upskill themselves by outsourcing domestic and caring work to immigrant, black and brown women in ways not open to women from the Global South. Placing the metabolising of negative affect on to these bodies can lead to what Berlant (2011) refers to as a 'slow death', meaning the ritualised and regular wearing out of particular communities and bodies.

Returning to the verbal exchange between the elite Afghan man and the Gurkha security contractor, the Afghan man can let off steam and perform a strong and aggressive masculinity to make himself feel better and to show his powerful presence. This affective performance is not open to the Gurkha. The Gurkha must stand and absorb this negative affect. It stays within him. In my subsequent interviews with other racialised security contractors, this very type of verbal encounter was articulated as one of the most significant points of wearing out – making these workers feel worthless and undervalued.

Taking affective labour seriously as a key form of labour in the service economies shows that emotional, spiritual and mental costs abound for those charged with producing positive affect and absorbing negative affect. Indeed, when taking into account affect alongside the other reproductive work, Whitney's (2017) and also Gutiérrez-Rodríguez's (2010) work prompts us to ensure we do not conflate all reproductive work. Rather, care work and domestic work often have different social markers attached to their value, as do the different bodies who do this kind of work. Care work continues to be professionalised and coded as feminine, whereas domestic work is still largely deprofessionalised, deskilled, 'dirty', emotional, and physical waste disposal work that is associated largely with brown and black women (Whitney 2017, 650).

Such dirty work in the security industry follows the similar racial and gender social hierarchies that feminist political economists have been discussing for decades.[18] In many of the various empirical cases within the textile and global care industries, both race and gender act as social markers that not only devalue the labour that these men and women from the Global South do, but also devalue their bodies – using them as affective waste-metabolising machines. Like feminist scholars such as Whitney (2017) and Peterson (2005), who caution us to think through how racial and gender hierarchies are re-established in how work is divided and valued, we also need to be mindful that private security work is not homogenous and similar hierarchies are re-established in who is tasked to do what security work – and at what costs to their own bodies and wellbeing. Like the 'women's work' that naturalises care work and labours of love as belonging to women's bodies, both gender and race are a form of labour (Whitney 2017, 654). This form of labour is also not exclusive to women and the work they do. Returning to the abusive encounter between the Gurkha and the elite Afghan man, the expectation on the part of the Afghan man that the Gurkha would absorb negative affect and not physically react to verbal abuses, the expectation of the latter standing stoic and being resilient, weighs down most heavily racialised security bodies. Labour of resilience and submission are thus naturalised on to Gurkha bodies. They stay in the worker's body and metabolise.

Overall, Whitney's (2017) affect as byproduct, alongside Brennan's (2000) affect as waste, prompts us to think about how affects produced for commercial purposes are not just about producing affect for the client's 'state of mind' or for a safe and secure atmosphere. Racialised and gendered security workers must also absorb negative affects, such as the anger and frustration of their clients and colleagues who let off steam. But who is allowed to let off steam and who must endure and absorb these affective wastes in sustaining a calm and secure atmosphere is heavily raced and gendered. Gurkhas would never let off steam toward their white colleagues nor toward their Afghan or Western clients.

Colonial legacies and the associated affective economies underpin and normalise these political economies of war. They are fundamental to maintaining a surplus in the global military workforce and reinforcing global hierarchies. Like the postcolonial military scholarship before me (Teaiwa 2011; Ware 2012; Barkawi 2017), my research illuminates understandings of militarism as a mobilising logic and feeling that supporting global warfare/security operations remains vital to waging war, but this operates differently in the everyday when taken outside the European/Western context. Beginning with the 'imperial encounter' opens conceptualisation on how militarism has enabled an uplift in economic and social status through (foreign) military service. Such analysis situates martial race as a disciplining and aspiring bonding discourse, and foregrounds the colonial bonds between 'ethnic' and 'British' soldiers forged through the act of war fighting. It is a bond that remains foundational to how Global South security workforces access security markets today.

It is these intersecting structures of imperialism, militarism and colonialism that produce what Ware (2012, 269–70) refers to as 'colonial military labour circuits' of the (cheap) surplus security labour forces utilised by both private security companies and the British military (Chisholm 2014a; Mynster Christensen 2015). Indeed, gender scholars within PMSC scholarship have shown how pathways to employment with PMSCs often occur through the same military colonial ties that have bound British officers to their ethnic/martial race soldiers (Barkawi

2017, 38–9) – with retired Western military officers championing and facilitating the employment of retired colonial soldiers and other militarised men of the Global South (Chisholm 2014a).

Affect and emotion enable a racialised and gendered devaluing of particular workforces as well as naturalising and inscribing labour roles on to them. This also enables a broader acceptance of the security market's status quo as normal – unfortunate, maybe, but certainly not political. It obscures the politics that underpin the archetypes of global security as white men and why Gurkhas remain their trusted martial race counterparts – men who, as Chapter 5 details, pick up the dirty work of private security. When thinking about how affect and emotions might stick to some bodies in different ways and how both position bodies in gendered and raced spatial positions, we see the ways in which hierarchies of global security workforces are sustained, naturalised and felt as 'just the market'.

Affect, Militarism and the Everyday

The following chapters anchor the above concepts in concrete practices and observations located within the everyday of security actors. I am inspired by Zoe Wool's (2015) exploration of the ordinariness observed in the everyday in her research on the after-war lives of US veterans in a Walter Reed rehabilitation centre. Like Wool's work, in this book, I position the analysis with individual militarised bodies who are caught between the extraordinary and the desire for the certainty of ordinary. My research departs from Wool's in that I begin with the martial, militarised Gurkha communities across Nepal, whose quest for the ordinary is set against a colonial geopolitical backdrop that marks everyday life with a high degree of uncertainty that involves accessing the materials necessary to keep life going. Ordinary is thus a future-orientated hope set against much uncertainty, not only within the socioeconomics of Nepal, but also for those martial contractors on the periphery of global security markets. The ordinary located in the everyday describes banal activities as a way to ground international processes and dynamics in concrete social interactions. These include how Gurkhas interact with Western security contractors and Western clients, how they move around a city and where their work is physically located. It involves the daily reproductive and domestic work that Gurkha wives do to keep their families going while Gurkha men work overseas, sometimes for up to two years at a time. It also includes the (largely Western) security clients and how they interact with Gurkhas, what security work they value and expect from them, and how this differs from what they expect from other security contractors.

The everyday is also a space in which concrete market relations are felt, experienced and practised.[19] The everyday is a perpetually 'fuzzy' and 'imprecise' concept (Elias and Rai 2019, 204). It remains appealing because it enables us to reorientate where we see 'the international' and who we see as important actors worthy of study. It also allows us to draw upon 'interdisciplinary dialogue' that can take our understanding of global security in novel directions (Elias and Rai 2019, 204). Feminists such as Enloe (1993, 2000) and Sylvester (2012) (amongst many more) use the everyday as an analytical entry point to study questions of war and insecurity. Enloe (1993, 2000) convincingly shows the investments that states make in everyday lives (and, indeed, in the lives of women) in order to wage war or advance militarism. Sylvester (2012) highlights how war is mediated through sensing, feeling and affectively connecting to war. Describing these varied everyday activities brings to life the concrete ways in which these different security actors shape, but are also shaped by, the global private security industry. Drawing upon the everyday as a key analytical entry point broadens who we see as involved in global politics and where. In understanding global security, it moves us from looking at the chief executives of PMSCs and state leadership also to include households, the clients, the displaced and the peace kept, for example.

The everyday is also marked by racism. This book is informed by, and builds upon, the exemplary scholarship of Marsha Henry. In particular, Henry's (2015) discussion of everyday peacekeeping is informative. Here, she describes how peacekeepers originating from Eastern Europe and the Global South carry with them multiple and contradictory identities as they manage the opposing demands placed upon them. These demands are mediated through what is expected of them as (racialised) peacekeepers within the UN working context. She engages with the concept of military capital to show how these peacekeepers draw upon different military logics and experiences to demonstrate their value within the global peacekeeping economy. This work builds on her 2012 'Peacexploitation?' publication that explored how the UN made use of gendered and racialised labour from women peacekeepers in the Global South to continue to extract workforces rendered cheap through global gendered, racialised and imperial structures. I build upon Henry's work by demonstrating the colonial histories that continue to stick to particular women and men. In doing so, I explore the various racial logics Gurkhas employ to increase their own value as security contractors, as well as manage and make sense of their own competing identities as providers and protectors.

As the following empirical chapters will demonstrate, the everyday makes visible the multiple spatial dimensions of the global security industry and illuminates the multiple actors involved in producing and valuing security practices. The everyday offers conceptual space to see how these concepts are made meaningful, given the various contexts, situated knowledges and positionalities of particular security actors. These include the everyday of the recruitment agents who market Gurkha talent through colonial tropes of martiality to the global industry; the security company directors who further champion Gurkha martial value; the security clients who place value on specific aspects of Gurkhas' security work; the Gurkhas themselves who emotionally and intellectually invest in their specific roles in the industry; and finally, the wives back home who offer indispensable emotional and affective labour in the broader service of the security industry.

The Gurkha subject offers a telling example of how affect, militarism, colonial histories and colonial political economies saturate the security industry. Still, they have yet to be systematically explored in broader discussions of security markets, and that is where my research comes in. I draw upon the entanglements of these aspects of security life specifically to render visible the emotional and affective care work being done by security contractors and spouses, and to uncover how this care work becomes naturalised on to brown and black bodies in the industry and how it is also devalued and not understood as core security work. I also use affect to explore how people, particularly those located at the peripheries of these markets, continue to invest affectively in the industry, despite the expectation that they will sacrifice so much for so little reward. Hope and happiness are central to keeping life going for communities who face incredible challenges whilst working in and supporting PMSCs. Affect animates how militarism is felt, sustained and structurally experienced for communities positioned on the periphery of global security markets. It materialises and is rendered meaningful in ambiguous and conflicting ways in everyday security spaces.

Bringing the everyday lives of Gurkhas and their families to the fore of my analysis shows that militarism does not have the same intellectual and affective investments or histories globally. While much is learned about militarism through the well-established feminist and critical military studies work, it remains predominantly located in European/ Western empirical cases and theorising. Militarism outside of these spaces is deeply entangled with caste, religion, imperial histories and, in the case of Gurkhas, economic precarity.[20] Militarism in the everyday, then, requires paying attention to how intersecting oppressive structures and logics condition how people negotiate global security markets, and how they invest in and understand their own militarised roles within these markets. It is the entangled colonial and military histories between the British and the Gurkha that have structurally and affectively shaped both security groups within global security markets, a thread to which the discussion now moves.

Notes

1. By this I mean that affective bodies include how bodies experience and navigate the world through what Värynen and Puumala refer to as 'sensuous effect' (2015, 238); the way in which the 'body senses pulses and rhythmically navigates' space and time, often unreflected and instantaneously (2015, 238).

2. Here I take note of and am indebted to the substantial feminist literature on the body and war. These include the work of Tidy (2019), who shows how the caring body features in sustaining nationalism. MacLeish's work (2013) specifically shows the trauma and scars that mark US soldiers and their families in the military community of Fort Hood. Väyrynen and Puumala (2015) detail how war connects bodies in different times and spaces, but also how war becomes normalised through daily rituals and routines. Overall, with this scholarship, I am committed to bringing bodies into the study of war to show the concrete and materiality of war, showing how war marks and makes bodies, and highlighting the diverse bodies that come to participate and experience war.

3. Feminists have drawn upon affect to develop further a standpoint for feminist analysis looking into power relations. See, for example, Clare Hemmings's (2012) work on cognitive dissidence and becoming a feminist, Judith Lakamper's (2017) work on cognitive dissidence and the foreclosure of solidarities, Sara Ahmed's (2010) work on affective aliens in the promise of happiness and Linda Åhäll's (2018) affect as methodology.

4. The affective turn in IR has brought important feminist criticism. This turn tends to treat affect as preconscious and rooted in biology, subsequently ignoring how affect is already gendered and raced (Åhäll 2018).

5. Both IR and feminist scholarships have a long tradition of drawing upon the concept of the everyday to locate the people-focused micro and banal practices of security and peace.

6. There is significant overlap in the two concepts within feminist scholarship and, indeed, in examples such as the domestic worker or the flight attendant; both affective and emotional labour describe the everyday work they do and how they are valued as economic and gendered subjects. The differences in concepts and terminology are rooted in the fact that they arise out of two distinct feminist intellectual traditions (Whitney 2017, 20). In feminist philosophy of

emotions, affect takes centre stage in working through how emotions work, how they circulate and how they become embodied through 'sticking' to different bodies. Sara Ahmed's (2004) 'Affective Economies' is exemplary of this type of theorising, where we locate emotions not as 'inside us', but rather in how they circulate, the affect surplus they produce and how they 'stick' to certain bodies.

7. To be sure, I am not interested in drawing clear distinctions between 'affect' and 'emotion', a move that tends to situate affect as 'outside' the realm of the social and as pre-personal (Hemmings, 2005; Ahmed, 2014; Pedwell and Whitehead, 2012; Åhäll, 2018).

8. See, for example, the works of Ahmed (2004) on 'structured feelings', Berlant's (2011) 'affect in crisis ordinary' and Åhäll's (2018) gender as affective structured feelings.

9. Ahmed (2004), in particular, talks about how 'the stranger', 'the immigrant' and the 'refugee' become saturated with affects of disgust and fear as they circulate in broader narratives around the state and citizens. This saturation occurs as these affects attach to the subjects and circulate in discourse – the more they circulate, the more affect they accumulate.

10. Attributes of fierceness alongside loyalty and bravery can be found in the following books written on Gurkhas: Christopher Bellamy's (2011) *The Gurkhas: Special Force*; Christopher Bullock's (2009) *Britain's Gurkhas*, Edmund Candler's (1919) *The Sepoy*; J. P. Cross and John Chapple's (2007) *Gurkhas at War: Eyewitness Accounts from World War II to Iraq*; Tony Gould's (1999) *Imperial Warriors: Britain and the Gurkhas*; Robert Hardman's (2010) 'As a Gurkha is Disciplined for Beheading a Taliban: Thank God They Are on Our Side!'; and John Parker's (1999) *The Gurkhas: The Insider Story of the World's Most Feared Soldiers*.

11. A kukri is a curved, bladed knife that holds practical, symbolic and mythical value. It is a symbol associated with Gurkha martial discourse and is described as their weapon of choice in battle (Gould 1999; Caplan 1995).

12. See, for example, the works by Åhäll (2018; 2016), Welland (2018), Gregory (2019), Howell (2015), Crane-Seeber (2016), and Chisholm and Ketola (2020).

13. See, for example, the works by Åhäll (2016), who draws upon militarism as affect to detail the hidden politics of militarisation, materialised through subtle movements, bodies and emotions; Crane-Seeber (2016), who explores how militarism is often pleasurable for soldiers; Dyvik (2016), who highlights how this pleasure is also experienced affectively through how we encounter military memoires; Welland (2021), who locates militarism as an affective relation binding US female military veterans to the joys of military service at the same time as experiences of sexism and racism; and Robinson (2016), who examines how affect in popular culture remains vital to the normalising of militarism as a logic and militarisation as a sociopolitical practice/process that is also at times exciting and pleasurable.

14. See Whitney (2017) for a detailed exploration of the key literatures and seminal texts in affective and emotional labour theorising within feminist and political economy disciplines.

15. Emotional labour was first documented in Hochschild's (1985) *The Managed Heart: Commercialization of Human Feeling*. Hochschild's exploration of flight attendance shows how this emotional labour is required to make passengers feel safe and to foster a cheery atmosphere.

16. Whitney's (2017), Hochschild's (1985), McDowell's (2009) and Wolkowitz's (2006) works on embodied labour in the service economy are exemplary.

17. See, for example, the work from Hardt and Negri (2001), where they highlight that under post-Fordism global economies, there is no longer a distinction between productive, material and reproductive labour. All labour takes on a form of biopolitical capital.

18. For striking examples of the gendered and racialised nature of global labour and how the devaluing of labour occurs through feminisation and racialisation processes, see the works of Henry (2012) on racial hierarchies in peacekeeping, Chisholm (2014b) on racial hierarchies in private military and security companies, Chisholm and Stachowitsch (2016) on the Gurkha security household labour in supporting recruitment into private military and security companies, and Whitney (2017) on racial hierarchies in global care and domestic labour chains.

19. Feminists and critical military scholars have drawn upon the everyday to conceptualise the ways in which emotions and affect feature in how global politics, security and war (Hutchison 2017; Åhäll and Gregory 2015; MacLeish 2013; Rashid 2020; Gregory 2019; Welland 2018; Baker 2020).

20. See, for example, the work by Henry (2017), Rashid (2020), Ware (2012) and Baker (2020) for substantive anti-race/critical race studies scholarship that highlights how militarism and militarisation materialise, are affectively experienced and are aesthetically represented in diverse ways.

CHAPTER 2

Bringing Martial Race to Market: Imperial Encounters, Militarism and the Making of Gurkhas

I was sitting outside in a small courtyard in the Jamsekal district of Kathmandu. It was just after lunch on a mid-summer afternoon and the sun cascaded through the tree leaves and branches that bordered the brick walls of the compound. There was a slight breeze in the air. Roshan sat down beside me as he handed me a cup of milky tea. I had gotten to know Roshan through my work with the security company at which he worked as a recruitment manager. His primary role was to recruit and assess local Gurkhas from the Indian army. Roshan was British, having received his citizenship when he served with the UK military during the 1990s. He spoke English with a subtle accent, with a pronunciation that most British people, attuned to regional accents and their association with class, would consider posh.

As we both gazed into the hazy blue sky that day, Roshan began to tell me a story about when he was selected to take an infantry battle course in the UK during the 1990s. He was stationed and trained in Hong Kong at the time and was surrounded by other Gurkhas and British Gurkha officers. He recounted how exciting it was to travel to the UK and how gruelling and frustrating the training was. As the physical fitness instructors and trainers barked orders in their Geordie or Liverpool accents, he and his other Gurkha colleagues tried their best to understand what they were being told to do. The instructors thought Gurkhas could not grasp basic military commands, rather than reflecting upon issues comprehending regional accents. 'We learned the Queen's English in Hong Kong, and we could not understand what these guys were saying and so we had difficulty following commands,' Roshan explained as he chuckled. I laughed along with this. As a Canadian migrating to the UK, I personally could relate to the difficulties of understanding the various regional dialects. (Fieldnote, Kathmandu, May 2017)

Introduction

The experiences of race and class and how these get lost in translation due to regional accents are certainly compelling stories to reflect upon. But what is important here is that this type of lost-in-translation experience was interpreted by the British national trainers to be a deficiency with Roshan and his Gurkha colleagues. The Gurkha men were written up in their assessments as being unable to follow basic military instructions. Instead of reflecting upon why Roshan and his Gurkha colleagues were not able to follow commands, their trainers allowed the Gurkhas' racialised bodies and colonial histories of being underdeveloped martial subjects to underpin how their capabilities were perceived. The common wisdom was that Gurkhas simply did not have the aptitude for this kind of military work.

Roshan's encounters with racism as a serving Gurkha illuminate the role that colonial history continues to play and how such histories, as Sara Ahmed (2004) says, 'stick'. This history shapes both Gurkhas as indigenous martial men and their British officers as the key people to know, mentor and develop these men from the hills of Nepal into successful military soldiers. For Roshan, being a Gurkha very much conditioned how his own experiences were mediated, classified and coded as a soldier with the British army. Such discussions connect to the broader experiences of military migrants working for the British military that Vron Ware (2012) demonstrates through rich empirical research. Ware articulates how the British military is structured through colonial histories and how these histories very much inform how men and women from Nepal and Fiji experience the British military. Like Fijian soldiers in the British military, Gurkhas are understood as being good, but as too literal. Gurkhas, according to their British officer counterparts, cannot follow basic commands. Gurkhas, it is said, require a particular type of leadership. All of these statements, voiced to me during multiple interviews with security contractors and security company managers, speak to a common sense around Gurkhas' natural place in military hierarchies.

The rest of this chapter proceeds with asking how Gurkha military histories shape the men's colonial present in the global security industry. I begin to account for how martial race – a racist governing logic through which the British came to know and understand their own superior positions alongside those indigenous communities that they deemed amenable to military labour within a broader colonial infrastructure – was central to producing these military gendered hierarchies. Martial race was the determining logic of who Gurkhas were and how they became valuable as soldiers, first for the East India Company and then, post the 1947 tripartite agreement, for the British military, the Singaporean police and the independent Indian army. Numerous historians and military scholars have written fascinating archival accounts of the ambiguities in the discourse and practice of martial race in India (Condos 2017; Das 2018; Barkawi 2017; Streets 2004; Caplan 1995; Sinha 1995; Enloe 1982), in Southeast Asia (Teaiwa 2005) and throughout Africa (Kirk-Greene 1980). This scholarship accounts for the contested nature of the logics behind the practice of governing indigenous soldiers during colonialism.

The second section of this chapter locates martial race as social capital within the current political economy of security recruitment in Nepal and in accessing the security market. I highlight how hierarchies of Gurkhas materialise differently, and show how security company owners and recruiters compete over who is in the best position to know, and to market, the so-called authentic Gurkhas. The final section brings in perspectives from the Gurkhas themselves and looks at how they make sense of their martial race in accessing global security markets. This section illuminates the distinctions between Gurkhas and their specific military training and how these distinctions are rendered more visible, not only in how the market establishes hierarchies and value, but also amongst Gurkhas themselves. Overall, this chapter highlights how martial race histories are drawn upon to offer currency for Gurkha security labour in today's security markets – labour that continues to be ordered and valued through their military relations with the British.

Martial Race and the Making of the Gurkha

The concept of martial race continues to be at the fore of historical and contemporary imaginings and reinterpretations of Gurkhas and their relations with their Western counterparts. Martial race is an array of ambiguous logics and practices, which Gurkhas, white British Gurkha officers and colonial administrators have all engaged with to varying degrees and in many contexts (Rand and Wagner 2012; Das 2018). Situated within the broader colonial administration policies and practices in India, martial race was not only about distinguishing 'martial' from effeminate, 'non-martial' local populations, but also about articulating 'who was currently fit for recruitment from those who were previously so, and hint[ing] at those who would be sufficiently [suited to a] martial future' (Singh 2015, 13). The ideology behind martial race was rooted in a long-standing belief that some communities were more inclined to violence and war, and thus better suited for military service than others (Singh 2015). The concept arose out of a colonial white imperial gaze, which perpetually depicted the indigenous soldier as exotic and raw (Das 2018). How martial race was applied and interpreted on the ground, though, was more ambivalent and haphazard (Rand and Wagner 2012; Singh 2015; Barkawi 2017).

The origins of the concept were first documented during British colonial control over India and then exported to other colonies (Killingray and Omissi 1999). Both France and Britain used martial race logics in varying ways on the local populations of their respective colonies, and, in the case of the US and Canada, on their First Nations populations (Holm 1996; Parsons 1999; Killingray and Omissi 1999; Des Chene 1999). Although classifying indigenous soldiers through a racial and caste lens was used as early as the late eighteenth century (Condos 2017), the Great Indian Uprising,[1] in 1857, historically marked the moment that the concept of a martial race began to be used as a key military strategy in order for the British to find trustworthy local soldiers (Barua 1995; Roy 2001). Pseudo-ethnography and ethno-photographic projects, alongside handbooks on martial race, flooded the market. British officers wrote about their regiments through the prism of castes and races. Such artefacts and pseudo-scientific inquiries continued post 1857, throughout both world wars and well into the establishment of independent India. This anthropological focus offered a framework through which Gurkhas and other martial raced communities could be understood in ethnological terms (Das 2018; Des Chene 1999). Pragmatically, using locals (or martial men from neighbouring regions) to police colonial states on behalf of the colonial administration was also a cheaper option, with less potential for the political backlash that could come from using more British nationals (Marjomaa 2003; Killingray and Omissi 1999). Consequently, building armies out of colonialised labour was an integral strategy for colonial powers (Enloe 1993, 79), and Gurkhas were a preferred indigenous group to recruit from, specifically after the Great Indian Uprising in 1857.

The intent was to create an ethnicity whereby military vocation was an integral identifying feature amongst the men in that group. By doing so, the British could draw upon a class of martial recruits who could be counted upon as reliable upholders of the colonial system (Enloe 1982, 25). Yet how the British identified which groups were martial and which were not remained largely undefined, with the decision-making process resting instead upon on the foundational knowledge and recruitment practices of both British officers and Nepalese local recruiters (Des Chene 1991). It was this very flexibility and ambiguity that left these so-called martial races adaptable to a variety of socioeconomic and historical contexts, as well as able to function to inspire, include, exclude and intimidate (Streets 2004, 4). In the UK, the martial race functioned as an inspirational tool for the image of British masculinity and racial superiority. In India, the concept of martial race served as a tool to exclude certain populations deemed untrustworthy and unsuitable for serving the British Empire (Sinha 1995; Streets 2004, 4). In both cases, gendered and racial imaginings of these men were crucial to constructing their particular soldier class. Indigenous groups of men deemed martial were thus positioned as the ideal colonial subject, and the men were constructed as opposites to Indian nationalists. They were said to be everything the Indian nationalist was not: brave, loyal and physically fit, with masculine prowess. Gurkhas were positioned in a privileged space amongst other Indian soldiers, soldiers otherwise referred to as sepoys. Because Gurkhas were understood not to have immediate political ties to India or a commitment to the cultural caste system, they were compared more to European soldiers, such as the Scottish Highlanders (Streets 2004). Gurkhas further entrenched their valued status when they sided with the British during the Great Indian Uprising (Streets 2004).

Discovering Gurkhas and the Anglo-Nepalese War

The British first encountered Nepalese men, later to become known as Gurkhas, during their expansion and colonisation of India in the late seventeenth century (Caplan 1995, 15; Coleman 1999). During this time, Nepalese foreign policy advocated self-sufficiency and isolation; the British knew little of Nepal or the people who inhabited the country (Coleman 1999). The Anglo-Nepalese War (1814–16) raised an awareness of the Gurkhas' status amongst the British. One British officer described the Nepalese enemies to the British as 'brave, sufficiently tractable and capable of sustaining great hardships' (Kirkpatrick, cited in Coleman 1999, 13). These men were named and understood through their battle pursuits. Whilst lacking in the equipment and military finesse of 'gentlemen British warriors', they were described as kind to their British prisoners and yet fierce in battle, where they illustrated brute determination (Coleman 1999). These descriptions, like earlier discourses around the Indian sepoys, emphasised the Gurkhas' bravery and gentlemanliness (Sramek 2011, 146). It was during this war, and the defeat of the Nepalese military forces, that the British first began to recruit Gurkhas into their ranks, but it would not be until much later that Gurkhas would receive the admiration of the British, detailed in their martial tropes of bravery, fierceness and loyalty (Caplan 1995, 19).

In order to build armies out of indigenous labour, the British had to persuade local rulers and the local labourers themselves that military service with the British was an attractive prospect. As a broader colonial project across India and what is now Pakistan, they had drawn upon local experts to recruit soldiers (Rand and Wagner 2012; Rashid 2020), and their recruitment of Gurkhas was no exception. To access new recruits from Nepal, the British focused on the borders of India, relying upon Gurkhas to go to villages and collect the men that the Gurkhas saw as suitable for military service (Des Chene 1991). Not surprisingly, the Nepalese government took issue with the British not involving them, and, indeed, for taking men from within their borders for foreign military work. They actively discouraged this type of recruitment by collecting and redistributing land known to belong to any Nepalese men serving with the British (Caplan 1995, 34). Despite this, the British managed to recruit Gurkhas into their ranks through the promise of financial gain (especially in comparison to the Nepalese policies, which left them impoverished) (Caplan 1995, 33), along with the opportunity for international travel (something valued within their communities) (Des Chene 1991). Far from being biologically determined for military service, the Gurkhas were thus recruited into the British military due to an East India Company military need, as well as the economic situation that the recently defeated Nepalese soldiers and their families found themselves in.

Like those of other martial race communities, Gurkhas were not passive subjects in this recruitment process. These communities, within both Nepal and what is now Pakistan, benefited economically and socially from participating in this colonial practice as colonial soldiers and recruiters (Rashid 2020). Gurkhas were called upon actively to collect the members from their villages that they viewed as appropriate for military service with the British (Des Chene 1991). Additionally, through their employment with the British and Indian armies, Gurkhas were able to provide economically for their families and communities. Caplan argues that villages to which Gurkhas returned home after their service experienced substantial social changes, which are directly attributable to Gurkhas' remittances arising from their military service (1995, 36–53). Caplan documents how Gurkha families built large homes, supported the start of local schools, and created new financial outlets for their communities to draw upon (1995, 36–53). They also brought back international knowledge and gifts that were valued within their local communities. By bringing back financial wealth and new cultural knowledge, Gurkhas were able to challenge the social hierarchy founded upon the social constructs of class and caste within Nepal, often to the frustration of Nepalese elites (Caplan 1995; Des Chene 1991).

Definitions of Gurkhas played an important role in recruitment. They were recruited from a specific geographical region of Nepal called Gorkha. At the time, this region consisted of people from four main ethnic backgrounds: the Magars, Gurungs, Khas and Thankurs. These so-called martial ethnic communities, identified by the British through these family names, also remained an important factor in identifying and constructing the Gurkha and where the British would focus their military recruitment drives (Parker 1999). The hills of Nepal were thought to produce rough and rugged men, which also had a role in determining their martial credentials (Parker 1999). These factors all played into producing a homogenous description of Gurkhas as men with a shared history, biology and geography. Once recruited, the men were regimented into particular military lifestyles that served to give them communal pride (Gould 1999; Streets 2004). The dress and rituals encouraged by the British developed over time. The British negotiated the process with great care, keeping in mind mutinies in the past and being keen to avoid disrupting the culture and traditions of the indigenous soldiers, such as by rejecting the use of leather in military uniforms to refrain from offending those who were Hindu. The mixture of dress and tradition therefore combined oriental and occidental traditions (Roy 2001). The Gurkha soldiers in turn performed the unfamiliar rituals and ceremonies demanded by the British military officers (Streets 2004).

Ever since the initial 'discovery' of the Nepalese hill men, the British, in collaboration with local Nepalese men already in service with them, have worked to construct detailed and homogenous descriptions of Gurkhas that persist to this day. Definitions of who Gurkhas are and their particular histories continue to be deeply political in contemporary British recruitment practices. Advancements in the socioeconomic status of Gurkhas and their families have often meant relocating to bigger city centres, where their sons and daughters receive private education. This urbanisation of Gurkha communities, alongside the UK military's employment standards requiring a higher degree of education upon entry, has meant that British officers can no longer recruit 'raw', talented young men from the hills of Nepal. In fact, as I learned in my conversations with many British Gurkha officers who actively recruit throughout

Nepal for the British military, the urbanisation of the 'hill men' has come as a disappointment. One British officer working at the British camp in Pokhara lamented to me during my last visit to Nepal in 2017 that young Nepal recruits have lost their 'raw' martial race through urbanisation.

The martial race attributes of Gurkhas were developed through a trial-and-error process within larger ideas of enlightenment and a Victorian enthusiasm for scientific classifications (Parsons 1999; Barkawi 2017). Climatic conditions, behavioural characteristics and physical qualities were all considered when classifying people as martial (Barua 1995; Lunn 1999). Asian men were measured, weighed and assessed, based on ideas of martial performance and cultural heritage (Tuker 1957). These classifications were further supported by sociological and anthropological research, along with military writings on the men (Caplan 1995). Within these Victorian practices, particular colonial masculinities also featured in dividing up military labour and were deeply connected to a larger racial hierarchy and civilisation/colonial policies (Sramek 2011; Sinha 1995). Being positioned as hierarchically closer to the European soldiers, Gurkhas' masculinities were captured in a preconceived can-do, flexible attitude toward the military demands on their lives. For Gurkhas, the military vocation came first (Caplan 1995, 25; Streets 2004). The racial and gender hierarchy not only positioned Gurkhas above the high-caste Indian sepoys from the Bengali army, but also assumed that the British would always remain at the top of the hierarchy. Therefore, both the British Gurkha officer and the Gurkha were constructed through colonial masculinities. Gurkhas were written about in sweeping colonial contradictions – they were fierce, yet innocent and playful, and maintained great physical prowess, yet were backward and simple. These colonial gendered tropes were rendered popular through photography and written descriptions, illuminating the exotic masculine sepoy for the benefit of the colonial gaze, and this continued throughout World War I (Das 2018). Such masculine tropes of the professional and gentlemanly British Gurkha managing the raw martial prowess of the Gurkha continues today in the branding of this 'security package' (Chisholm 2014a), a relationship I explore further in Chapter 3.

To reinforce British racial superiority over his ethnic soldiers, the British officer had to conduct himself with a high degree of professionalism and gentlemanliness in order to demonstrate British cultural and military authority to the indigenous military labourer (Caplan 1995, 61–3; Sramek 2011). His role was to lead the colonial armies by example. In turn, sepoys were to be ruled, and 'this rule could only come from the British for without the restraining influences of the British race, all would degenerate into anarchy' (Peers 1991, 568). Caplan discusses at length how representations of Gurkhas as martial raced men also assumed that British national Gurkha officers were naturally a part of the commanding class (1995, 55–86). British Gurkha officers at the time were disproportionately trained in public schools in the UK and carried a belief in being a chivalrous gentleman, as well as a belief in the white man's destiny as a governing race (Caplan 1995, 61–3). These men's cultural and professional upbringing thus reinforced their belief in their own superiority and natural suitability as the mentors of Gurkhas, as well as other indigenous soldiers.

In this colonial military force, the British officers have been positioned as the superior raced, masculine leaders, and the ones with the professional training and ability to mentor the indigenous soldiers. They underwent and continue to undergo specific leadership training, where they are required to learn the local indigenous languages and to spend periods of time in their soldiers' homeland and communities. This practice continues today. Tristan Forster recounted his own pseudo-ethnographic study of a particular Nepali village, conducted as part of his training to be a Gurkha officer (Interview, 28 August 2012), while Ian Gordon, the other security company manager I spent time with, recounted his fear of not being able to master the Gurkhali language well enough to command respect from his soldiers. In both cases, the British military institutionalised the British officers to lead with empathy and paternal care. However, this British performance has often been haphazard, and British officers have struggled to lead the Gurkha men through an ethnographic understanding of them, and of their caste, religions and geographical distinctions. The goal has been for Gurkha officers to have a fluent command of local dialects and languages, as well as cultural competencies around those of the Nepali so-called martial communities in order to lead Gurkhas, which many have failed to achieve (Barkawi 2017). Despite on-the-ground practices that have illuminated the ambivalence of these policies, it is this construction of martial logic that has positioned the British as the superior (natural) race and the Gurkha as the exceptional, loyal and almost-European soldier.

The loyalty of Gurkhas needs to be contextualised through military historians' writings on Nepal's economy during the time of initial recruitment of Gurkhas into the British military. These military historic writings illuminate the particular economic and social structuring that occurred in Nepal before and after the Anglo-Nepalese war. Prior to the unification of Nepal, the country consisted of many kingdoms, and slavery as a form of labour had long been practised within Nepal prior to the encounter with Britain. The active use of this type of labour was observed in the policies of Prithvi Narayan Shah, the Gorkha commander of Gorkha (a geographical district in Nepal), who encouraged servitude in his military ranks with the promise of land to his soldiers. For many young Nepalese men who were indentured to landowners under a monarchical system, this was an attractive means to further their own social status (Whelpton 2005). Not only did these soldiers receive land, but indentured labour was also enforced to increase cultivation productivity for the benefit of the military (English 1985). During Prithvi Narayan Shah's rule, those who did not meet the necessary cultivation production numbers were sold into slavery and lost access to their land. The numbers were significant. According to 'one officer of civil service in Garhwal, during the Gorkhali control over this region, two hundred thousand men, women and children were sold into slavery' (English 1985, 68).

This type of forced military labour also featured in the Nepalese defence forces during their operations against the British in the Anglo-Nepalese War (Coleman 1999, 21–2). Compulsory unpaid labour had deep roots in the Nepalese political economy, referred to as the Jhara system (Regmi 1976, 156). Irregular soldiers who were forced Nepalese labourers comprised a large number of the irregular fighting force. Under the Nepalese Jhara system, men from the ages of twelve to eighty were obliged to report for duty with two months of their own rations and their own rifles. The Jhara system was an economic system administered by the ruling Nepalese, who exacted compulsory unpaid labour from the peasants of Nepal. Such labour included military armed labour and logistical support for the military, such as by being a porter or building bridges. In return for their unpaid labour, the Jhara workers were often granted security through land-holding rights, along with an exemption (either partial or full) from paying taxes or homestead rents, though cultivation taxes were still required. The Jhara was used for irregular or more urgent needs, whereas the Rakam system was utilised for regular unpaid labour needs, which were specific to the location/village the Jhara worker belonged to (Regmi 1976, 156–7). Consequently, these men were given little to no remuneration for their service. Instead, men who served long enough with the Gorkha army in internal conquests during the unification of Nepal were given land. Conquered young men and Jhara workers were recruited to perform manual labour tasks on behalf of the military officers to whom they were assigned (Coleman 1999;

Regmi 1976, 157). Their labour was performed in exchange for food and was invaluable to military missions.

The Nepalese defeat in the Anglo-Nepalese War marked significant shifts in the political and economic positions for the men taking up arms against the British. The end of the war resulted in a defeated regular and irregular Nepalese army. Many of these men were faced with various economic and land policies after the Anglo-Nepalese war, after which castes such as the Brahmans, Thakuris and Chetris were privileged over the Gurkha castes (the Gurungs, Thapas and Magars), leading to increased land and wealth distribution inequalities (Caplan 1995, 28–33). These land and tax policies were coupled with the Brahmans, Thakuris and Chetris actively discouraging the Gurkha castes from joining the Nepalese military. Economic and military recruitment policies, as discussed by English (1985) and Caplan (1995), forced many Nepalese hill people into abandoning their lands and migrating to India to avoid the harsh restrictions of the administration. With few options for alternative means to support themselves and due to the social pressures and shame of being conquered, many men could not return home (Des Chene 1991). Joining the British military appeared to be their only option.

It is within this context that Gurkhas were willingly recruited en masse to serve with the British colonial army. Drawing upon these aspects of Gurkha history, critical scholars such as Enloe (1982), Caplan (1995), Parsons (1999) and Streets (2004) have re-examined the roots of martial loyalty – not in terms of martial biology, but in the realm of economic necessity. These writings work to demonstrate how the representations of Gurkhas were reflected in a struggle over access to newly emerging colonial economies and political identities. But perhaps the economic incentive remains a bit overstated. As Caplan (1995) documents, Nepalese men identified as Gurkhas had been migrating as military labourers long before the Anglo-Nepalese war and the British recruitment drive. Thieme and Wyss (2005) also document, and the following two chapters support, a belief amongst Gurkha communities that it is a rite of passage for Gurkha men (and women) to migrate for economic opportunities. What these studies suggest is that, in additional to economic incentives, there is a cultural incentive for them to work abroad as military labourers. These same economic inequalities and cultural and historic practices of military migrant labour continue to frame Gurkhas' willingness to participate as TCN labourers, underpinning the struggle over who can access Gurkha subjectivities within PMSCs.

The significance of the ways these new colonial economies, coupled with the cultural practices of migration labour, disciplined the subjectivities of the newly constituted martial men (and their communities) should not be glossed over. Whilst men like Gurkhas, understood as martial by the British, were complicit in the production of their martial races, and, as such, were also able to challenge socioeconomic positions back in Nepal, some men fared better than others in their new role as perpetrators of colonial violence. Most men who engaged with martial roles were, at some point in their careers, situated in highly dangerous places and expected at times to enact violence (Lunn 1999). As a result, many Gurkhas dealt with their martial gendered bodies and expected roles during violent encounters in conflicting ways (Des Chene 1991). For them, it was vital to believe prior to going into battle that one would not live. Being afraid of dying would mean that they were poor martial soldiers (Cross and Chapple 2007). This is a reminder of the psychological and emotional impact that the experience of being martial and participating as military labourers has had on many men deemed to be Gurkhas.

Legacies of Martial Race

Although employing martial race as an actual military logic fell out of favour and was ultimately rebuked for its dubious scientific and anthropological knowledge claims, it still appears as an important marker for community and personal identities for those who share these martial histories. Indeed, these logics operate as central in how the Gurkhas and their families throughout Nepal articulated their own identities and how they connected with their broader communities when I interviewed and spent time with them. Moreover, Gurkhas continue to be revered for their heroic pursuits amongst Westerners and those in the Indian military alike (Khalidi 2001–2), and the Indian army continues to use martial race logics in its recruitment of Gurkhas (Barua 1995; Marjomaa 2003). The legacy of Gurkha communities throughout Nepal and their economic and cultural footprint continue to be notable.

The retired Gurkhas that I spent considerable time with during my stays in Nepal were active in their local communities, building local libraries, cooperative banks and hospitals. Gurkha wives talked about how their husbands' foreign labour enabled them to send their children to British boarding schools, and to 'separate' from their in-laws' homes to build and live in homes of their own. The social capital of being a Gurkha or the wife of a Gurkha is also noteworthy. Both often offer

Figure 2.1 Retired British Gurkha pointing at medals on display in a living room area, in Pokhara, Nepal, November 2018. Photo credit to Robic Upadhayay.

financial assistance to the broader community and practise the high degree of autonomy that economic wealth brings them. The entire social fabric of these military communities is underpinned by the intergenerational foreign military service of Gurkhas. Boys are raised to aspire to become Gurkhas as a rite of passage and girls are groomed to become Gurkha wives, so much so that many young Nepali women choose careers in education or nursing, in the hope that they can easily transfer these occupations to the UK when they marry a British Gurkha.

These martial race histories also remain integral in understanding Gurkhas' roles in global security today. Martial warrior vignettes reinforcing racial and gendered tropes of Gurkhas, detailed at the beginning of this chapter, reappear in more contemporary stories. For example, Parker references the Gurkhas' unsophisticated nature in a humorous story of Gurkha learner drivers (1999, 21). Retelling a story told by Corrigan, a former British Gurkha officer, Parker describes how many British Gurkha officers during their time in Nepal avoided using the same roads as Gurkha learner drivers. As the story goes, the learner drivers attempt to come to attention when passing the officers and this 'is not necessarily conducive to safety on the Queen's Highway'. While intended to elicit humour, this story is also typical of what Des Chene (1991) describes as vignettes designed to reinforce the Gurkhas' subaltern and underdeveloped status. In the story related by Parker, the Gurkha is most concerned with displaying his adherence to military rank and hierarchy, even at the expense of road safety. These stories tell us that Gurkhas are both brave and naturally fierce warriors, but also that they remain simple-minded and naïve, and therefore require the British Gurkha officer to mentor and manage them. As such, the stories not only are about Gurkhas, but also say a great deal about the British officers and their role. It is the retelling of the entangled histories between the British officers and Gurkhas that continues to bind them in the present, as both find their way into global private security markets (Chisholm 2014a, 2015a). Martial race, then, remains an important shared history for Gurkhas and Gurkha officers. This history entangles the men together in what was referred to in interviews during this research as the 'Gurkha family' and demonstrates both the emotional and the financial incentives involved in becoming a Gurkha.

Gendered Hierarchies, Colonial Affects and the Marketing of Gurkhas in Global Security

Nepal continues to be an impoverished country with severely limited employment opportunities. Faced with few educational and labour opportunities, it has a long history of state-sponsored, international migration of its citizens for economic reasons. Statistics from the International Labour Organisation (ILO) indicate that out of the 26.495 million people in Nepal, nearly 2 million are formally working outside of Nepal (ILO 2014), double the global average of economic foreign migration (Shrestha 2017). As of July 2011, unofficial government documents had recorded 2.08 million Nepalese migrants leaving Nepal and India for temporary work internationally each year (Sijapati, Limbu and Khadka 2011). Nepal is a country rooted in economic migration and relies upon the remittances sent home by these labourers. Men, women and children all migrate to India, the Middle East, Hong Kong, Japan, the United Kingdom and Central Asia to pursue economic opportunities (Seddon 2005; ILO 2014). However, as the regulations surrounding the migration of Nepalese people are underdeveloped and poorly managed, these Nepalese citizens are vulnerable to human trafficking and forced/bonded labour.

Gurkhas are situated within this economic environment but, compared to their fellow citizens, they are in a position of structural privilege.

The social capital and material wealth that result from becoming a Gurkha can be brought back to communities throughout the country that struggle with reproducing everyday life, a reality that has been acutely observed (Chisholm and Ketola 2020; S. Sharma 2020). This is so much the case that the British Gurkha selection process, which occurs once a year, continues to attract roughly 4,000 young Nepali men aged 17–21 to the broader training centres of an industry that profits from their hope of becoming a Gurkha. The global demand for martial (disciplined) labour, coupled with the limited economic opportunities for Gurkhas, makes Nepal an ideal ground for recruitment of TCNs into private security. Gurkhas have a long history as military migrant labourers. They tend to migrate internationally for economic reasons and continue to work in a militarised field where their military skill sets can be utilised, a motivation also reflected in many former soldiers' participation in the security industry (Thieme and Wyss 2005). For Gurkhas, labour migration is seen as a way of life and as honourable work (Thieme and Wyss 2005). Additionally, because of their martial race reputation, the men are typecast, so it is difficult for them to find employment in any other national or international industry (Kochhar-George 2010; Thieme and Wyss 2005).

Foreign migration of security labour from communities deemed martial is not new. Those men who were deemed martial from their colonial encounters and service have drawn upon their own martial identities to access security work across the British empire in the late nineteenth and twentieth centuries as military police labour (Condos 2017; Metcalf 2007). Such imperial circulations of military labour have grown more global in contemporary security markets. According to the Nepalese agents and security company owners I interviewed, their martial race status and global reputation allow Gurkhas to fill a niche role in security, including as unarmed static guards in the Gulf States, as state protection providers in Brunei and Malaysia, as global cruise line security with companies such as Princess Cruises, and as security contractors in Iraq and Afghanistan. Notably, the actual number of Gurkhas working in private security is not known. According to a representative of the Nepal Ministry of Labour, 1,198 Nepalese men were formally employed in Afghanistan in 2010.[2] In 2008, a Swiss Peace report documented roughly 4,000–6,000 TCNs working in Afghanistan (Joras and Schuster 2008). FSI WorldWide, a Gurkha security company operating within Nepal, claims to have 3,000 Gurkhas employed globally, and IDG, another Gurkha security recruitment company in Nepal, claims to have 2,500 Gurkhas working globally.[3] In 2016, in a personal interview, a representative of Nepal's Department of Foreign Employment (DoFE) unofficially estimated 3,500–4,000 Gurkhas to be working internationally; however, considering that FSI WorldWide and IDG Security alone record that number on their payrolls, the number of Gurkhas seeking employment abroad is likely to be much higher. Overall, recorded numbers offered remain outdated, anecdotal and contested. This is largely the result of both security companies and nation states (both home and host countries) not keeping accurate records. Moreover, even when records of foreign migration are kept in Nepal, definitions of what constitutes security work are contested and numbers of Gurkhas are unavailable.

Adding to this statistical problem, many Nepali Gurkhas are recruited through India, thereby bypassing Nepalese governing institutions altogether. These informal recruitment and employment practices related to Gurkhas are not something unique to them, but speak to other literatures that track the migration patterns of men and women from the Global South, including other migrants from Nepal. For migrant workers in the Global South, accessing employment through informal networks is central to their migration. This unregulated access to international employment can increase opportunities for men and women, but at the same time makes them vulnerable to exploitation and bonded labour (Sijapati, Limbu and Khadka 2011). This is in part because, while Western companies rely upon their lower-priced services, these same companies do not have immediate access to these labour pools. Instead, most Western companies depend upon in-country recruitment agencies. Because migration levels are high in Nepal, local recruitment agencies are a big business in the country. In the same interview conducted with the DoFE representative in 2016, I was told there were 769 registered recruitment agencies. While the Nepalese government attempts to regulate these agencies, growing anecdotal evidence suggests that many practise extortion and bonded labour in order to garner more profits. For instance, during my interview in 2012 with Tristan Forster, CEO of FSI WorldWide, he mentioned a US government contract he took over from a well-known Western PMSC, where many of the TCN contractors staffed were working in-country with a visa for travelling, not working. These contractors had incurred substantial debt with local agents to enter the country for work and faced regular threats from those agents to repay the loans. In addition, Gordon and other Gurkhas interviewed, such as Jitendra and Roshan, referred to a local community called 'the warehouse', where Nepalese men who had gained entry into Afghanistan on traveller instead of work visas were held in precarious political and economic positions until they could find work. In these cases, as Bishal, another Gurkha, informed me during his interview, the men wait to be 'rescued' by PMSCs based in Kabul; they rely on these PMSCs to give them a job and obtain the necessary work visa for them, as there is no Nepalese embassy in Afghanistan to appeal to. For such men, being 'rescued' has become even more of an acute need with the recent transfer of power to Taliban in Afghanistan and the mass evacuation of people who have worked for foreign companies.

The issues of forced and bonded labour,[4] which plague labour practices in Nepal, as well as adult bonded labour, are largely unexplored (Sijapati, Limbu and Khadka 2011). Practices of both bonded and forced labour were raised throughout my interviews with Gurkhas and Gurkha security company owners. While British Gurkhas could largely escape these practices, Indian Gurkhas and men from Nepal being represented as 'Gurkhas' but with little to no military training were more vulnerable. These stories have given rise to another struggle, which is over who and what constitutes a Gurkha. The ideal around who a Gurkha is remains contested but, in general, security practitioners I talked to defined a Gurkha within private armed security as a Nepalese national with British or Indian military training, or Singaporean police training. In unarmed security, who can lay claim to the identity of Gurkha is more expansive. Recruitment agents in interviews described Gurkhas as Nepalese men and women with Nepalese police or military experience.

Throughout my interviews with security practitioners in Kabul, the men who did not have formal Indian or British military or Singaporean police training were reported to have faced high levels of exploitation and extortion by rectruitment agents, with the promise of obtaining work abroad. Many, as indicated above, had accumulated debts, were isolated from larger communities within Afghanistan and were in the country illegally, having gained entry on a tourist and not a working visa. While documentary tracking of these practices within the industry remains limited, desperate economic situations within Nepal are likely to be the primary reason why men and women are willing to take on particular forms of labour that make them vulnerable to exploitation.

Despite, or perhaps because of, Gurkhas' economic and peripheral political positions in global economies, these men are seen as the ideal Global South security contractors by PMSCs. As with other globalising industries that exploit the economically impoverished positions of men and women from the Global South, making these labourers more adaptable to precarious work (Phillips 2011, 63), PMSCs seek Gurkhas under the same impoverished economic conditions – conditions that make Gurkhas more amenable to particular forms of security labour. This work remains indispensable in global security operations. As Barker (2009, 2015) illustrates, TCNs' supportive labour is a central and fundamental feature of contemporary US military operations. She argues that the raced and gendered subjectivities of men from the Global South, coupled with their economic plights, reinforce a colonial-style division of labour whereby race foregrounds divisions between the US soldier/Western contractor and the non-white, mas-culine, supportive labourer. Economic conditions coupled with raced practices in the production of a Global South labour force also appear in private security. Gurkhas' position at the periphery of global eco-nomics, coupled with their 'martial' race, conditions these men to take up more precarious work. During my interviews with Gurkhas and British Gurkha officers who were now security company directors, it was made clear that Gurkhas continue to be seen in terms of their raw martial talent, and as needing to be managed by men who know them and understand their abilities in order to get the best out of their labour. This was captured best in an interview excerpt from the CEO of FSI WorldWide, Tristan Forster, one of the security company directors and former British Gurkha officers I spoke with at length around the uniqueness of Gurkha security labour:

> It all comes down to the training. The raw material is key and outstanding, if you are recruiting from the right areas and the right people. The trick is the training that turns that raw material into someone who is incredibly disciplined and proud. If you go into Nepal, into the hills, you will meet guys and girls, very tough, not a huge amount of discipline, not forward thinking . . . similar issues you would find in [inhabitants of] developing countries . . . then you bring to it this tradition, this history. Had the Indian army never recruited the Gurkhas, who knows what sort of honour and bravery would have been observed today. But certainly, wherever we've taken these guys and trained them, they have been outstanding and continue to be outstanding on military operations and peace training. (Interview, 28 August 2012)

As I will discuss in the following chapter, it is this colonial logic of raw martial talent being managed by the British Gurkha officer, who is in the best position to know and mentor these martial soldiers, that continues to underpin the 'uniqueness' of the Gurkha security package (Chisholm 2014a).

Martial Race from the Perspective of Gurkhas

The previous sections of this chapter largely focused on how the British have imagined Gurkhas and operationalised martial race as part of a colonial administration practice around the recruitment and management of indigenous military labour. I then explored how such histories are taken up in the broader imperial circulation of these military labourers and in contemporary recruitment and security branding in PMSCs. In this final section, I pay attention to the voices of Gurkhas to uncover how they understand these histories. By doing so, I further demonstrate how this history and the way it is interpreted and is given meaning remain ambiguous and immediately connected to the broader socioeconomic contexts in which martial race is situated.

Gurkhas continue to draw upon this martial race history in defining their own value in the security industry. Perhaps unsurprisingly, the Gurkhas I interviewed and spent time with drew less on the contradictory colonial tropes of innocence and playfulness and more on the trope of martial prowess. They used the language of discipline and bravery to showcase their military attributes. These men also spoke of heritage, particularly in terms of their surname being associated with martial race histories, to articulate how being a Gurkha is hereditary – thereby demonstrating that not just anyone can become one. One is born into a Gurkha family. The latter point indicates that, for these men, it is not just anyone that can be defined as a Gurkha. It is due to this exclusionary concept, coupled with their military attributes, that these men saw themselves as exceptional and thus proudly asserted their identity to me. Their use of the language of surnames and family heritage, and even geographical birthplace, was also designed to differentiate between themselves and the broader Nepali community. The Gurkhas viewed their own community as needing specifically to have a military/police service background and international experience. In a focus group with Gurkhas working as security contractors in Afghanistan back in 2010, when I asked what a Gurkha was, they responded:

> We are Gurkhas because we are working in security and we have worked in the army . . . our ancestors, our father and grandfather, mostly they joined the British army and the Indian army. So, it's our blood, in our blood cells, to protect the different parts of the world. (Focus group with Fabian, Puk, Tek and Jitendra, 11 May 2010)

These Gurkha histories are also affectively experienced. The focus on natural and intergenerational military aptitudes has continued to be reinforced in the multiple conversations I have had with Gurkhas over my years of research into their lives and experiences. Again, to return to Jitendra's statement, quoted at the beginning of Chapter 1, it shows how affective relations hold these men in dangerous situations: 'I was afraid. But I also knew I was a Gurkha and Gurkhas do not run. I had to be strong. It's in my blood.'

Some, like Randhoj, poke fun at the colonial legacies of Gurkhas. A retired British Gurkha, Randhoj was in the process of obtaining UK settlement status for himself and his family when I met him in 2010. Randhoj was a great storyteller, easily able to draw his audience into the various details of military history, his own childhood and the broader cultural politics within Nepal. While he and I were visiting the British Gurkha museum in Pokhara, we were confronted with a series of black and white images of Gurkhas standing next to and in close proximity to their colonial British officers. The imagery and curating of the museum had reinforced what Das (2018) describes as a colonial imperial gaze on the men – capturing their exoticism and rawness. As we both gazed at an image of a physically taller white officer standing in front of some smaller Gurkha men who were in formation during a military inspection, Randhoj told me another story about the famous exotic Gurkha:

We were on parade and standing in formation waiting to be inspected by our British officer. He had brought his wife along to see the Gurkha men he'd been working with for so long. She had never seen a Gurkha in person before. As he moved along, inspecting each soldier, his wife by his side reached out to touch one of us, saying 'Oh, how cute.' Quickly, our officer rebuked her in a sharp tone: 'Don't touch the Gurkha.'

While we both laughed, for me, his playful retelling of the 'Don't touch the Gurkha' story demonstrated the absurdity of the Gurkha colonial trope. Randhoj's retelling turned the confronting colonial gaze depicted in the images we both looked at back on itself. This story, a culmination of multiple stories of Gurkhas that Randhoj told me over the months we spent together, produces a much more complicated history of what it means to be a Gurkha. Randhoj, like all the other Gurkhas I spent time with, no doubt affectively connected to this intergenerational history. As we continued to move through the exhibit, we paused at the sign above the doorway and he read out the words: 'It's better to die than live like a Coward.' Here, Randhoj smiled as his body stiffened a bit. I could feel his pride and I stood quietly beside him, smiling with him. Perhaps obviously so, Randhoj and other Gurkha men I spoke with over the years related more to the martial prowess and bravery than the infantilising 'rawness' articulated by the British officers.

Throughout my interviews with and observations of Gurkhas, the men were committed to upholding the intergenerational legacy of Gurkhas as brave, loyal, and disciplined. Expressed not only when they explained why they stay in and endure inhospitable and dangerous places, the Gurkha subject also mattered in how they articulated themselves as fathers and husbands. I have written elsewhere how Gurkhas in Afghanistan described their security contracting work as a sacrifice – one that they did not want to pass along to their sons (Chisholm 2014a).

During my time in Nepal with Gurkha families, Gurkhas and their wives would joke that they would encourage their sons to become Gurkhas only if they failed at school or at business. Indeed, it is only when I began to ask Gurkhas how they understood themselves beyond the military martial myth – as sons, as fathers and as husbands – that I began to understand the sacrifices and the trauma that these men experience as part of their military labour, and why they might not want the next generations to continue with this type of military work.

Figure 2.2 Young Nepali man training at a local Gurkha training centre in the hopes of becoming a Gurkha, in Jhapa, Nepal, August 2017. Photo credit to Robic Upadhayay.

It was when I began to ask the men questions about being a father, son and husband that I also began to learn about the emotional toll of being a Gurkha. The men had experienced long separations from their families and endured feelings of sadness when, on their return home, their young children had run away from them because they did not know who they were. They also managed broader anxieties around balancing pursuing military service (and dangerous deployments) with their commitments to family life, and being the breadwinner weighed heavily on them.

Despite these hardships – and always running parallel with them – there are feelings and experiences of privilege. In all of this, there is a political economy that underpins how Gurkhas understand themselves as martial men. Because of the financial and social wealth that becoming a Gurkha can bring in accessing global security markets, there is a lot at stake in declaring oneself a Gurkha. Becoming a Gurkha is a game changer for young men and their communities. It can wrest people out of poverty and significantly improve their life choices and their options around what 'the good life' might mean for them and for their families. Determining who gets called a Gurkha in global markets is something that security company owners, local recruiters and Gurkhas themselves all have a vested interest in. Consequently, through these contestations, a hierarchy of Gurkha materialises – as does an associated value. While there is certainly a pervasive homogenous Gurkha global reputation that persists, not all Gurkhas are the same; nor do they all have equal access to global security markets. How British Gurkha officers rank Gurkhas and how Gurkhas understand their own value as TCN labourers do not always align. In many ways, these hierarchies are reproduced through a language of authenticity and military training, but established hierarchies reflected in the market are also resisted. It is through this resistance that we can observe the potential for agency in the disruption of the homogenous Gurkhas as a martial raced logic.

In the majority of my interviews and throughout my fieldwork, an overwhelming hierarchal classification of Gurkha persisted within the security industry context. That is, the British Gurkha was considered the most valued, then the Singaporean police Gurkha, followed by the Indian Gurkha. The valuation of these tiers of Gurkhas rested upon the amount of economic wealth and immediate association with the British that these separate services could bring. The prestige of being a British Gurkha was, and remains, sustained through the potential not only for financial wealth, but also for international travel and the ability to reside in the UK. The intense selection process for becoming a British

Figure 2.3 Young Nepali men smile at a local Gurkha training centre, in Jhapa, Nepal, August 2017. Photo credit to Robic Upadhayay.

Gurkha also reinforces the martial masculinities and exceptional status a Nepalese man will be afforded if he is successful.

For the men, coming from the Singaporean police, the Indian army or British military and having overseas experience, combined with the appropriate Gurkha family history and bloodline, meant that they were Gurkhas. Yet, I also observed privilege amongst Gurkhas in how the men accessed the market – through either agents or direct contacts – and/ or in how they viewed the monetary value and labour opportunities afforded to each tier of Gurkha. Access immediately privileges those British Gurkhas who have personal connections to the Gurkha officers who have become security company directors.

Distinctions amongst Gurkhas begin to arise when they first attempt to access the security market. It is during this initial phase of access that the men become aware of how security markets distinguish between Gurkhas and value some more than others. All the Gurkhas I interviewed had often begun their journey into contemporary private security through word of mouth from others working within the industry. In order to gain employment with foreign companies, most of the men interviewed had to be vetted locally and some had utilised a local agent. This is a common practice for any migrant labourer (Thieme and Wyss, 2005). But finding the right agent can be risky and the stakes of getting it wrong are high. The agencies act as the mediator between the international employer and the Gurkha seeking employment. They promise the employer authentic Gurkhas, based on the popular martial raced history, and promise the Gurkhas a chance to continue to work abroad. Many Gurkhas pay a considerable amount of money to agents and to employers to access international work. This type of experience with agents is being increasingly documented by academics studying Nepalese economic migration practices (see, for example, Thieme and Wyss's 2005 discussion of the use of agents in labour migration).

Because of the risk associated with agencies, finding the right agent is important. Sante, an Indian Gurkha, believed that agents registered in Nepal were the ones to be trusted. He stated that a lot of Gurkhas are taken advantage of when they pay agents: the 'agents [are] getting a bunch of money from these men and these men's families to get over here and then have little opportunities ... The Nepali Gurkha is so happy that someone will get him a job and will immediately trust on him.' Sante stated that it was important to be vigilant, but also highlighted how the Nepalese Gurkha is perhaps the most disenfranchised of all the Gurkhas, having no formal contacts with military Gurkha officers outside the Nepalese army. Because of this tier of Gurkhas' peripheral position amongst Gurkhas, I was told during interviews with Indian and Singaporean police Gurkhas that these men are seen as the most vulnerable and most inexperienced in the perils of the marketplace. The Nepalese Gurkha is therefore the one most likely to be exploited because of his perceived innocent and trusting nature. Fabien, another Indian Gurkha, approached entering the market in more fatalistic terms. He stated that finding a good agent depended a lot on luck:

> Sometimes it's promised to get a good service and sometimes it's ok and sometimes it is not. Sometimes [a Nepali contractor] is staying at a local camp and we need money, and we call our family please send us 1,000 dollars [USD], we are hungry. Sometimes there are visa problems, and he is in jail. (Interview with Fabien, Kabul, Afghanistan, 7 May 2010)

Fabien positioned himself and other Indian Gurkhas at the periphery of security markets and subsequently saw himself as vulnerable. While British Gurkhas have immediate access to (white) security company owners, for most Indian Gurkhas the agent remains the vital link for contract opportunities.

Being associated with the British through the Singaporean police or British military means more immediate connections with the security companies. While the men described themselves in interviews as all part of the same Gurkha caste or community, British and Singaporean police, because of their military affiliations with white Westerners, are more privileged amongst all the Gurkhas when it comes to accessing the security industry. Not only is the difference amongst Gurkhas realised once they attempt to gain access to the security market, but it also becomes inflated once the men begin work within the security market. These differences mirror the tiers of Gurkhas and the impact on what jobs the men can procure. Throughout my observations of Gurkha security contractors, it was the Gurkhas trained by the British military and Singaporean police who managed to obtain the managerial positions over other Gurkhas. Indian Gurkhas almost always were in positions of static guard or convoy protection.

Gurkhas legitimised these differences. When speaking with me one to one, Jitendra commented that 'the British do more training, so the training side, [is] very good in British' (Interview, 3 May 2010). Kitendra furthered this notion by stating that 'they [the Indians] are better in battlefield, but tactically the British are better because they have more training and newer equipment' (Interview, 12 May 2010). British Gurkhas and Singaporean Gurkhas were also said to be better suited for managerial roles: first, because these roles require a good command of the English language in order for the men to be able to converse with country managers and clients; and second, due to the managerial skills these Gurkhas gain in their respective military or police training. Indian Gurkhas, I was told, are more suited for static guard work because of their military training, which, according to the men, makes them more amenable to working long and tedious hours in harsh climates. They have the physical stamina to perform well under these pressures, whereas, Kitendra and Jitendra both stated, British and Singaporean Gurkhas lack this stamina but have the intellect to conduct managerial skills. Thus, hierarchies exist not only between Gurkhas as they access the market, but amongst Gurkhas and other TCNs and Western contractors.

Conclusion

Different challenges for both Britain and Nepal came after the Anglo-Nepalese war. Out of these, recruiting the desirable and sought after so-called martial race Gurkhas remained a problem for the British.

While the Nepalese government worried about training and arming Nepalese citizens to fight for another national army, the British were able to influence the Nepalese government with financial incentives to recruit Nepalese nationals en masse during both world wars, to fight in Europe on Britain's behalf (Coleman 1999; Gould 1999). The legacies of Gurkhas' martial race histories and their over 200 years of military service continue to mediate who they are as security contactors and their value to global security markets.

Many Nepalese men have chosen to seek employment with the British colonial armies partly because of the financial benefits inherent in doing so (Parker 1999). There is a certain degree of coercion embedded in this choice that arises through entanglements of colonial economic structures and affective relations to militarism and military service (Chisholm and Ketola 2020). It is within this position that the British have recruited the 'willing' and 'loyal' Gurkhas. Despite the economic and political influences that contextualise Gurkhas' participation as martial warriors – first in the British colonial army, and now in both the British and Indian armies and in private security – for many Gurkha and British officers I interviewed, Gurkha martial race history has a strong resonance in their daily lives. Indeed, this affective bind reinforces the Gurkha security package, dividing security management and security protection work in an almost seamless way between the British officers and Gurkhas. It is this relationship, and how it manifests in the Gurkha security family, to which we now turn.

Notes

1. How this event is referred to is deeply political and contested. In general, the uprising has also been referred to as a 'war of independence' a 'rebellion' and a 'mutiny'. For a detailed account of this uprising and its multifaceted nature, as well as the British response, read Clare Anderson's (2007) *The Indian Uprising of 1857–58: Prisons, Prisoners and Rebellion*.
2. This statistic is based on an interview I conducted with a public service representative within the Nepal Ministry of Labour in May 2010.
3. Statistics from IDG Security website, 'About Us', available at: <https://idg-security.com/about-us/> (last accessed 13 September 2021).
4. The ILO defines forced labour as all work and services that are 'extracted from any person under the menace of any penalty and for which the said person has not offered himself/herself voluntarily'; see ILO conference 89th Session and International Labour Office, *Stopping Forced Labour: Global Report under the Follow-up to the ILO Declaration on Fundamental Principles and Rights at Work,*

Geneva 2001, cited in Sijapati, Limbu and Khadka (2011, 14). Bonded labour is a form of forced labour, in which the labourer participates in a 'hybrid of credit and labour agreement, whereby the provision of labour serve[s] as a collateral for a loan' (Sijapati, Limbu and Khadka 2011, 26).

CHAPTER 3

Locating Love in the Gurkha
Security Package

Our heritage is founded in the culture, expertise and values of the Brigade of
Gurkhas of the British Army. As the Gurkhas say, 'Hami Jasto Kohi Chhaina'
(There is nobody quite like us). We now employ more than 2,500 people
including former Gurkhas as well as experienced security guards from around
the world. They are united by a common commitment to IDG's Code of
Honour. The Code lays out our combined responsibility to the personal,
familial and social welfare of all of our staff and ensures that only the very best
security specialists wear the IDG badge.[1]

In the previous chapter I explored how martial race histories came to
matter in producing Gurkhas as racialised soldiers – valued for their
martial prowess, their unfettered loyalty and, at times, their childlike
and playful nature. I showed how these histories, within a hierarchy of
men and masculinities, naturalise Gurkhas as perpetually the subaltern,
causing them to be understood and valued in terms of how they measure up against the fully developed and professional white British military officer. In this chapter, I investigate how these histories underpin
contemporary global security markets. Imperial encounters continue to
be affectively felt in everyday security encounters between Gurkhas and
their British Gurkha officers, now security company owners. In short,
Gurkha histories are affectively lived in the present and this chapter
explores how.

Affects of honour, duty and reciprocity manifest in ways that reinforce
Gurkha recruitment and security company owners' own self-imaginings
as the liberal-minded and ethical guardians and custodians of Gurkhas,
as well as the protectors of their heritage within security markets. These
same affects, structured within the same shared colonial histories, also

create Gurkhas as dutiful security contractors. Such gendered and racial-ised tropes enable a seemingly timeless and clear division of labour and expertise that each of the two groups takes on and affectively invests in, being bound by a friendship marked through colonial military service. This chapter examines the affect of love and friendship, how it binds this community as a family, and the ways in which both British Gurkha officers and Gurkhas invest in and experience this relationship.

A particular focus of this chapter is placed on the politics of this friendship between British Gurkha officers, now security recruitment company directors, and Gurkhas. I look at how expressions of friendship and love sustain colonial security relations within this Gurkha security family and make possible – even celebrate – colonial management styles and structures. To do this, I centre my analysis predominantly on two Gurkha security company directors: Tristan Forster of FSI WorldWide and Ian Gordon of IDG Security. I draw upon my interviews with them, along with a multitude of Gurkhas who worked as security contractors in Afghanistan.

This chapter makes use of Ian's and Tristan's own accounts of how they understood who Gurkhas are, how they expressed their love and friendship for them, and what it meant to be part of the Gurkha family within the broader global security industry. I then compare these expressions of love with those of Gurkhas I have come to know and have spent considerable time with over the years. These Gurkha men similarly expressed love and gratitude for being afforded an opportunity to work as security contractors, an admiration for these former military commanders and a duty to protect and serve them with a high degree of loyalty.

The comparison shows how the Gurkha family continues to draw meaning from a particular colonial ambivalence, whereby the Gurkha security package remains an exclusive familial bond – Gurkha officers maintain a fatherly, managerial and patronising style of leadership, while Gurkhas take on the role of the 'dutiful' and protective sons. Familial protective language, from the standpoint of the British Gurkha officers, insulates and protects Gurkhas from the harshness of the (racist) secu-rity markets, while, from the standpoint of Gurkhas, it obliges Gurkhas to provide physical protection to their white officers, shielding these officers from the physical dangers that come with doing security work. It is through these enactments of friendship within everyday security practices that we see not only the importance of gendered and racial hierarchies, but also the role that emotions and affect play in sustaining these hierarchies.

Both hierarchies materialise in two subjectivities that I call the protective Gurkha officer father and the grateful and dutiful Gurkha son.
These friendships are never on equal footing, but rather continue to be
haunted by the colonial structures and gender hierarchies embedded
in the related histories. Drawing specifically upon the work of Sherene
Razack (2007) and how we feel (steal) the pain of others, this chapter
begins to get at the politics of love and empathy within this particular
colonial structure, showing how such friendships can often be exploitative, toxic and harmful.

The Politics of Affect

To question the role that affect plays in militarism and security is not
new. Linda Åhäll and Thomas Gregory (2015) edited a collection on the
topic of emotions in and around war, one of the first volumes to document the diverse ways in which emotions shape how we experience and
think about war.[2] Catherine Lutz (2019) compiled an entire section of
a reader on militarism dedicated to the emotional lives that are bound
to this concept. *Dying to Serve*, by Maria Rashid (2020), is an empirically
rich book on how emotions around a particular colonial history sustain
military service in Pakistan. Zoe Wool's (2015) book, *After War*, is a
haunting account of US veterans at a medical rehabilitation centre in
the US. Her descriptions of the everyday lives of veterans and their
families at the centre are saturated in emotions and affects of hope,
fear and joy, arising out of and in connection with their own personal
relations to US militarism. Catherine Baker's (2020) edited collection
shows the diverse (and global) ways that people embody and affectively
experience militarism, and Kenneth MacLeish (2013) offers an empirically rich account of how affective investments in militarism sustain
military families and serving soldiers at Fort Hood, a large base in the
US. Other scholarship of note includes Julia Welland's (2021) work
on the affective entanglements of militarism, gender and nationalism
within Ms Veteran America, and Nicole Wegner's (2021) exploration of
militarism as affectively underpinning two Canadian military commemoration events. Collectively, these works have illuminated the diverse
practices and spatial–temporal politics in which militarism is sustained
as a feeling and carries an enduring affective relation to how we as
communities come to place ourselves in the world. Paying attention
to affect ultimately shows us how the enduring emotional binds we all
hold to militarism and the politics of demilitarisation are not part of a
straightforward or easy pathway.

Megan Mackenzie (2015), Jesse Crane-Seeber (2016) and Aaron Belkin (2012) have also explored the politics of emotions that bring together (mostly male) soldiers in an exclusive comradely bond within the US military. Mackenzie's (2015) *Beyond the Band of Brothers: The US Military and the Myth that Women Can't Fight* explores in great detail how the myth of the band of brothers endures, affectively and emotionally conditioning 'gut feelings' about the exclusion of women from fighting and the natural place of war for men and male bonding. Belkin (2012) demonstrates, through examining the practice of military hazing, how homosociality is central to male bonding in the military, regardless of whether if it is coded that way amongst serving US soldiers. Crane-Seeber (2016) also draws upon queer knowledge, and kink in particular, to explore how male soldier bonding is predicated on practices of submission and subordination as much as domination. Where Crane-Seeber explores how military bonds are formed and sustained through kink performances of submission to military order and domination of civilian counterparts through performances of hypermasculinity, Mackenzie's (2015) *Beyond the Band of Brothers* explores this bonding through gendered feelings around who should serve in the first place. She illuminates how 'gut feelings' around women's participation in combat roles as 'feeling wrong' endure; keeping women out of combat service. Such feelings are anchored within the broader band of brothers' myth that has historical and contemporary resonance and that underpins the naturalised and gendered tropes of what Elshtain (1982) refers to as just warriors and beautiful souls. Combat, in other words, continues to be about men and men's manhood. The role of emotions in sustaining heteronormative exclusive military groups, as well as (re)productive military labour, contributes to my exploration of what the affect of love does politically in sustaining what I call the Gurkha security package. I make use of these rich and diverse literatures to explore how military colonial legacies structure particular feelings of love that produce and sustain gendered exclusions and divisions of labour within this security package.

Specifically, I locate love within the martial race histories that bind Gurkhas and their British officers in a colonial relationship. This is similar to Mackenzie's (2015) historical tracing of the politics of military friendship – in Mackenzie's case, the band of brothers destabilises this politics as a timeless, natural exclusive military community. Instead, she highlights the gender politics that underpin who has access to this kind of friendship in the first place. Like Wool (2015), MacLeish (2013) and Rashid (2020), I trace the politics of love in everyday security encounters.

Both MacLeish and Rashid's work contributes to how I show that the myth of this martial relationship continues to find purchase in contemporary security practices and to shape the current relationships between British Gurkha officers and Gurkhas. Military love constructs a sense of exceptionality, or the feeling that 'there is nobody quite like us'.

Love binds this family together in a way that those outside the Gurkha family, including myself, can look in on, appreciate and write about, but never quite understand. Such sentiments were expressed by Maria Des Chene (1991) some thirty years ago in her own ethnographic work on Gurkhas. I explore this military love through the metaphor of family – one that is rooted in gendered colonial hierarchies, but that is also rendered strange – to queer these hierarchies and tropes in everyday performances. Queering Gurkhas' friendships with their British officers gets away from understanding these friendships only through an already known and familiar colonial trope. It enables a refocus on the spaces and temporalities of other ways of being in(side) this family that always run alongside and parallel to this colonial relationship. While the protective Gurkha officer father and the dutiful Gurkha son tropes certainly exist, they are not the only way that men in the Gurkha family experience this friendship – often, as queer scholars remind us, experiences are more fluid and context-specific. For example, both Gurkhas and their British officers draw upon performances of masculine protector and affects of love to keep safe and protect one another from the harshness of security markets and from the physical dangers of the work. Consequently, Gurkhas come to assert themselves as security experts and acknowledge their own value outside of this colonial narrative.

My use of the metaphor of family to describe this relationship and the specific tropes of protective father and dutiful son is intentional. Describing the Gurkha security family in this way moves away from the band of brothers metaphor to describe a friendship forged through military service. I feel that descriptions of brothers and brotherhood are suggestive of a somewhat equal relation. The Gurkha security family friendship is not equal; nor is it founded on sentimentalities of equality. The Gurkha security family, with its tropes of protective father and dutiful son, illuminates a clear gendered division of labour and hierarchies, producing Gurkha officers as the all-knowing and fully developed 'fathers', who guide and mentor the Gurkhas as passive dutiful 'sons'. Importantly, these tropes are temporally fixed. There is never a moment where the 'son' graduates to the head of household, to care and protect his ageing father. Both 'father' and 'son' are bound together through affective relations of love and gratitude. This loving family obscures, and even celebrates, colonial models of leadership and representations of Gurkhas – as honourable men, yes, but also as men who become infantilised as they are marked as being in need of protection from and within security markets. Indeed, it is the feelings and affective connections to these racial ideals of whiteness that British Gurkha officers (and broader Western communities) hold that come to matter. The self-perception of the British is as the civilised liberal subjects, as the professionals, and as the best suited to lead and be the champions to end racist structures that continue to perpetuate and drive broader colonial, global, economic, security and development models.

The understandings of colonial histories and contemporary relations that I present in this chapter are indebted to the diverse and vibrant postcolonial work across IR, international political economy and development studies. More specifically, the foundational work of Sherene Razack (2004) and her invaluable critique of Canadian white imperialism and military operations are informative for uncovering how we come to think about and practise affect through imperial global modalities. These embodied affective relations underpin the work by Lisa Tilley and Robbie Shilliam (2018), where they engage with the materiality of race/racialisation in global markets and international political economies. The scholarship by Alexander Anievas, Nivi Manchanda and Robbie Shilliam (2015) also offers important insights into the breadth and depth of how 'the colour line' remains central to thinking through and practising global politics.

At the same time, I do not advance a critique of the colonial binary of Western privilege/Gurkha exploitation – although, of course, this structure does matter, and I have written about it extensively elsewhere (Chisholm 2014a, 2014b, 2015a). To highlight only the structural exploitations of Gurkhas would render silent the rich and nuanced relationships these communities have had, and continue to forge, in contemporary moments. It would smooth over the messiness of daily life, where openings of friendship do exist, and obscure the important role that affect plays in binding communities, which IR more broadly would see as involving an immutable divide between the insider/outsider and the privileged/dispossessed (Pin-Fat 2019). These histories continue to be (re)imagined and affectively lived through an ambivalence that is also marked by a long history of friendship, love and reciprocity (Gandhi 2006), forged through regimental and colonial histories. Gandhi's use of friendship challenges the binary of colonised/coloniser, and instead focuses on how such binaries are blurred through friendships and mutual connections that colonial structures have often obscured. Drawing upon Gandhi's (2006) and Pin-Fat's (2019) works, I trace the role of love and friendships between Gurkhas and British officers as a way of accounting for how these affects bind them together in the making of the 'Gurkha security package' (Chisholm 2014a).

Love in the Military

I first met Ian Gordan, the director of IDG Security – a Gurkha security company who supplied Gurkha labour to the United Nations, in Kabul, Afghanistan – when he made a country visit. In preparation for this visit, Rabindra, the lead Gurkha for IDG operations in Afghanistan, hurried the other Gurkha men who were in the compound into a military formation in the small courtyard in front of the house. When Ian arrived through the vehicle gate and got out of the SUV, he was greeted by the men standing at military attention, hands by their sides, in their IDG security uniforms. Ian smiled as he walked past the men, taking time to ask them questions in Gurkhali, to exchange laughter and shake their hands. Each man, upon Ian's inspection, stood to attention. Their bodies stiffened and their chests expanded as they saluted him and then quickly snapped their saluting hand back along their side, staying at attention, until Ian had passed to the next Gurkha. Ian had a relaxed nature about him in response to this militarised performance by the Gurkhas. He did not return the salute. He simply smiled and put out his hand to be shook. I was to the side of this exchange, standing beside the country manager, Steve. We were the 'spectators' of this pseudo military inspection parade. Initially this struck me as odd and unnecessarily militarised. Performing this role upon the arrival of a security director was drastically different from the other security contractor interactions with their director's visits that I had witnessed. (Fieldwork note from Kabul, May 2008)

My first reading of this interaction was one of overt military hierarchy, which immediately reinforced Ian's white colonial privilege and the Gurkhas' subordination. Before getting to know Ian, I was guilty of placing upon him a rigid trope of a colonial officer saturated in self-indulgence and privilege. I have softened my reading as I have become much more aware of the complexities of the martial race military family and the affective investments that both Gurkhas and British Gurkha officers like Ian hold. Over the years, Ian has expressed to me anxieties around also wanting to be accepted and recognised as a valid military and security professional by his Gurkha community. Receiving (as much as giving) love and forming a friendship with Gurkhas was a way for Ian to secure his own position within the regiment. He needed

Figure 3.1 Ian Gordan and Gurkha security contractors who work for him, at a lunch I was invited to, in Kathmandu, Nepal, April 2017. Photo credit to Amanda Chisholm.

Gurkhas to accept him as a legitimate leader. Tristan Forster, the second security director introduced at the start of this chapter, has also communicated in our various conversations the difficulties in acting as anything other than a colonial officer, specifically in front of older generations of Gurkha men. During a conversation with Tristan over whether Gurkha officers can ever be anything but colonial in their relations to Gurkhas, Tristan commented on the view of older generations of Gurkhas that any deviations in such behaviour are not appropriate or becoming to a British officer.

The histories between the men therefore haunt what relationships are possible and structure what behaviours and what kinds of interactions are intelligible. Even if Ian wanted to act in a more familiar and brotherly way, this probably would have been seen as inappropriate behaviour by the Gurkhas he previously served alongside in the Singaporean police, and by the Gurkhas he now contracts in private security. Over the years, Ian Gordon has consistently expressed an enormous respect for Gurkhas, as well as detailed knowledge of and reverence for the culture in which these men and their military service are situated. This is clear from how he organises his company and from the language and images he uses on his website to project a particular imagining of his company, as well as from the casual stories he shared with me. Ian exhibits a loving affective investment in a colonial nostalgia around British Gurkha heritage – a heritage, as the opening quote illuminates, that is fed directly into the marketing of these men as exceptional, in that there's nobody quite like them in private security.

The foundations of these colonial military hierarchies are reproduced by Gurkhas as well. Not only do they appear in particular behaviours – for example, how the men came to formation for Ian – but also they are part of investments in the martial celebrations of Gurkhas as fierce and loyal and as dutiful to their British officers. The Gurkha men I conversed with and spent time observing in different environments were grateful for the work Ian offered them, and they shared an affection with him not only as their employer, but as someone who championed Gurkhas' value as security professionals in global security markets. They, just as much as British Gurkha officers like Ian Gordon, referenced the colonial histories of Gurkha military service as underpinning this military friendship.

Indeed, humorous and harrowing stories of military bonding and friendship were openly shared with me by both British former Gurkha officers and Gurkhas. Through these stories, sentiments of bonding, forged through this shared and exclusive military service, were illuminated. Ian detailed the significance of winning Gurkha soldiers' approval and the British officers' anxieties around performing in a way that was understood as becoming in a Gurkha officer in order to fit in and be taken seriously by their respective regiments. For their part, Gurkhas shared stories of their own playful and fierce nature, and the need to prepare and mentor their British officers culturally, as well as the gratitude they felt for the mentorship they received and the championing of their military value. In all of these stories, references to colonial and military hierarchies formed the backdrop to these relationships. The accumulation of these moments I have witnessed has made it apparent that there is a mutual affection that binds these men well after their military careers are over. Love, as observed in acts of reciprocity, of duty, of honour and of gratitude, underpins the familial relationships between the British former Gurkha officers and Gurkhas.

My critique of the limits to love and generosity when they are rooted in a colonial legacy of white supremacy and civility is not intended to highlight the personal failings of any individual. Inspired by Haraway's (2016) *Staying with the Trouble*, this chapter grapples with how love and friendship, while they are certainly possible and important, cannot completely overcome the structural racist and gendered legacies on which they are built. Moreover, if left unreflected, enactments of love can often obscure and further perpetuate colonial violence, even if this is unintended.

As I write this, I am reflecting upon how my own friendships with Gurkhas and the haunting of my histories with colonialism continue to shape these relationships – many of the men continuing to refer to me as 'ma'am', despite my informing them that they can just call me Amanda. I also continue to make sense of how my own interest in Gurkhas' experiences has been viewed by these men through the narrative of Joanna Lumley – a white woman championing the virtues and rights of Gurkhas on their behalf. It is these very colonial structures that impact how and the ways in which the individual affectively invests in friendships, and in the Gurkha family. As this chapter shows, affective investments in sustaining the nostalgia for the colonial Gurkha heritage are much stronger amongst those who are the most privileged: the British Gurkha officers. Such loving connections to this colonial past (and contemporary) present result in more ambivalent relations when considered from the perspectives of Gurkhas.

I therefore approach the concept of 'love' with scepticism and nuance. Not only am I unconvinced of the benevolence of friendship, but, like Ahmed (2014), Halberstam (2011) and Berlant (2011), I remain sceptical of love always being a good thing. In the name of love, we can enact brutal violence against those who we deem to be not one of us and a threat to our values (Ahmed 2014). In the name of love, we can also be at once an honourable and loving family member and an exploitative and cunning capitalist entrepreneur (Berlant 2011). As well, in sharing in others' empathy and grief out of love, we can actually steal the pain of others, using their pain to reaffirm our own humanity (Razack 2007). Here, I am concerned with what love does to obscure (and endure) the structural inequalities that persist from the colonial nostalgia referenced by British Gurkha officers, as well as many Gurkhas themselves. In fact, this particular friendship illuminates the various contradictions of violence and support involved in the production of love and friendship in creating and sustaining the Gurkha family in global security markets.

Feminist research has long shown how emotions and love are central to why people (mostly men) will endure hardships and hostility and continue to fight – often for the love of their fellow (male) soldiers. Feelings of love and bonding endure long past formal military service, as observed with Gurkhas and former British officers. MacLeish (2013) locates the politics of love in the ambivalence of the everyday making and enduring of life at a large US military base, Fort Hood. Love is 'a basis for making, breaking and being subjected to rules' of war (MacLeish 2013, 143). In its various formations, love carries feelings of 'personal and autonomous obligations' (MacLeish 2013, 144) that give love a governing power. In this research, MacLeish shows how love takes on a heteronormativity form in producing military families, as well as a homosociality structure in binding soldiers in brotherhood and an aspirational and ideological love for country and army service. Love in the context of US militarism organises and reproduces military labour, animates uniformity in the 'army family' and gives meaning and purpose to violent death (MacLeish 2013, 144). In the face of potential death, the men's brotherhood is forged. In my own observations of and conversations with Gurkhas over the past decade, I have found that, more often than not, there is a friendship with another who has served with the British, the Indian army or the Singaporean police. To be a Gurkha carries enormous social capital within Nepal, but it also binds former servicemen together in mutual admiration and friendship because of a shared understanding of their collective military and service.

Such friendships arising through (colonial) military service are not novel to Gurkhas or British officers. Expressions of love, intimacy and empathy between and for bodies in war underpin the friendships and comradery between all soldiers (Bourke 1996), and also others who are touched by war more broadly (Das 2006). This form of friendship through shared military service has a long history. Das (2006) explores, for example, how intimacy and expressions of love materialise in World War II writings. Mutual admiration and friendships within the broader Gurkha regiments that include British officers and Nepali nationals are rendered clearly in most popular military celebratory books written about Gurkhas.[3]

Intimate acts of prolonged embraces in and out of war bind male soldiers in moments often described as homoerotic, but as coded within heterosexual frameworks. The intimacy of prolonged embraces between two soldiers, as one lies dying in war, as Das (2006) argues, forever connects the living to those comrades now dead. For Belkin (2012), the acts of homoeroticism are not only found in war, but are located in the preparation for war. He describes these practices of various hazing rituals involving anal penetration between soldiers in the US military. These acts of intimacy and expressions of love help to form homosocial bonds between male soldiers. While I did not witness homoerotic expressions of friendship such as those detailed by Belkin (2012) or

Das (2006), hugs, handshakes and pats on the back were common greetings amongst Gurkhas and British former Gurkha officers. For me, what a queer reading of this kind of friendship highlights, though, is how fluid concepts of gender and sexuality have been, and continue to be, in war.[4] Expressions of friendship between Gurkhas and British Gurkha officers are never timeless or just one thing. A queer reading enables me to see, for example, how both Gurkhas and their British officers/security managers draw upon performances of masculine protectors (detailed below) as a way to assert their own empowerment and all the while infantising each other, to justify their need to protect.

In the loving bonds described as band of brothers, or comradeship, friendship or brotherhood, and in loving expressions called cohesion, morale and esprit de corps, what becomes clear is the intensification of male bonding amid the constant anxieties of death, illness and dying bodies (Das 2006, 114; MacLeish 2013). Joanna Bourke (1996) describes the everyday banality of male intimacy in war, including hugging and bathing together, as enabled bonding that is never coded as homoerotic. Such loving bonds matter for militaries. As MacLeish illustrates, it is 'precisely this potential for harm or death that demands [militaries pay] unparallel attention to and [ensure their] involvement in other people's lives' (2013, 146). This is because such loving bonds, understood in grammars of cohesion and group morale, are instrumental matters of life and death for militaries (MacLeish 2013, 146). Acknowledging the role of love and intimacy in forming these bonds in war compels us to 'reconceptualise masculinity, conventional gender roles and notions of same-sex intimacy' and brotherly or familial bonds post war (Das 2006, 115). For my purposes, exploring love and friendship within Gurkha communities leads to a better understanding of how both colonial models of leadership and representations of who Gurkhas are as martial subjects continue to find purchase in global security.

Building a Security Brand Like No Other: The Gurkha Security Package

Accessing the global security markets from Nepal is tricky and riddled with potential for significant financial loss in paying for work that does not materialise – or, if it does, the pay and working conditions are significantly less advantageous than what was promised. Gurkhas continue to rely on their relationships with former British Gurkha officers to gain access to security work and achieve a decent wage, as well as safe working conditions. Ian Gordon and Tristan Forster run two security recruitment companies that are leading the way in maintaining a high commitment to ethical recruitment practices that ensure contractors and their families do not pay to access foreign employment, and that the type of work promised to them in Nepal is in line with the work they do in the host country.

These two companies recruit and employ former Gurkhas from both the British and Indian armies and the Singaporean police. Ian is a former British officer who managed Gurkhas working as Singaporean police officers. After retiring from the military, Ian set up his own company as a way to bring Gurkhas and their experience to security markets. In one of our many conversations, Ian expressed the outrage he felt after learning that, upon their retirement, Gurkhas – including many of his own former soldiers – found it very difficult to find security work or any other kind of work, even in a booming global security industry. It was then that he decided to start his own company as a way to bring these men and their military honour to the security market.

Like Ian, Tristan, a British ex-Gurkha officer, expressed a similar nar- rative around his motivation to start his security recruitment company. In multiple conversations, he repeatedly told me, 'These men are good men and make great security contractors.' I observed that Tristan and Ian each position their leadership roles both as educators of the value of Gurkha security labour and as protectors of Gurkhas, specifically from the racism and exploitation of the market. By offering cheaper and reputable security contractors from the Global South to global security markets, both IDG Security and FSI WorldWide continue to thrive.

It is within this broader political context of exploitative foreign labour practices in terms of payment for work and poor living and working conditions that Gurkhas enter global security markets. They rely heavily upon men like Tristan and Ian, including their social capi- tal, to secure employment. Tristan and Ian both have championed the virtues of Gurkhas' (racialised) labour to PMSCs, government embassies and international organisations such as the United Nations. Their com- panies are also underpinned by a commitment to ethical recruitment involving the rigorous screening of contractors, the welfare of workers being built into their contracts and zero fees for Gurkhas who wish to access work. This combination of professional and (cheap) contractors alongside a commitment to human rights and labour rights makes these companies desirable to Western governments, commercial entities and the UN. Consequently, the two security company owners have devel- oped a security package 'like no other' and successfully created a market for Gurkhas. Many Gurkhas I spoke with were quick to acknowledge this support and extend their gratitude for the ability to find work after retiring from the military.

The former British Gurkha officers and Gurkha security contractors form what I have called the Gurkha security package in global security markets. In previous work, I sought to explore how racism and the martial race histories of Gurkhas sustained material inequalities and exploitative relationships between Gurkhas and their white managers (Chisholm 2014a). I detailed the ways in which both Gurkhas and white managers bought into these racialised logics. This chapter extends this analysis by exploring the role of affect in sustaining broader structural and discursive logics around Gurkhas' value as security contractors. This security package is marketed in global security markets as a security community, whereby Gurkhas' value as security professionals comes through their association with the British. They become known to the broader security community through their martial race histories, which condition these men as racialised contractors, whereby their experiences of the industry are marked through racial logics. Such logics also reinforce a particular Global North/South division of labour. White Westerners assume managerial and leadership roles, with the privilege of claiming who and what gets articulated as security expertise, and those from the Global South take on the poorly paid and more physically dangerous work (Chisholm 2017). But where do the politics of love and friendship fit in the making of this Gurkha security package?

Loopholes of Love and the Global Security Market

To understand the role of love in binding the Gurkha security package is also to see how love is central to the way that military bonds and broader cohesions are established and endure long after military service. Love and friendship certainly do exist between British Gurkha officers and Gurkhas, but the two are not on equal terms. Rather, this friendship is coded within a broader colonial nostalgia that positions the British Gurkha officer as the natural and timeless leader – a champion of Gurkhas and their value, rooted in their love for the Gurkha family and Gurkha histories.

I first met Tristan in the bar/lounge of the Victoria Service Club, a members-only hotel and conference centre for serving and retired British and Commonwealth soldiers and their families. Tristan is charismatic and has an infectious personality, and I instantly warmed to him. We sat in the club and talked about Gurkhas and what it was like to be a British Gurkha officer for over three hours. The conversation kept getting more animated as he entertained me with stories about his own personal connections to Gurkhas as a child and then getting to know them through his military regimental history. It is a bond like no other, he said. Telling me about his initial pseudo-anthropological research, conducted as a core component of his Gurkha officer training, and his struggles with learning Gurkhali in order to lead his men, Tristan reflected upon these experiences and how they rooted a deep affection for the Gurkha communities and the Gurkhas whom he served alongside and led. I smiled and nodded along as he shared various anecdotes. As the aforementioned feminist work on military bonding has recounted, Tristan's love for Gurkhas and regimental pride came through his military service and the stories he shared with me. This love was the reason for Tristan setting up his own security recruitment company. He saw a gap in the global security market, in that companies were looking for (cheap) Global South contractors, and he realised that he could champion the security expertise and professionalism of Gurkhas in these markets. He told me: 'I believe in these men and their skill and was horrified to learn that there was no market for them after their military service.'

Like Ian's company, IDG Security, FSI WorldWide also brands itself and its origins as arising out of the founders' military personal connections to Nepal. Notably, these connections and the brand fall within the colonial imaginings of Gurkhas. FSI WorldWide's 'Our History' page explains how Tristan and his colleagues came to form the company:

> During their time in the Army, they developed a deep sense of respect and admiration for the people of Nepal which led to FSI Worldwide being built on the determination to help former Gurkhas find rewarding employment.[5]

It is Ian Gordon's and Tristan Forster's love for Gurkhas and for Nepal that has been the reason for them both to start their businesses. They continue to champion particular versions of themselves and of Gurkhas, and they profit from colonial understandings of who these men are and where their value as security contractors arises from. Love for Gurkhas, and for Gurkhas' histories, explains these men's origins within the security industry. The market, then, becomes a space from which to project this love. The market is a space of opportunity to champion the Gurkha men, as well as a potential threat in terms of exploitation.

Against the racial harms alongside the economic potential of the market, both Tristan and Ian act as male protectors of Gurkhas, shielding them from the perils of a private security market willing to exploit Gurkhas and tarnish their reputation. They become the father figures of the Gurkhas, providing economic opportunities for their former military soldiers and other Gurkhas, saving them from impoverishment, but also educating the market on Gurkhas' value. Yet running parallel to this story of love and unfettered admiration is also one of market advantage. Championing Gurkhas' value through the very racialised logics (colonial histories) that render them always subaltern opens up security markets to these men, while at the same time closing down conditions of possibility beyond the racialised martial security contractor. Appealing to Gurkhas' value through their martial histories opens up global capitalist markets largely predicated on race-to-the-bottom labour practices and a continual racialising and feminising of workforces to make Gurkhas cheaper in order to maximise profits for the potential clients of IDG and FSI. Gurkhas are desired because they are cheap labour that is knowable and trustworthy through its association with British Gurkha officers. Expressions of love by both Tristan and Ian in championing the value of these beloved military Gurkha colleagues sit uneasily alongside their engagement in already exploitative markets, where they profit from the very racial tropes that expose these men to harm in the first place.

Love in this context needs to be understood within the broader political economy in which it is situated and given meaning. Berlant's (2011) work on love in capitalist structures is informative for thinking through Tristan's experiences and his articulations of his activism in promoting Gurkha labour, as well as tackling racist markets through ethical recruitment practices. Berlant shows how love can be a 'bargaining tool' that invites others to join one in making a better life, but how it also provides a loophole (2011, 180). For Berlant, the loophole comes through the locating of love in the private sphere, the family, which is bounded and separated from the outside capital space. This loophole allows us to be selfless, sacrificial and magnanimous (in private spaces), as well as calculating and cunning (as required and valued by the market). Such a separation between the instrumental capitalist self and the loving private self enables 'a disidentification with what's aggressive in [our] pursuit for desire and interest in all spaces, and to see [ourselves] as fundamentally ethical because [we mean] to have solidarity with some humans [we know]' (Berlant 2011, 181). Such an interpretation of love enables a reading of British Gurkha officers, who can both show love and draw upon racial logics as a marketing strategy that renders vulnerable the very men for whom they express love and whom they wish protect.

Both Ian and Tristan, as security company directors, thus demonstrate this 'love with a loophole'. They do so by privately, in homes, hallways and social and professional spaces, showing solidarity and expressing a commitment to making the lives of Gurkhas and their families better. At the same time, in order to run profitable global companies and create a niche market, they continue to draw upon racialised and colonial logics in their branding campaigns and discussions with global clients and market actors. This love of Gurkhas and admiration and respect for them as a military community can co-exist through this love loophole with profiting from racialising their value as security professionals. This is possible because love is kept in the private sphere, contained within the Gurkha security family. The market remains on the outside of this family – as a space of possibility where Ian and Tristan and their companies continue to expand and grow with emerging markets that need (cheap) security labour.

The market, though, is a space of harm. As such, Tristan and Ian in this context justify insulating Gurkhas from the same markets in which they themselves advance Gurkhas' racialised worth. They foster the notion of a Gurkha security family. In the words of Ian, 'there is nobody quite like us', meaning that they can protect Gurkhas from exploitation and racial mistreatment by being the men that protect and represent them. Love thus functions in contradictory way in the market. It is located in an insular security unit whereby British Gurkha officers come to speak on behalf of and profit from Gurkhas. However, love also features inside this military friendship, a relationship founded upon a familial gender hierarchy located in the tropes of father and son.

The Gurkha Security Family

Vocabularies of love affectively connect to and are given meaning through these Gurkha racialised histories. Tristan Forster and Ian Gordon both referenced Gurkha military regiments as a Gurkha family: a family with the male British national Gurkha officer as the head of the household. They used paternal language to describe further how the British Gurkha officer intimately knows Gurkhas through long histories with the 'Gurkha family', and discussed how it is through this knowledge and history that the officer is best suited to mentor and lead. The love that binds this Gurkha family creates and fosters spaces of exceptionalism. Love and other affects have particular military histories that give them the appearance of being natural, and even lend a sense of celebratory nostalgia. Such affects not only build an exclusive community, but also create exclusions. Love and friendship within the Gurkha community are also gendered.

Being a part of this family also produces what Mackenzie (2015) calls gut feelings, which are rooted in an affective relationship to militarised masculinities. Not only do these gut feelings reinforce a strict, racialised, colonial hierarchy amongst Gurkhas and their officers, but they also encourage a male exclusive space. These feelings, as Mackenzie (2015) argues, are considered valid, or even as more valid than any empirical or factually based evidence applicable in the debate over women's (and trans persons') inclusion. In the case of Gurkhas, this military family and Gurkha military service, women feature only as the grateful and, as the next chapter will highlight, happy housewives, mothers and daughters. This family is exclusively male, and the Gurkha officer assumes the 'natural' role of head of the household. This naturalness was captured in one of my interviews with Tristan Forster:

> The way the brigade of Gurkhas likes to induct its officers. It goes back to the days of colonialism where you had the East African rifles, brigade rifles . . . you had British officers working with native troops and trying to get the best out of both parties. You didn't have the officers just standing around and giving order[s]; you had them integrated in the community. It was very important for the officers to learn about the culture of where the men come from. It is taken very seriously. If you fail your language course or you don't have the personality, you don't get on well with the Gurkhas from a different culture, then similarly you are not going to last long. It is brilliant, because you end up getting officers that are ideally suited, worthy of commanding these men. (Interview, London, UK, 1 September 2012)

The quote above comes from one of the interviews I conducted with Tristan over a decade ago as I was still learning about who Gurkhas are and their colonial histories. Yet this style of leadership continues to hold in how both IDG and FSI manage their security contractors. In the quote, Tristan describes the training of British Gurkha officers in a timeless way – a management style of leadership through anthropological methods dating back to colonial times and still finding purchase in the British military today, as well as within private security. Leading with empathy and care for the men one commands was key not only for Tristan, but also for the other Gurkhas and Gurkha officers I have had conversations with. Within the Gurkha community, the Gurkha officer is positioned as the leader who leads through love and a thorough knowledge of the culture his men come from. Describing Gurkha officers in this way brings to the fore a colonial nostalgia where friendship and love are viewed as necessary.

This military bonding is also deeply racialised and embedded in imperial projects of white supremacy, as Razack's (2004) examination of Canadian Airborne Regiment operations in Somalia and the killing of a young Somalian boy attests. The writings of numerous colonial military historians such as Das (2006), Ware (2012) and Barkawi (2017) all highlight this imperial project. For the Gurkha security family, racialised violence materialises in such a way that colonial hierarchies and racial imaginings of Gurkhas continue to underpin their broader recruitment and management. Love brings forth a colonial style of family, but it also positions British officers as the rightful heads of the family – heads that lead through a particular version of love and empathy.

Leading through Love

Both Tristan Forster and Ian Gordon's perception of themselves as leading through fatherly love comes first from knowing who Gurkhas are and spending time and energy with these men and their broader communities. Tristan described Gurkha officers and their management style with a vocabulary of love and empathy:

[Gurkha officers] are very sensitive in the sense of really understanding how to get the best out of their men. They have equally been good at operating with local nations in whichever country you might be in. That sort of patience, [not meaning they] don't get the job done, there is professionalism there, but they can do it and bring the guys along with them. [Gurkha officers have a] very good leadership and management style, [are] very fit, very dedicated, very exceptional in their thinking and attitude. [They] enjoy travel and enjoy working with other cultures. The Gurkha regiment get a lot of people applying and [there are] not that many positions, they can be picky. Just really good people generally. All of the Gurkha officers, to a man, I am very fond of today. (Interview, London, UK, 1 September 2012)

This quote highlights the perceived exceptionalism of Gurkha officers who lead through empathy, sensitivity and a cultural understanding of Gurkhas. This brings us back to a colonial nostalgia that knowing Gurkhas is how one can best manage them. Both company owners spoke of their leadership through empathy and of knowing their men, knowledge honed through their Gurkha regimental experience, as a way to get the best out of Gurkhas.

Tristan shared his belief in the unique positioning of British Gurkha officers in terms of their abilities to recruit and manage Gurkhas properly. His marketing of Gurkhas implicitly positioned him as the authority over and guardian of Gurkhas. He established his own authority by creating himself as the ideal Westerner who could understand and manage Gurkhas, bringing out the best of their abilities. Returning to our first conversations back at the Victory Service Club in London, UK, he described his upbringing by way of giving a history to his cultural competency and natural suitability to lead:

> I guess I grew up as an ex-pat kid in amongst all sorts of different environments. Whether it was Hong Kong Chinese or India, I had lived overseas with different groups and loved learning languages. It just somehow felt like home to me . . . I guess I sort of had it in my blood in a sense. I met Gurkhas as a kid in Hong Kong and when [we] were in India and just sort of had this very strong affection for them when I had met [them]. My parents tell a lovely story about me, whenever we went to visit the Gurkhas, not seeing me, because I was off with the lads and never wanting to leave, because I enjoyed bonding with them.

In relating his childhood travels in non-Western communities, Tristan positioned himself first as a child growing up knowing Gurkha men. It was then through his professional training in the UK military as a Gurkha officer that he moved from being a child among the Gurkha to being more of a father figure.

The self-positioning as a father figure inadvertently leads to management practices that reproduce colonial hierarchical power relations. In one situation I observed, Ian Gordon was berating a Gurkha for behaving in a way he viewed as 'unbecoming for a Gurkha'. I was later told by the British country manager that the berated Gurkha was suspected of stealing money. The country manager did not believe that this Gurkha had actually stolen anything, but Ian told me later in an interview that, in holding his Gurkhas to a high ethical standard, he felt compelled to discipline any conduct that could be suspect. His discipline came in the form of a semi-public verbal altercation in the Gurkhali language with the Gurkha contractor. During this altercation, the Gurkha stood quietly with his head bowed, while Ian stood facing him and speaking very sternly before pointing in a direction where the Gurkha immediately walked. The observation reminded me of a military dressing down. For me, the performance reinforced the militarised hierarchy and discipline expected within this particular security company. The public berating in Gurkhali was intentional.

Paternal love materialises in holding individual Gurkhas to a high moral standard and also in the care work of clothing the men. I remember sitting in the IDG security office in Kathmandu, where Ian and his in-country recruitment manager, Padam, were mulling over a new shipment of Gurkha security uniforms. They exchanged a colonial hat back and forth, discussing the fabric's texture, as well as its firmness and ability to absorb sweat in the heat of Afghanistan. While great attention was paid to the hat's usability, there was no acknowledgement of the actual colonial design and what optics this design would carry with it as the men who wore the hats performed their security work. This illustrates that the broader discussion of fashion and uniforms generally goes unreflected. Instead, manner of dress is often used as a way to 'celebrate' the colonial roots of Gurkhas and of the security companies. It is taken as common sense that one should celebrate this heritage, without acknowledging the racialised imagery of Gurkhas that is saturated in, for example, the style of hat chosen as part of a uniform.

Tristan also drew on the metaphor of fatherly love to describe his role with and relationship to Gurkhas. This management style is demonstrated on FSI WorldWide's website, which discusses how, through mentoring Gurkhas, Tristan and his likeminded former Gurkha officer colleagues are able to manage and nurture them in such a way as to get the best out of them. According to the website, this management style comes from men who are familiar with and committed to the potential of the Gurkha. Here, the company highlights its commitment to ethical

Figure 3.2 IDG Security uniform for Gurkha contractors in Afghanistan and Kathmandu, Nepal, April 2017. Photo credit to Amanda Chisholm.

recruitment practices and affirms that these practices carry the ability to get the best out of everyone – that is, everyone non-Western – as opposed to just Gurkhas. As on IDG Security's website, the audience is informed that it is the Gurkha officers who are in the best position to know who the genuine Gurkhas are and manage them properly. Thus, the client can be assured they will get contractors who perform as the legendary Gurkha does.

Tristan's and Ian's reflections on their positions within a broader nostalgia of belonging to Gurkha families speak to the colonial military administration discussed in the previous chapters. Leading through anthropological methods positions the British Gurkha officer as the best to 'know' and to 'manage' Gurkhas. British Gurkha officers are purported to have the necessary empathy and cultural competency, obtained through long-term immersion in Gurkha communities, that are required to manage Gurkhas – through putting themselves in the shoes of the Gurkha. Using such language of management through anthropological practices reinforces the colonial masculinity script that Caplan discusses at great length (1995, 55–86).[6] These vocabularies work to reproduce colonial and gendered father figures within security markets through discourse. The Gurkha officer is the protector/authority figure and the Gurkha is his loyal serving soldier. As I observed during the 'parade' mentioned at the start of this chapter, these performances also work to exclude the participation of the outsider, who is relegated to be a spectator of a colonial family that is reimagined and reproduced in private security settings.

Through uniform choice, website branding and everyday encounters, both Ian and Tristan continue to reinforce the importance of colonial heritage in shaping themselves and their relations to Gurkhas. Defining Gurkha as a 'colonial' package ensures, for both men, that they control what Gurkhas are and their own positions of authority to speak for and on behalf of them. In interviews, both men detailed how maintaining control over defining and marketing Gurkhas also means that bonded labour and the exploitation of Gurkhas can be reduced. Both positioned themselves as personally responsible for changing the exploitative practices of Gurkhas in security markets. Having placed themselves as the protectors of Gurkhas from the dangers and harshness of the market, while at the same time infantilising them, the two security company owners viewed them as unable to act with agency outside of these market structures. By positioning Gurkhas as prone to exploitation and abuse, both Tristan and Ian also enable their own roles as protectors well beyond helping Gurkhas to gain access to security work. In attempting to hold a particular Gurkha standard to the outside security market, they also practise a broader patronising management style that includes how Gurkhas dress, at what times they eat and how they conduct themselves, in a way that is much more 'hands on' than what I observed with any other security contractors' arrangements. While their commitment to improving the conditions of Gurkhas' economic positions is not in question, such a positioning of themselves as the fatherly protectors of Gurkhas tends to obscure how these same men reproduce colonial myths of the Gurkha family in order to privilege and benefit financially from the marketising of Gurkha labour in global security.

If we return to Ahmed's (2014) reading of love as an affect that excludes and binds, we can see how both Ian and Tristan use vocabularies of love and affection to foster an exclusive Gurkha family – one that is forged through a shared 200-year military history that naturalises the men as the head of Gurkha regiments and Gurkha security families. Expressions of love act as reasons for insulating Gurkhas from the exploitative harms and racism of the global market. Love positions Ian and Tristan as the authentic knowers of Gurkhas, as their champions and their custodian father figures in security. Consequently, it also reinforces an infantilising relationship whereby Gurkhas are forever bound to these men and their companies both to access the market and to ensure favourable conditions for their labour experiences. Via exclusive marketing campaigns such as 'there's nobody like us' and managing through love and empathy, Gurkha officers position themselves as the rightful guardians of Gurkhas for the rest of the market to observe and to celebrate, all the while continuing to profit from ongoing colonial imaginings of these men and their capabilities.

Love, then, becomes the foundation of how Gurkhas and British officers understand their sense of exclusivity, in that the space of exclusion and source of ontological security from the outside sustain the Gurkha security package (Chisholm 2014a). This package brings value to Gurkha labour through the coupling of two distinct security bodies – the British Gurkha officer and the Gurkha – in a package that is, according to Tristan and Ian, every bit as good as 'Western security'. In previous work (Chisholm 2014a), I drew upon this package to highlight how colonial histories have actively shaped how Gurkhas access the market and the hierarchies of security labour that this mechanism raises – rendering these men 'almost but not white'. Love, located in a colonial military history, binds Gurkhas and officers in an exclusive family. Fostering a sense of exceptionalism through the tagline of 'there's no one quite like us' is only one aspect of what love does. Love creates a cohesive and exclusive security community predicated upon and celebrated through a colonial nostalgia of Gurkha heritage and military service. But love also enables former British Gurkha officers like Ian and Tristan to champion and naturalise their own privileged roles as managers and custodians of Gurkha labour while profiting from this racialised labour. British Gurkha officers are, however, only one side of this Gurkha security package story. Love, in all of this, is like that of the heterosexual love marriages Halberstam writes about (2011, 34–8). Love is normalised and naturalised through colonial structures and histories, and at the same time, it seeks to situate itself outside of these politics – to be experienced and seen as timeless, natural and pure. This chapter now turns to explore how Gurkhas themselves understand and navigate their colonial heritage and affective relationship with former Gurkha officers in the colonial present of security markets.

Dutiful Love and Protecting the British Gurkha Officer

I first met Sherba Harder, or Tiger, as he was introduced to me, in 2008. Sherba was a Gurkha with the Indian army and had been working for IDG in Afghanistan for a few years. He was warm with me and I always

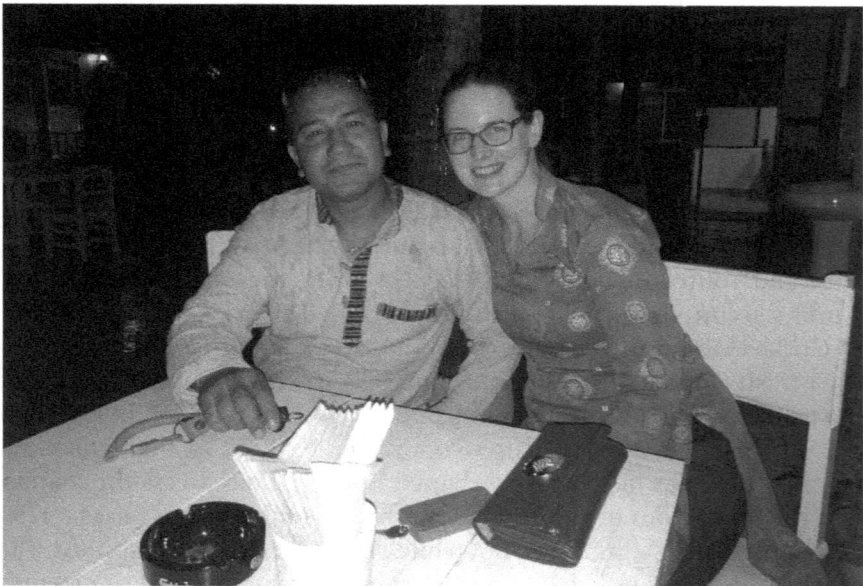

Figure 3.3 Amanda Chisholm sitting with Sherba in Pokhara, Nepal, April 2017. Photo credit to Amanda Chisholm.

felt safe and protected around him. Although I felt close to Sherba and over the past decade have shared meals in his family home and been taxied around Pokhara on the back of his Enfield motorbike, there is still a formality around how he interacts with me. We have shared lots of laughter and he allows me to grab his arm as I recall an exciting or funny experience we shared in Kabul, smiling as I talk, but the same familiarity in spoken and tactile form is not returned. In fact, some four-teen years later, he still refers to me as 'ma'am', despite me continuing to ask him to call me Amanda. Despite this, I feel a closeness to Sherba and I believe it is reciprocated. I begin with this experience of my own relationship with Sherba because I think it highlights the profound role of colonial legacies and how they structure encounters. As for Ian and Tristan, my own whiteness and privileged position as a Westerner, a foreigner, afford me a social decorum that cannot be overcome. This does not mean friendship is not experienced. It means that such experi-ences are always interpreted and embodied within the broader colonial, gendered and caste/class structures in which they are embedded.

In many ways, Sherba has embodied the ideal Gurkha security con-tractor. Both Ian and Tristan commented on how he was loyal and had a friendly disposition. The country manager for IDG at the time also relied heavily upon him for day-to-day security activities. He silently worked in the background, without complaint, doing regular perimeter checks and ensuring that the broader logistics around work and transportation for the other Gurkha contractors in the compound were in order. He also carried out the bulk of the monotonous and physically taxing work of a static guard, in addition to the emotional labour of ensuring that particularly myself and the other women in the compound felt safe. He did the latter through investing in us as human beings, getting to know about and asking about our families and bringing us cups of tea. Such labour, as Chapter 5 demonstrates, sticks to the brown and black bodies of security contracting. We came to expect this kind of (often thankless) work from men like Sherba. While not formally acknowledged in any contracts or key performance indicators, this emotional work is vital to making clients feel safe, and it is disproportionately placed upon men like Sherba.

Sherba always expressed gratitude to Steve (his country manager) and to Ian for giving him the opportunity to work as a security con-tractor. This work enabled him to provide financial support for his family back in Pokhara, Nepal. He took his work seriously. In one exchange I had with him while we were making tea, Sherba exclaimed that white managers were smart and worldly, and so it made sense that they were in leadership roles. In the same conversation, he also stated that it was important that he and other Gurkhas keep these men safe, located in the high walls of compounds in front of their computers, writing intelligence briefings and standard operating procedures, while Gurkhas were in more immediate physical spaces of danger. 'We know the culture here. They do not,' Sherba explained to me. 'We have street smarts.' Gurkhas' own value, then, came through their ability to keep Western men (and clients like me) physically safe through their bodies (by standing guard). Sherba also explained that when it came to on-the-ground local knowledge and ability to blend in and relate to locals through similar dialects and cultural understandings, Gurkhas had these skills, while us white people did not.

Where British Gurkha officers like Ian Gordon and Tristan Forster would assert their own masculine protector self-image in insulating Gurkhas from the economic harshness of global security markets and the broader global recruitment industry, Gurkhas projected a self-image of a dutiful and physically protective son. Here, Sherba drew upon protector masculinities to reclaim a sense of value and worth that being placed as the subaltern 'protected' leaves no space for. He used this masculinity to enable a repositioning of his own role within the broader security industry, which, as demonstrated in the opening vignette, clearly positions these men in extreme spaces of insecurity with very little protection. Indeed, I was often told how Western men were book-smart and had the necessary international knowledge and experience to manage companies and clients, but that they were unaware of cultural contexts and did not have the street knowledge required to keep them physically safe. Repeatedly, I was told by Gurkha security contractors during my time in Kabul that because they could speak Urdu and Farsi, they had a better working knowledge of the security risks across the city. Like Ian and Tristan, who juxtaposed their protector father roles to keep Gurkhas safe against the dangers and harshness of racist and exploitative markets, Gurkhas positioned themselves as the physical protectors of security managers due to their ability to know about potential physical dangers and to keep their managers physically safe in Kabul.

While Gurkhas like Sherba certainly have to navigate more structural disadvantages in accessing and experiencing the security market, they are not passive subjects; nor do they see themselves as needing the level of patronising 'care and wellbeing' management provided by their Western security managers. In my other interviews with Gurkhas working in Afghanistan, there was a great deal of frustration expressed over the amount of scrutiny of their regular movements around the city,

Figure 3.4 Gurkha men at the Tribhuvan International Airport, Kathmandu, ready to fly to Afghanistan, in Kathmandu, Nepal, November 2017. Photo credit to Robic Upadhayay.

the clothing they had to wear and their regimented eating times. Such frustrations were brought up when I asked them how they felt about being treated differently from their white Western colleagues. While the pay differences and contractual leave time were more accepted, the high degree of management of their personal rhythms and eating, sleeping and leisure routines was not so easily countenanced.

Yet these frustrations appeared to be overridden by the understanding that their access to global security markets occurred directly through their relationship with the same managers who were in charge of their 'wellbeing'. As such, many Gurkhas just shrugged their shoulders and explained away these frustrations to me in interviews, expressing once again the gratitude they felt about having this work and the way they felt it was their duty to perform their jobs well. This indebtedness to British security company directors like Ian and Tristan can often reinforce colonial relationships, whereby the Gurkha feels compelled to reciprocate the security directors' actions with a display of uncompromising loyalty. As Jitendra commented when detailing to me how he pursued work initially in Angola during the 1990s with a former Gurkha officer, 'My old commander request[s] me, ok you come here. Ok I will go, sir; I will obey your orders.' Jitendra followed this statement with descriptions of the dangerous work he felt compelled to perform and of being exposed to violent situations where he was not sure he would make it out alive. Jitendra's duty to perform the work requested of him was also echoed by Gurung in his interview. When I asked him about being exposed to dangerous situations and whether he had a choice as to whether or not to participate, Gurung responded: 'In our profession we cannot choose to [not be exposed to danger] . . . if I am told to go out, I can't ignore [that]' (Interview, 6 May 2010).

Here, a sense of duty is mixed with a feeling of being affectively bound to the long and rich heritage of the brave Gurkha. However, this gratitude for work and willingness often to uphold the Gurkha martial reputation unquestionably and habitually is not without its limits, and not all frustrations can be absorbed into the overall gratitude for this security work. Unlike for Tristan and Ian, military service for many Gurkhas I spoke to was not a calling as much as it was a necessity. While men like Jitendra expressed gratitude and a duty of service, they also mentioned that their own work as a Gurkha was a sacrifice to open up more possibilities for their children, so that they would not have to look to military service in order to support themselves and their own future families. As such, the calling of being a Gurkha is one that is not very often viewed with a rosy nostalgia – the way that Ian and Tristan thought of it. In fact, just as the broader structural logics that work to privilege Gurkha officers were not always lost on Ian and Tristan, the Gurkha men I spoke with also recognised how their own histories were taken up for their further exploitation as security labourers. As Rohan said,

> the security companies are getting the contracts because of the Gurkha. They convince their clients that we are good, but we have been cheated by these same companies. This is because they are using your name and yet you are treated completely different. (Interview, August 2010)

Again, such feelings of frustration tend to exist parallel to expressions of gratitude. This shows that the relationship between Gurkhas and the men who offer their social capital by obtaining access to these markets for them is not a straightforward one. Unlike the warm, celebratory military history that Ian and Tristan drew upon when detailing their own reasons for investing in global security markets and their personal connections to Gurkhas, the Gurkha men I spoke to felt a deeper ambivalence.

In my more recent visit to Nepal in 2016, I began to ask Gurkhas to reflect upon their security service as fathers, sons, brothers and

Figure 3.5 Interview with a Gurkha family, in Pokhara, Nepal, November 2017. Photo credit to Robic Upadhayay.

husbands. Strangely, up until recently, I had never thought this line of questioning was important. I was wrong. What it revealed was a deep sense of contradiction around the concept of military service. Many of the men I conversed with had experienced a high degree of frustration, pain, grief and loss that ran parallel to the feeling of celebration for what it means to be a Gurkha. Being a part of the global security industry takes the men away from their children, their parents and their wives for extended periods of time, as well as exposing them to physical danger. Despite the expressions of love and gratitude, the men were very much aware of the structural conditions that marked their experiences as significantly different from those of their country directors or other white security contractors. And many felt the injustice of this, while continuing to be grateful for any employment opportunities. I have written about how Gurkha security contractors very clearly understand the colonial and racial structures that disadvantage and devalue their security work (Chisholm 2014a). This immediately materialises in the more regimented eating times, the required uniforms and the lack of mobility around Kabul and other cities, when compared to Western contractors. Such parallel feelings of pain and gratitude are best observed in an excerpt from my interview with Rabindra and his wife, Sunika:

At that time, I had to go join the army because of financial problems we
had at home. I didn't join the army because I wanted to, and after joining
I felt like I have left my young children who are very small, and I am also
very newly married, and I left my wife home. I felt like I really made a mistake
and that I shouldn't have joined the army. All the time during the training,
which lasted for eleven months, I always felt like that. But that also [was]
when I was free and used to think about things. (Interview, Jhapa, Nepal,
2016)

Rabindra detailed his pain while we were surrounded by excitement
in the room. His daughter was getting married the next day to a high-
ranking Nepali military officer. Both Rabindra and Sunika were happy.
They were happy at the financial security such an arranged marriage
would bring for their daughter and the status of the marriage. The next
chapter will explore more about what this happiness does and means,
but to mention it here is also to illuminate that Gurkhas' desire to work
as security contractors cannot just be understood as their 'calling' as
martial raced men. Asking Gurkhas to reflect upon their military service
as fathers, as sons and as husbands illuminates the tensions of both
joy and pain that run parallel in their relationships to their security
managers and their role as security contractors. When I asked Rabindra
to reflect further upon his service and how he coped with missing his
family, he stated:

We are men, we have somewhere or other to work, everyone knows that.
We must have discipline, and we do find people who motivate us, like our
seniors, but we still feel it is difficult. And in our free time, we do share with
each other what is going on within ourselves as everybody has left their
families and there for working purposes. Everybody there is working for their
families . . . our main option is to separate work from family, to not think of
family when we are working.

These various vignettes of love and mutual friendship articulated
in a sense of duty and gratitude to one another certainly foster a sense
of exclusivity – a space that only Gurkhas and their officers can truly
share. But this Gurkha family is also filled with ambivalence in terms
of how specifically Gurkhas feel inside this friendship. Expressions of
love for Gurkha military history and service bring Gurkhas and officers
together emotionally in an exclusive 'there is no one quite like us' bond.
Outwardly, to persons like myself, the 'us' requires a sense of exceptionalism that is ultimately held against the insecurity of the global markets

and violent environments in which this Gurkha family resides. It leaves people like myself and others on the outside, curiously looking in and relying upon men like Tristan and Ian to explain Gurkhas to us – as, of course, many Westerners do not have the opportunity that I have had to spend time with Gurkhas and their families.

In this context, the positioning of the Gurkha security family against the insecurities of the global market reinforces an affective investment by both Gurkhas and officers like Ian and Tristan, whereby empathy and concerns of welfare justify and legitimise patronising management styles, and Gurkhas feel an overwhelming need to express duty and gratitude for the opportunities provided to them. Yet when we look inside this relationship, we also see a high degree of ambivalence for this kind of security work. Open expressions of outward gratitude and duty to serve run parallel with personal desires, articulated in interviews as a wish for a different path and a different life for the next generation of Gurkhas. This Gurkha history, love and friendship also might be very much time-bounded, as this reflection of an encounter between the son of a Gurkha and Tony Bergin, a former British Gurkha officer, articulated to me suggests:

> During a holiday in the UK, I came across a son of a former Gurkha I used to command. After saying hello and exchanging pleasantries I asked the young man what he was planning to do for a career. The young man replied that he was signing up for the navy. I was surprised [at] his response. I asked this young man why he was not going into a Gurkha regiment and following his father's and grandfather's military career. He replied, 'Sir, if I may be direct?' I said, 'Yes of course,' to which he replied, 'I do not want to be told what to do by younger versions of you.' (Interview, August 2012)

Reading over this young man's response almost a decade later reflects, for me, how the rise in political and economic choice attached to UK settlement rights also affords Gurkhas, and their families, the ability to challenge colonial relations, and, in particular for this son of a Gurkha, to communicate their subjectivities differently. While this choice surprised Tony, for the son of the Gurkha, being afforded UK citizenship through his father's settlement rights allowed him to choose something other than participating in the Gurkha security family. As British Gurkhas and their families are awarded more political, social and economic rights through their residency in the UK, there is a surplus of retired Indian Gurkhas that are now taking their place in private security.

Conclusion

I have written elsewhere (2014b, 2015, 2017) about how expressions of race and racism manifest in the everyday, reinforcing a naturalisation of Global North/South divisions of labour, whereby Global South contractors are expected to sacrifice the most in terms of physical insecurity, whilst gaining the least. This chapter has extended this previous analysis in looking at the role of love as an affective relation established through martial race histories and military service, and how it works to reinforce these divisions of labour. Love, as it gets entangled with militarism, sustains as much as it obscures the colonial structural violence that underpins the Gurkha security package. Gurkhas and their officers draw upon particular versions of colonial histories to maximise their own material benefits while often obscuring the violence that such colonial relations uphold. The affect of love here reproduces at the same time as it obscures the colonial legacies that continue to underpin this Gurkha security family.

Nepalese men continue to engage actively in competitions of potential for security work, as demonstrated in the previous chapter. This chapter has revealed that even when these Gurkhas avoid the financial coercion and bonded labour of agents, there is a strong feeling of obligation to their former Gurkha officers to behave in an orderly and non-disruptive way – regardless of the labour conditions. Jitendra's story of risking his own life to pursue security employment for the financial benefit of not only himself, but also his white former Gurkha commander, demonstrates that such compulsions to perform as the dutiful Gurkha – choosing to take up dangerous work at the request of their former Gurkha officers – can be just as inhibiting and coercive as being a bonded labourer. The structural dimensions that condition expressions of love through duty and protection are not lost on many of the Gurkhas and their families I spent time with. In fact, when you ask Gurkhas to reflect upon their military service as fathers, husbands and sons, as the next chapter will explore in more detail, strong emotions of regret, pain and loss bubble to the surface.

Through exploring the personal accounts of Gurkhas and British Gurkha officers, this chapter has illustrated how affects of love and duty continue to bind both Gurkhas and British former Gurkha officers in colonial hierarchical relations. Security company owners have detailed how their love of Gurkhas, developed through their work as British officers, was the foundation for them starting their security businesses, with the aim being to ensure Gurkhas could access a lucrative market and be protected from labour exploitation. Gurkhas, in turn, draw upon their regimental duty and admiration for their British national former Gurkha officers as the reasons why they need to protect them physically from the harms and insecurities lurking in hostile terrain. In both cases, appeals to a protector masculinity are performed to give meaning to their own sense of self as empowered men, and give purpose to their security positions. Indeed, it is the affective tie to what it means to be a Gurkha and to not wanting to be the one to let down the Gurkha reputation that offer Gurkhas just as strong a pull to endure the economic and security hardships that come with being positioned at the periphery of markets.

Love as an affective relation continues to position Gurkha British officers as the natural guardians and custodians of the Gurkha name and reputation, and love also makes Gurkhas resilient in the face of hostility and danger. To understand adequately how gendered and racial hierarchies are formed and sustained by those marked as privileged and others as exploited, we must continue to think through how the entanglements of colonial legacies of militarism are structured, experienced and affectively lived. I now turn from love to focus on the affect of happiness in exploring how militarism materialises and is sustained within the 'happy' Gurkha security household.

Notes

1. IDG Security, 'About Us', available at: <https://idg-security.com/about-us/> (last accessed 13 September 2021).
2. See also Tom Gregory's (2019) *Security Dialogue* piece, 'Dangerous Feelings: Checkpoints and the Perception of Hostile Intent', where he draws upon affect to explore how it sticks to certain racialised bodies, rendering some more vulnerable and killable than others.
3. There is a surplus of books and journalist commentary, largely written by British national white authors, discussing the Gurkha military histories and who these men are as martial soldiers. This is not an exhaustive list, but some examples are: Christopher Bellamy's (2011) *The Gurkhas: Special Force*; Christopher Bullock's (2009) *Britain's Gurkhas*; Edmund Candler's (1919) *The Sepoy*; J. P. Cross and John Chapple's (2007) *Gurkhas at War: Eyewitness Accounts from World War II to Iraq*; Tony Gould's (1999) *Imperial Warriors: Britain and the Gurkhas*; Robert Hardman's (2010) 'As a Gurkha is Disciplined for Beheading a Taliban: Thank God They Are on Our Side!'; and John Parker's (1999) *The Gurkhas: The Insider Story of the World's Most Feared Soldiers*.
4. Here I am reminded of the queer writing of Melanie Ritcher-Montpetit (2014, 2017) and Catherine Baker (2016), as well as Spike V. Peterson (2010, 2014), who all use queer theory to render binary immutable concepts such as gendered

and sexual relations fluid and to highlight the spatial and temporal sexual hier-archies within global politics.

5. FSI WorldWide, 'Our History', available at: <http://fsi-worldwide.com/about-us/history/our-history/> (last accessed 7 May 2021).

6. See, for example, Caplan's Chapter 3, 'Officering Gurkhas: The Culture of Command', in *Warrior Gentlemen: 'Gurkhas' in the Western Imagination* (1995), for a historic examination of how Gurkha officers were central in the production and performativity of Gurkhas and integral to constructing the Gurkha family, regiments who were understood as separate from and exceptional to the rest of the Indian army.

CHAPTER 4

The Happy Gurkha Housewife: Reproductive and Affective Labour in Global Security Households

> I was really happy to become a Gurkha wife. We would have a good lifestyle, wouldn't have financial problems, we would not have problems to fulfil the basic necessities of life like food and clothing. (Songita, May 2017, Nepalgunj, Nepal)

Spouses of security contractors and the labour they perform are almost completely absent from conversations around global labour and PMSCs.[1] When Gurkha wives have entered into conversations, they have largely been understood as the grateful benefactors of a global security industry. Such an assumption assigns these women to the side-lines, unworthy of study. This logic pervades not only the global military and security markets,[2] but also the broader global labour recruitment industry, and, indeed, has influenced our understanding of who are actually the workers, as well as the knowledge producers within global markets.

Wives are rarely treated as active stakeholders and agents in the broader circulation of global labour.[3] This is an error. Such an over-looking of wives and families misses the ways in which global security regimes and markets continue to draw upon their emotional, affective and reproductive labour in order to exploit workforces. For example, Alison Howell's (2015) work describes the emotional work military wives of US soldiers do as integral to making these (mostly men) resilient as soldiers. Saskia Stachowitsch and I have detailed how colonial histories within Nepal have fostered community life patterns around foreign military service, making the recruitment of Nepali men into the global security industry straightforward and almost pre-destined (see Chisholm and Stachowitsch 2016). In addition, Rashid's (2020) *Dying to Serve: Militarism, Affect, and the Politics of Sacrifice in the Pakistan Army* explores how mothers grieving over the loss of their sons are constructed by the Pakistani state as irrational and primitive in order to maintain the narrative of the patriotic soldier's sacrifice for the state. Rashid's (2021) work extends this analysis by illuminating how the family household and the female kin both continue to be feminised sites that must be disavowed and protected by the male soldier. Importantly, while central to how the Pakistan military functions, this process remains ambiguous and negotiated through intimate encounters between spouses of soldiers and soldiers themselves. In each of these cases, women's labour and the household remain central to how security regimes function. Consequently, when we ignore the wives and broader households, not only do we miss vital labour that is indispensable to how global markets function, but we also maintain a single celebratory imagining of the market. We see the market as a space that brings an economic lifeline to these families, without also acknowledging the substantial sacrifices and coercive mechanisms through which they are brought into these market relations in the first place.

This chapter is structured to show, first, the concrete ways that Gurkha wives enter security market relations, and how they come to support the industry through their reproductive and life-building labour. Here, I draw upon two dozen interviews with Gurkha wives to show how structures of patriarchy, poverty and global markets condition possibilities of and for these women. The chapter then moves on to demonstrate how this labour is underpinned by the affective relations these women have with security service, and the role happiness plays in sustaining them as reproductive supporters of global security.

Throughout this chapter I privilege the experiences of Gurkha wives and their central role in global security markets, first with foreign military service and later with commercial security markets. I show how popular understandings of these women as (un)grateful benefactors/housewives of the security industry obscure the profound reproductive and affective labour they perform as a necessary part of how these markets function. This labour involves not only the care work necessary for sustaining family life, but also the labour that goes into sustaining and making a kind of life that continues to build communities where military service remains the fabric of these activities. Overall, I seek to account for the colonial and patriarchal structures that condition the women's everyday lives and the affective relations they have with military service as a central pathway to a good life.

The chapter features two vignettes arising from ethnographic interviews in 2017 with Neha and Sunika, two Gurkha wives from separate

Figure 4.1 Kiran, a Gurkha wife laughing during our interview, in Pokhara, Nepal, August 2017. Photo credit to Robic Upadhayay.

locations in Nepal. These women told different stories about what brought them to become Gurkha wives. Yet their experiences are reflective of the diverse backgrounds of women who become Gurkha spouses, and they show how women navigate the patriarchy, caste, ethnicity and regional structures that shape their experiences as women. Neha and Sunika's experiences were echoed in my interviews and observations with some of the other thirty women I spent time with throughout Nepal from April through to September 2017.

I focus on how these women drew upon the affect of happiness as a feeling they had, or expected to have, or even had once had and wanted to feel again, to make sense of their own experiences and their own world building whilst supporting global PMSCs. In this context, I am particularly interested in questions around how affect underpins how we build our own lives and pathways through the world, as well as those of our children, our spouses, our parents and our broader communities. Focusing on these affective relations as central to our world building gets at the everyday micro practices of living, of being and of connecting – what pathways we invest in, the ones we foreclose and the ones that remain unthinkable.[4] These affective relations often unreflectively draw us down particular pathways (Berlant 2011; Ahmed 2004, 2010; Halberstam 2011). They manifest in the ordinary and in the everyday. They 'do not have to await definition, classification, or rationalization before they exert palpable pressures' on and through us (Stewart 2007, 3).

Affects in the everyday can take us by surprise, but they also can be affirming. In many of my interviews, both myself and the women I was speaking to felt joy, as well as pain and excitement, as they recounted the experiences of their marriage, having their children and building their own homes. At times, we were caught off guard in interviews, the atmosphere flowing from joy to tension as wives recounted particular moments of trauma. These moments demonstrate how affects mark us, bubbling up from recalling a distant memory. These affects of joy, anxiety and dread can be fleeting, as well as enduring. They do not work through a prescriptive meaning (Wetherell 2015). Rather, they materialise 'in the way they pick up density and texture as they move through bodies, dreams, dramas, and social worldings' (Stewart 2007, 3). Affect in the everyday, then, tells us about the 'forces of things' that move us in particular directions, and away from others (Stewart 2007, 16). To demonstrate how affect moves these women and shapes the meaning they place on their own experiences, I turn now to the story of Neha and her recounting of her wedding day.

I Did Not Know I Was Getting Married Until the Morning of My Wedding

I dreamed with my childhood girlfriends that we would never get married. I loved my mother and father so much and I could not imagine leaving them to move into the home of my husband's. This was not a life I imagined or desired. I was happy. I found out on the morning of my wedding day that I was to be married. My parents explained to me in our home that I was to move into my new husband's family home that evening, a few miles away from where we were living. I had never met my husband or his family until that day. (Neha, Chitawan, 2017)

Neha's body slightly stiffened and she fidgeted on her chair across from me as she recalled her wedding day. Her husband sat beside her and put his hand out for hers. She did not appear to see his hands as she looked at me and continued her story. Neha and Jitendra had been married for twenty years. They looked happy to me, as they both had large warm smiles, greeting me and welcoming me into their home. Only moments before, I had asked them to talk about when they first met, a question that I thought would be a warm-up one, as they were laughing and sitting close together across the coffee table from me and my translator, Basanta. Yet, as Neha continued her story, the atmosphere changed. Neha appeared a bit unsettled, with her body tensing. I was taken aback, as I certainly did not expect this reaction. However, this probably shows my own inexperience at the time in understanding the toll of structural and cultural practices that shape and constrain women across Nepal – in this case, arranged child marriage. The room felt heavy as Jitendra, Basanta and I sat quietly and listened.

'We don't tell girls they are going to be married ahead of time because they will run away,' Jitendra told me in a matter-of-fact tone, as a way to explain Neha's testimony. I was at a loss for words. I moved on to my next question.

All of the Gurkha wives I spoke with remembered the day of their wedding vividly. That day had marked a profound change in their everyday lives. Not only do these women become wives at a young age, but they also immediately move into the home of their husband's family. They become, simultaneously, a daughter-in-law and Gurkha wife-in-training. In my interview with Hira, she described her own anxieties around not only getting married at the age of sixteen, but also moving into a new family home over an hour's walk away from her parent's home: 'I was worried about how will I work? How can I make [my

Figure 4.2 Neha, a wife of a Gurkha working in Afghanistan, laughing as she greets us prior to our interview, in Jhapa, Nepal, August 2017. Photo credit to Robic Upadhayay.

in-laws] happy?' (Interview with Hira, Pokhara, Nepal, 2017). During this time, the young bride is really dependent upon her new in-laws to ease the transition. In Hira's case, she said she felt supported and was able to form emotional connections with her new sisters, who were of a similar age.

It is a profound transition for these women, and patriarchal familial practices at the time supported this. The Gurkhas I spoke with, when they began their foreign military service, would send their salary to their parents, particularly if they were in a new marriage, and their wives would receive an allowance administered through their in-laws. This allowance would teach them how and where to spend the money sent home by their husbands. For some women like Hira, this arrangement is a supportive one, while for others, it is a difficult adjustment. Issues around alcoholism and domestic violence in the new household are common, and this affects the integration of these newly married women into their in-laws' home. There is also a great amount of loneliness and many feelings of isolation as the young wife adjusts to life with a new family. Many of the women meet these new family members only on their wedding day. Between the homecomings and departures of their husbands – which usually occur once every twelve months in private security and sometimes even less in the Indian army – Gurkha wives learn to 'mark time' by staying busy with daily chores to keep their mind occupied and away from thoughts of loneliness.

To be sure, Neha's story is not in isolation. Amid the tales of success, achievement and celebrations of being a Gurkha wife, there are also stories like Neha's, which highlight the role that patriarchy, conservative culture and caste all play in shaping life for women in Nepal. While Neha was eighteen when she got married, many women I spoke to were much younger. Child marriages are common in Nepal. Human Rights Watch (2016) has indicated that 37 per cent of Nepali women marry before the age of eighteen and 10 per cent before the age of fifteen, despite Nepali law stating that women need to be twenty years of age to marry. The same report highlights the cultural and economic reasons underpinning this practice. A 2017 UNICEF report points out disparities in numbers of child marriages based upon geographic differences between rural and urban areas, and among educated versus uneducated girls. Nepal has one of the highest rates of child marriage across Asia (UNICEF 2017). For many of the women I talked with, while they were not children when they were married, they did feel a pressure to marry from their parents and other family members. According to Acharya (2008), marriage is a profound cultural and social institutional practice across Nepal. This is so much so that even women aspiring to higher education accreditations and professional careers still need to get married and to balance their career aspirations with reproductive duties and responsibilities for the family. The fact that women are located as mothers, wives and daughters-in-law continues to impact the ways in which they become integrated into more formalised economies, as they have to maintain both reproductive and public (paid) roles simultaneously.

Neha's marriage story was one of anxiety and surprise. Other women I spoke to were given more advanced warning. Some, as the story of Sunika and Rabindra will highlight, have the opportunity to choose for themselves who they marry and how. However, as Dhanamaya said to me, 'We had a saying in the family that we have to get married to a Gurkha army man' (Interview, Jhapa, Nepal, 2017). Dhanamaya's arranged marriage was something she was neither excited nor anxious about. She knew what a Gurkha was because her father was one. Marrying a Gurkha was just something that she learned was expected of her. Others like Hira recounted getting married as a somewhat negative experience: 'I don't know exactly what I felt, I was too young when I got married, but I do remember that I cried a lot and said I don't want to go' (Interview with Hira, Pokhara, Nepal, June 2017). In all of these cases, regardless of the feelings associated with it, marriage was a social arrangement women were expected to participate in.

To understand the social reproductive fabric that sustains Gurkha communities and the broader Nepali communities, we must also understand how patriarchy, caste systems and capitalism all function together in shaping the experiences of wives. Social reproduction within Gurkha households materialises through these specific contexts of capitalism, colonial histories, caste-based cultural systems and militarism. Indeed, capturing the realities and experiences of Nepali women involves exploring how both security and political economy influence their lives (Kunz 2017). Within global private security, the actual care and household provisioning work done by wives arise through a complicated picture of governance that not only involves what the market demands, but also how household work is framed through these particular contexts. In fact, Seira Tamang (2009), a leading feminist scholars who writes and publishes internationally on women's issues in Nepal, convincingly highlights how it is impossible to talk about a unifying Nepali woman or women's experience, given that social markers of caste and region, as well as political party affiliation, have significant cultural and material influences on how women's experiences are shaped. These differences are further entrenched by foreign aid and development schemes, which often pit feminist advocacy groups and non-governmental organisations (NGOs) against one another in competitions for funding (Tamang 2009).

Nepal is a conservative, caste-based, Hindu-governed country that once was also a monarchy. The country has experienced numerous political structures, including the removal of the monarchy, the establishment of a democratic constitution, the Maoist 'People's War' and finally the new constitution and restoring of a democratic state. Amid the changing politics, Nepal has continued to be a Hindu, conservative, patriarchal state, led and developed by elite Hindus located in Kathmandu who are mostly men. In the drafting of its six constitutions, women have largely been absent as decision makers and their experiences and gender rights have rarely been considered. The most recent constitution document, implemented in 2006, did make significant concessions to address women's equality and rights, including those of women from Dalit, Adivasi Janajatis (indigenous) and Madhesis caste communities (Tamang 2011). While women and women's issues appear to be more visible in the constitution, everyday life for women in Nepal does vary significantly, depending upon where they stand. Caste, regional, religious and social economic statuses continue to matter just

Figure 4.3 Songita and her daughter laughing during an interview, in Pokhara, Nepal, November 2018. Photo credit to Robic Upadhayay.

as much as gender. Indeed, it was Tamang that reminded me of this over coffee, during a sunny afternoon in Kathmandu. One cannot speak about women's experiences without paying attention to how these multiple and intersecting power relations materialise. Indeed, the life story of Yogmaya Neupane,[5] as retold by Lyytikainen, Yadav and Wibben (2020), alongside those of the multitude of women I encountered and spent time with throughout my numerous trips to Nepal over the past decade, attests to the fact that Nepali women's experiences are deeply conditioned by multiple axes of power relations that reach well beyond gender.

Despite the varying experiences of women, they continue to conduct the bulk of the reproductive and household work, even if they enter into politics or full-time professional careers. Women also struggle to gain access to resources, as well as ownership of land and political and legal rights, and face social stigma around menstruation, which is still understood as unhygienic and results in menstruating women being physically separated from the family. Women continue to experience child marriages and violence around dowries, and face high levels of domestic abuse once married. Women's integration into formalised economies continues to be gendered and focused on micro credit and deskilling economies such as textile work (Achyara 2008). By deskilling, here I draw upon the feminist political economy work by scholars such as Enloe (2000) and Peterson (2004) to mean economies in which the concepts of 'care work', 'labours of love', 'women's work' and 'naturally suitable' are stand-ins for the idea that their labour requires no professional training. As such, by naturalising the skill it takes to partake in these labour activities, we deskill and devalue the labour. Consequently, women already come into market relations with their labour devalued.

Women's access to the global market through migrant work, and thus to the means of supporting themselves and their families, is also severely restricted. While economic migration contributes over 25 per cent of Nepal's gross domestic product, women make up only a fraction of this (formal) workforce. Grossman-Thompson (2016) claims that, according to Nepal's DoFE, less than 4 per cent of the work permits granted for foreign work are for women. However, the DoFE and other international migration organisations suggest that these figures are not accurate, and that the numbers will be considerably higher when informal access to foreign work through India is considered (Grossman-Thompson 2016). Women's ability to pursue this type of work is governed by both paternalistic state laws and gendered cultural beliefs around women's honour and the (gendered) dangers of foreign labour. Again, Grossman-Thompson (2016) talks specifically about the justification for the ban on Nepali women seeking domestic employment overseas, based upon paternal 'protector' gendered logics. Indeed, in my own fieldwork and conversations with DoFE officials and recruitment agents, there were echoed sentiments along the lines of 'We need to protect women from being assaulted or killed overseas by other foreign men, so we ban their access to foreign work entirely.'

It is within this broader context of patriarchy, the caste system, geographies and the gender politics around coming out of a civil war that Gurkha women and their experiences are situated. Gurkhas traditionally derive from the Rai, Gurung, Pun and Tamang castes; however, they have also been described as having their own unique martial race caste, which has afforded them and their families flexibility in social and economic standing through their military service and international experience (Des Chene 1991). The economic and social influence and affluence that Gurkhas and their families are afforded continue to make this type of military life desirable (Nepal 2020; Chisholm and Ketola 2020) – so much so that becoming a Gurkha wife is often considered a game changer. Young girls in Gurkha settlement areas such as Pokhara grow up with the aspiration of becoming a (British) Gurkha wife, with the goal being to migrate to the UK with their future husband. Often, these young women aspire to training in the health and education sectors, seeing these career paths as easily transferable to economic life in Britain. Despite the extensive difficulties around integration and a sense of belonging experienced by women who have migrated there (Choudhary 2015; Low 2016; Ware 2012),[6] the dream of life in the UK is one that pulls in young girls as much as it does the young men I spoke with throughout Nepal, who were training in the hopes of becoming a British Gurkha.

For those women who become the wives of Indian or Singaporean police Gurkhas and continue to stay in Nepal, their economic, political and social prospects are much higher than those available to their civilian counterparts.[7] These material and social benefits were not lost on the women I interviewed – with many commenting that while life might be hard at times, they continued to see their lives as blessed through their association with military work. In fact, becoming a Gurkha offers an economic and political lifeline not only to the young men who continue to try out during the annual selection process (see my Introduction), but also to their families.

The life of a Gurkha wife in Nepal, as the opening quote from Songita states, is one of financial security. Such security in the context of Nepali everyday life, which is marked by a high degree of insecurity, is remarkable. Gurkha wives' lives are largely considered to be ones of luxury with very little work (Pariyar, Shrestha and Gellner 2014), regardless of whether this perception is rooted in a lived reality. Consequently, wives and family members have a large stake in their male family member becoming a Gurkha. It is because of this broader socioeconomic context that I want to turn next to the story of Sunika and Rabindra.

I Forced Him to Become a Gurkha

'I forced him to become a Gurkha.' When Sunika made this declaration, I felt the room go heavy. Only moments earlier there had been a buzz in the air. Basanta and I had arrived at the home of Sunika and her husband, Rabindra, earlier that morning to find a variety of people rushing around, all preparing for the wedding of their oldest daughter the next day. She was marrying a Nepali army officer, Rabindra had declared with pride as we walked through their front door. Sunika stood inside waiting to escort us to their living room, a space with less activity, where we could sit and talk. I had just opened up my notebook and my iPad, and offered what I considered to be a warm-up question: 'So, what made you want to become a Gurkha?' I had posed the question to Rabindra, but Sunika replied. In that moment when Sunika spoke, I was surprised and caught a bit off guard. I had been researching Gurkhas for nearly a decade and had never come across a wife who had forced her husband into foreign military service. In that moment, I also realised that I never actually asked such questions in the presence of wives. I looked over to Rabindra in my search for a follow-up question. He was seated on the other side of the living room with his head down. He was quiet. Basanta also sat quietly beside him. 'This is the first time I've heard a story like this, Sunika,' I said, with a surprised tone. She then began to tell me about their pathway to military service.

Sunika and Rabindra had come from a hilly and remote area of Nepal, called Panchthar. They had moved to Duran because of the number of insurgent activities between the Maoists and the Nepali military and police forces during the 1990s and early 2000s. 'It was not safe for us to continue to live there,' Sunika told me. She went on:

> At that time we were kids. I was 17 and he was 20, and we didn't really think too much before getting married. But I liked him as he was very handsome, and more than that we got along well, we had some common interests. It has been almost thirty-two years we have been married and till now there is nothing bad or serious that has happened to us and our relationship.

Sunika recalled being a young girl in her village and watching through a window of the local school as a child, the teacher writing on the chalk board and the students sitting in rows of desks, writing. She wanted that life. Her family could not afford to send her to school. She was the oldest and had to work to support her family and her young siblings. Later, she had found herself and Rabindra constrained by poverty once again. At that point, they were married with two small children.

> I only knew that in the village there was a bit of shortage of money in the household and I wanted to really send my children to an English boarding school. I only know [the] Nepali language and some alphabet too. This is the one thing I regret, not getting an education. I wanted a different future for my children. I wanted them to go to school, so I told Rabindra he had to try to become an Indian army Gurkha when they came around for recruitment. We needed money. We had nothing.

I looked over at Rabindra while Sunika continued. He nodded along to Sunika's words, and then said:

> I didn't join the army because I wanted to, and after joining I felt like I had left my young children who were very small, and I was also newly married and had left my wife at home. I felt like I really made a mistake and that I shouldn't have joined the army. All the time during the training, which lasted for eleven months, I always felt like that.

Rabindra said that he eventually got used to this military work pattern and relished the two months off a year that he was given by the Indian army to go home and be with his family. He added, 'That was the system I was used to, and that way I served the army for about sixteen years.'

A lump in my throat was beginning to form and it was difficult to swallow. Rabindra and Sunika held on to their quiet pain, the way Neha and Jitendra had, but differently. Rabindra recounted what had been lost for him as a father and husband over the time of his military service. But these verbalised thoughts were fleeting. They were actually unthinkable. Instead, as I found in my interview with Neha, in speaking further, Rabindra drew upon happiness in the present and in the future, and what being associated with foreign military service had afforded them.

Neha and Jitendra's and Sunika and Rabindra's stories were not tales of the celebratory life of Gurkhas that I had read so much about – and, indeed, had my own emotional investment in – in over a decade of researching this community. These are stories of both pain and joy that run parallel. They are the stories of families building a life and life pathways amid the structures of caste, poverty and patriarchy that condition what kinds of life are possible. But my questions were different ones.

I was asking these husbands and their wives, and also the children of these Gurkha men and spouses, to reflect upon Gurkha service not as soldiers, but through a family prism, as spouses, parents and their children. Upon reflection, I am not surprised now that the answers to what life was like as a Gurkha and as the spouse of a Gurkha were so different.

Sunika began to speak again:

> It wasn't the wrong decision. I was happy thinking that now my daughters will get to study. It had been only eleven days after the birth of my youngest daughter when he had left for the army. I was happy on one side. But after he went, he sent his first letter, which I still have kept with myself. He had written in the letter that in the army they were treating him like an animal. My child was around five months, and I was cooking food when I read the letter, and at that particular moment, all I could feel was pain. I will never forget that day.

I leaned in and listened closely, my eyes fixated on Sunika. Basanta and Rabindra were also quiet, as we all focused on Sunika. 'How did you respond to that letter, did you ask him to come back or remind him of the importance of his sacrifice?' I asked. She answered:

> I couldn't reply to the letter. I wanted to write the letter and sat down to do so, but then again, I thought, what if I write something serious and he comes back? I couldn't have him do that, because everyone in the house, his mother, his father, cousins, relatives, even the neighbours were really happy that he went into the army. No one ever saw the sad part of it. I felt it, his mom felt it. So, I never replied to his letter. I just kept it with me and kept all the pain within myself. I couldn't even tell him to come back, nor could I write a reply to him.

Sunika had tears in her eyes. So did Rabindra. In fact, so did I. She quietly wiped the tears away, as I asked, 'Did you have anyone to talk to about this? It sounds so very difficult. Who were your support systems?' She explained: 'Gurkha wives know this pain. But you cannot tell civilians. They will think you are crazy. You are a Gurkha wife. You are blessed. Why are you complaining?'

Indeed, being a Gurkha wife is largely associated with affluence. It opens up opportunities to what would otherwise be impossible. Like becoming a Gurkha, becoming a Gurkha wife is also a game changer. Gurkha wives have been written about as one of the most empowered groups of women in Nepal – being able to make financial decisions and to take a lead role in the community on behalf of, and in the absence

Figure 4.4 Interview with a Gurkha family, in Jhapa, Nepal, November 2018. Photo credit to Robic Upadhayay.

of, their Gurkha husbands. With Nepal being a conservative patriarchy with its conservative social values, women's choices are often very constrained otherwise, and having access to finances that enable one's everyday life not to be marked by precarity is profound. It allows these women to have a life. Sunika recalled the difference between her life as a Gurkha wife and those of other wives:

> Farmer wives' lives are hard. They don't even have the basic necessities of life. It's difficult for them to even get one meal a day sometimes. But for us, that is not a problem. Life is easier for us. We can even pay for our children's education.

Financial and social affluence clearly opens up possibilities. This fact had led to many of the wives I interviewed generally looking positively upon their lives as Gurkha wives.

Such positive orientations to life in a militarised community do not take away from the pain experienced – however long ago. This reality often bubbled up in my interviews, perhaps because I was someone outside of their immediate lives, but also curious about their experiences. It happened in multiple interviews I conducted with wives. Sometimes the story told was about dealing with an alcoholic and abusive mother-in-law at an early age, and before the young couple had the financial means to separate physically from the in-laws' home. Sometimes wives talked about a huge sense of loss of community and the hopes of starting a new community, and other times the conversation was simply about adjusting to everyday life in the absence of one's husband.

These moments are hidden from the broader celebrated Gurkha wife story. Yet they illuminate what the happy Gurkha wife story obscures: that is, the patriarchal structural violence and the toll that the military pathway exacts on families. Neha's and Sunika's stories illuminate how women come to participate in, and are affectively connected to, global security as Gurkha wives. They show the intense amount of emotional and affective work that goes into sustaining life and building their small life worlds while their husbands pursue foreign military employment. I will return to a broader discussion of affect later. First, I want to move to account concretely for the kinds of life-building and reproductive work these women do to keep life going for their families and communities – and in support of the global security industry.

Waiting and Weighting in the Everyday Life Building of Gurkha Wives

On 10 June 2016, thirteen Nepali (and two India national) security contractors were killed in a car bombing as they were being bused to work from their compound in Kabul. They had been contracted by Sabre Global UK, Ltd, a UK-based security company, to protect the Canadian embassy. When their bodies were flown back to the Triviyani International Airport in Kathmandu, they were greeted by grieving families and an outraged public. Both the security company and the Canadian government were absent from the airport. What was clear with the deaths of these men was that there was limited protection in their livelihoods and no insurance for their families upon their deaths. Their deaths led to another country-wide ban on migration to Afghanistan and Iraq (Sharma 2016). Over the next four years, the families of these contractors would navigate a series of international legal frameworks to seek justice, eventually settling out of court with the Canadian government for 20.4 million Canadian dollars (Nepali Times 2020).

The deaths of these men, the ways in which their lives were (not) protected and how their deaths were handled by security companies, Western companies and governments are not unique. While Western countries rely upon the security work these men and their families provide, they offer few assurances in return. Such a lack of reciprocity and the vulnerabilities of working in this industry are felt by Gurkhas and their spouses – and, indeed, throughout Nepal. The security industry's impact on Nepal first came to the fore on 31 August 2004 with the public execution of twelve unarmed (and non-military) Nepali farmers who were recruited to work in the hospitality industry in Amman, Jordan, but who quickly found themselves trafficked into Iraq, where their convoy was ambushed and they were subsequently gruesomely murdered. Their deaths were videorecorded and circulated globally (Tavernise 2004; BBC News 2004). The murders sparked outrage amongst communities throughout Nepal and led to a country-wide ban on Nepali citizens seeking work in the security industry (BBC News 2010). This is just one tragic case demonstrating the mounting death count of Nepali nationals in the broader global 'War on Terror' efforts led by Western nations (Gill and Sapkota 2020).

The stories above highlight the dangers involved in foreign security and other work. This potential for danger and the actualities of the risk of injury or death in this work remain in the background of Gurkha wives' daily lives. It is the tension between managing the anxieties that come with the realisation of the risk involved for their Gurkha husbands, the hardships of day-to-day life and the hope for a happy future that helps women to mark time as Gurkha wives. The very real possibility of death or injury, notably with little assurance of any welfare support, marks their lives and reinforces a general vulnerability; however, this is all set against the world making and future lives that both Gurkhas and Gurkha wives affectively invest in. Marking time between moments and seeking comfort from a future that has yet to reveal itself become important in this context. As two Gurkha wives said to me:

It won't always be like this. (Nega, Pokhara, Nepal, 2017)

We will be together in the future. (Punam, Nepaljung, Nepal, 2017)

Throughout my interviews with Gurkhas and Gurkha wives, I was told how the beginning years of their lives together were marked by the initial shocks and surprises of what life would be like. But, they all said, they got 'used to it' over time, and life, however hard, became 'normal', while they 'learned' to adjust to the rhythms of everyday life in a Gurkha security household. This speaks to a pattern of training young women that has gone on as long as Gurkhas have been working in foreign militaries. Young women marry, move into their in-laws' homes and

Figure 4.5 Gurkha talking to his family via video call the night before he flies out to Kabul for work, in Kathmandu, Nepal, November 2018. Photo credit to Robic Upadhayay.

are 'managed' into becoming good wives, and then mothers and carers, whilst their husbands are away.

Time marks how these families and individuals build their capacity to endure, but it also marks how everyday life is experienced. This life together in the Gurkha household occurs in stages. There is often an initial shock and feelings of isolation as the young wife moves in with her in-laws for the first time, after which her new husband generally returns for military work after a month with either the Indian army or the Singaporean police. Time is then marked through annual (but sometimes longer) military leave breaks, where the wife is involved in the homecoming celebrations and departure rituals. The time between departures and homecomings can be two years. The period at home is usually one month. In between these homecomings/departures, the wives continue to do all the reproductive tasks in the household, care for their in-laws, fill medical prescriptions, pay land and school fees, participate in community and religious and cultural events and plan future financial investments. Time is then marked again from when the husband and wife, typically along with their children, can afford financially to separate from the in-laws and build a new place, and make a new home, of their own. Finally, time is marked once again from when the Gurkhas retire from the military. For my interviewees, at this stage, work in private security is pursued. Between these various moments, the women mark time through keeping busy with their household work and raising children, interspersed with long periods of waiting. Most of the women I spoke with had years of experience as wives of army soldiers and so their transition to private security was pretty straightforward.

The biggest difference the women spoke about that set them apart from other wives outside of the industry was the long separations from their spouses, and at times, the related intense loneliness. In being physically separated from their husbands, all of the women's life building, involving having and raising children, caring for ageing parents and making financial decisions for immediate and short-term needs and for the future, is often done alone. When I asked what the most difficult thing was about being a Gurkha wife, the women I interviewed articulated the loneliness they felt initially, and, like Sunika, the inability to express this loneliness outwardly.

> When there is a problem I'm facing, it would have been nice to have been together with my husband. But because he is so far away, and then we cannot live together, that part is difficult. (Srimaya, Dharan, Nepal, May 2017)

The husbands also play a key role in facilitating the initial transition for wives from their own family home into their husband's family home. Songita reflected that her husband was her biggest source of support in adjusting to her new life as a Gurkha wife:

> He would write letters to me to explain his family, and then he used to console me, tell me to be patient, and then used to tell me that later we'd move to another place [separating from his family]. (Songita, Dharan, Nepal, May 2017)

Being a Gurkha wife is seen so much as a blessing that to be anything but openly grateful becomes nonsensical. Consequently, women will seek support from their husband's family members or their husbands. For the most part, the women I interviewed said that they needed to reorientate their loneliness into just being a good wife – meaning one who thinks of others. When I asked them about what makes a good Gurkha wife, I was repeatedly told that a good Gurkha wife is someone who keeps the house tidy, who is respectful and kind to her in-laws and her children, and who is a good host. I was also told by some Gurkha wives that they must be disciplined and courageous when faced with adversity, including long periods of being alone and experiencing loneliness. Keeping busy was cited as a way for wives to cope with their husbands being away, often in dangerous work conditions.

> I was so busy in so many things from cooking food, giving food to labourers that come to work on the farm, taking care of the household. Of course, I was worried [about my husband], but most of the time I was very busy. (Srimaya, Dharan, Nepal, May 2017)

> I had to console myself that he had to work in difficult situations to earn for our livelihood and for a better life. Therefore, I engaged in any work at home to relieve the distresses, but I shouldered this burden alone. (Tara, Pokhara, Nepal, April 2017)

Both Srimaya and Tara carried this burden alone and, like Sunika, were not able to share this more broadly within their friendships and family. Women like Songita marked time between the letters she received from her husband in the army.

> At the time we did not have the facility of phones. We would get letters once a month only, and I used to keep waiting for the letters. I would receive a letter and wait in anticipation of getting the next. (Songita, Surket, Nepal, June 2017)

Amid the intense feelings of loneliness and, at times, physical isolation, these women keep life going and keep the family together. They not only produce and sustain physical life (bearing children, caring for ageing parents), but they also reproduce a quality of life for themselves, their husbands and their children. This involves making financial decisions for a secure future, choosing boarding schools for their children and getting involved in community engagement activities, not only through giving money, but also in making decisions impacting the community. Perhaps most intangible is the profound work they do to teach their children to know and to love their physically absent father.

> We show [the children] pictures of [their father] and talk about him all the time. We tell them their father is working hard and sacrificing so they can have a nice life here. (Hira, Pokhara, Nepal, April 2017)

> Before their father comes home, we all plan together what foods we will cook for him. The children get excited about all the chocolates he will bring them. (Songita, Surket, Nepal, June 2017)

The wives are instrumental in emotionally managing both the homecomings and departures of their husbands for themselves and the children. These are deeply emotional times, as they only happen once each year on average. Planning for the initial arrival and for how the children and their father will settle in and become reacquainted is the responsibility of the wives.

> I encourage my children. Go to him. He's your daddy. They look at him from a distance at first, but he brings out candy and they are quickly on his lap. (Neha, Chitiwan, Nepal, April 2017)

Managing these emotions and working to ensure a loving and close family is important work. It sustains and reproduces life beyond physical living, but also secures qualities important for the family. The women's emotional work in showing the children who their father is, in demonstrating that his work is a sacrifice and is honourable, also ensures that the legacy and importance of being a Gurkha is carried to the next generation.

Certainly, the children I spoke with articulated love for their Gurkha fathers, but there is always a cost when forming social and familial bonds at a distance. Rabindra, one of the Gurkhas I spoke with, expressed the pain of the pull to be with his family and the reality of the work that necessitated him being away from them:

> There is always a tug-of-war within me between these two roles [of husband and of Gurkha] I have to play. I could not reduce one or exchange one with the other, because both are crucial. My coping strategy is to keep myself busy as a way to ward off stresses. (Rabindra, Jhapa, Nepal, May 2017)

Rabindra's testimony illuminates the tough choices men make when pursuing this foreign military labour. Throughout my interviews there was the same quiet tension in the recognition that being physically away from the home came at a cost. Wives quietly admitted to me that their children were not as close to their father. While they did their best to teach their children to know and to love their father, their love was often out of a sense of duty.

> My elder daughter was born when her father was abroad, so it was difficult for her to get close to [her] father as we were not living together. But slowly she got used to him. He would bring her chocolates. He was physically around with my youngest daughter, to raise her. They are very close. (Dhanmaya, Jhapa, Nepal, May 2017)

Gurkhas working in private security now have consistent access to WiFi when on duty and can be perpetually available through Facebook Messenger and WhatsApp. This immediate access enables the men to have regular contact and involvement in the everyday running of their families. In fact, unlike the UK spouses of security contractors I interviewed (see Chisholm and Eichler 2018), Gurkha wives spoke about ensuring that their husbands were immediately involved in the day-to-day running of their family 'back home'. Whereas the wives in military households within the UK generally manage the day-to-day running of households to let the male spouses focus on their security work (Chisholm and Eichler 2018), Gurkha wives continue to keep family life going, but they also involve the Gurkha men in everyday life – albeit virtually. Consequently, Gurkha wives ensure that Gurkhas remain a core part of the family, beyond being the breadwinner, despite them being physically away. This is a core strategy in building families and connecting the family members' life-building labour across different geographies.

All of this unpaid and often unacknowledged work that Gurkha spouses do in keeping families together, so that the broader security industry can extract the security labour it does, remains silenced, in part because it is understood as taking place outside the security market. It is through the logic of 'housewification', Mies (1986) claims, that this work is understood and rendered not as work, but as an activity. What Mies means by this is that when we locate the kinds of reproductive work these women do as taking place in the private home and we understand them not as workers, but as housewives, we view their reproductive work as 'activities' – as something that supplements the 'breadwinning' work of Gurkhas in private security. Thus, it does not become worthy of study or broader interventions. It is the kind of work that is considered natural work that women are born to do. Such a conceptual move feminises[8] this work, moving it away from something that has important market value, that involves skill, into a timeless natural division. This gendered process of housewification/feminisation, as Mies (1986), as well as Enloe (2014) and Peterson (2005), indicates, makes Gurkha wives' work cheap. We devalue this work when we see it as a supplemental activity to what we perceive as the real and paid work of Gurkhas.

Such conceptual separations and the broader devaluing of women and their work occur in military households in other geographic and political locations. In fact, the body of research accounting for women's military household labour is now quite extensive, as the beginning of this chapter highlighted. Located within critical military studies and feminist IR subfields, the scholarship is diverse. It includes feminist global political economy framings of the military, where the concrete (un)paid activities of military spouses involve both the outsourcing of military support for post-traumatic stress disorder (PTSD) and the broader mental health needs of soldiers returning home, and all of the social reproductive work inside the home. Such scholars seek to illuminate how, in all of these spaces, the everyday and the household play a key role in how states and non-state actors (Hedström 2017) are able to wage war.

The Gurkha spouses I talked to were taking on most of the reproductive work of the household. Their responsibilities, among others, were cleaning, cooking, ensuring children were fed and excelling at their studies, tending to the needs of ageing parents and parents-in-law, making investments in land and business, participating in cooperative banking schemes with other Gurkha wives, and planting and growing rice and vegetables. All of these daily activities are foundational to ensuring that family life is sustained. Consequently, the everyday lives led and concrete emotional and reproductive work done in Gurkha homes are similar to those of other security households. The ways in which military service demands this type of gendered division of labour and appropriates the household into the broader military fold continue to place primacy on waging war over other ways of organising family life.[9]

MacLeish's (2013) ethnographic reflections, arising from time spent with serving soldiers and their spouses at Fort Hood, the US military base, offer a glimpse of everyday life for this militarised community. Throughout the vignettes with various interlocuters, he demonstrates the affective tolls on US military spouses and reflects on who might have the harder job – those doing security work 'over there' or those holding the fort at home. These military families are called the unsung heroes, MacLeish (2013) proposes,[10] as a way of acknowledging what they do, whilst not addressing any gendered or racial structures that position people in these roles. MacLeish also shows how everyday life for soldiers and their spouses is bound together by death and the very real possibility of soldiers dying.

MacLeish (2013) highlights how the lives of US-national military spouses are governed by military temporal rhythms surrounding deployments. This is, in other words, not just an experience of Gurkha wives. Military wives in the US are also conditioned through the intertwining of both the 'wait and weight' (2013, 103) of everyday life, as MacLeish refers to it – the waiting for the phone call (or no phone call) and for homecomings, but also the weighting of the rug that may be pulled out from under them with the news that their military serving spouse or someone in their unit has died (2013, 95–6). MacLeish thus accounts for the heaviness that resides within military households and military spouses in his research. Their everyday life is framed by waiting for news of whether their military serving partner is dead or injured, and by how such dreaded feelings and anxiety bubble up, as much as the wives try to control it. These feelings are accompanied by long periods of absence and waiting for the serving partner to return. Overall, this marking of time 'becomes something qualitatively different, as a defining feature under which life is reproduced' (MacLeish 2013, 96). Such time counting and the practice of waiting between tours were very much felt and lived by the Gurkhas and Gurkha wives I interviewed, as they built their lives and families around homecomings and departures and the marking of time in between.

Alison Howell (2015) and Denise Horn (2010) both emphasise the ways in which militaries continue to rest very much upon and to appropriate the labour of these households. In many ways, the experiences and perspectives of the Gurkha spouses I spoke to resonate with the aforementioned studies, highlighting how aspects of the security household might indeed be global. But there are also historical and structural contexts that make the experiences of Gurkha wives particular. There were moments when I, as a security contractor spouse/partner, resonated with the work these women do, the emotional work they take on and how their lives are shaped through the security industry's rhythms and routines around homecomings and departures. Conversely, the ways in which these women navigated life choices that were structured through caste, the patriarchal Nepali state and the security market were experiences that I, along with other Western security contractor spouses like me, did not share.

Broader economies of war certainly structure the everyday lives of Gurkha spouses as well. Their life paths, hopes and dreams are fundamentally informed by the broader patriarchy within Nepal, the overarching gendered norms on what is acceptable and appropriate for women to do and how this is all further compounded by practices of caste relations. There are experts on this subject within Nepal who write about these entanglements, and notable scholarship includes the work of Tamang (2009).

In many ways, Gurkha spouses are often prepared for the absences, the waiting and the living with dread. With over 200 years of military history of Gurkhas fighting on behalf of the British empire and Indian army, women, just as much as young men, are conditioned to tread these life pathways. Many of the wives I spoke to were already very familiar with what a Gurkha was and what being a Gurkha wife entailed when they married. These women had built-in support systems, often moving in with their husband's family at the time of the marriage. Yet this support infrastructure can also lead to further isolation and violence for these women.

Feelings of dread and anxiety resonated throughout my interviews with Gurkhas and their spouses. The couples managed these feelings by maintaining regular contact through texting platforms such as Viber, Facebook Messenger and WhatsApp, and through life-building work, including planning for the future amid the harms and trauma byproducts of the security industry. And yet, the hardships were not their focus, and I must therefore return to how the women largely assigned meaning to these activities and to building a life within the context of their participation in global security. As two of the women shared with me:

We are happy. (Soniga, Pokhara, Nepal, August 2016)

We Gurkha families are very different. In our families, we get good salaries and are financially well off. We can afford things, and also get our children a good education. We feel a bit proud when we hear people calling us Gurkhalis. It is good. (Srimaya, Dharan, Nepal, May 2016)

So far, this chapter has focused on the concrete ways in which Gurkha wives support the global security industry and how they have come to do so. It has also explored why this work continues to be seen as conducted outside of security market activities – and is therefore largely silenced as work important for the security industry. Yet this supportive work is profound in terms of how life building is practised in the family, and for how and in what ways the security industry can extract labour from Gurkhas. Gurkhas can be away for eleven months of the year because Gurkha wives pick up the slack in the life-building work, in keeping families together and in supporting future generations at home. Indeed, as Basham and Catignani (2018) illuminate, such relationships extend to broader military communities in the ways that the military (and, by extension, the private security industry) remains a 'greedy' institution that continues to draw upon the flexible labour of households in order to perform its military functions.

Most of those who come to be Gurkha wives have experiences of poverty and feel a desperation for an everyday life that is not marked by a need merely to survive. To become a Gurkha wife is finally to be able to be financially secure and to be afforded space and time to plan for the future. But, as the stories of Neha and Sunika that opened this chapter also illuminate, this life is also about stories of trauma and violence. Despite these testimonies, all the women I interviewed and spent time with said that they were happy.

Happiness in these testimonies acts to sustain the attachments to militarism and to military pathways as fundamental in the broader world-building projects these women are involved in. To be finally happy and to secure a happy future for the children are all future-orientated goals that help these women make sense of their pasts and the contemporary moment. But what is happiness as an affective practice doing in these moments of life building?

The Politics of Happiness

I began this chapter with the narratives of Neha and Sunika because they capture the significant restraints and possibilities faced by Gurkha women – and, indeed, all women in Nepal. Both women told stories of significant trauma: trauma that was stuffed down, that was normalised, that informed their past and that continued to bubble up in their present. Yet, both women expressed enormous amounts of happiness outwardly. Happiness in both of their contexts was tied so much to broader structures of gendered power that work to naturalise women (and men) into a particular life pattern. As an affect, this makes some life pathways seem more desirable and promising than others.[11] Happiness was felt in the everyday world-building moments for Neha and Sunika. It could be observed in the buzz in the air and the excitement in the preparations for Sunika and Rabindra's oldest daughter's impending wedding. It was articulated in the solace and sense of accomplishment Neha and Jitendra expressed in their ability to send their children to a private boarding school and to secure a different kind of future for their children. This everyday life building is marked by what Stewart (2007, 1) classifies as 'shifting assemblages of practices and practical knowledges, a scene of both liveness and exhaustion' – a dream of a simple life where insecurities around food, water and housing cease. It materialises in what Wetherell (2015) refers to as 'affect as practice': that is, the routinised ways that bodies are moved, objects are handled, subjects are treated and things are described in the world (Reckwitz 2002, 249–50, as cited in Wetherell 2015, 148).

In this context, and returning to Ahmed's (2004) affective circulation, affects of hope and happiness accumulate around the object of the

Gurkha. Objects can be anything that triggers an emotional response. This includes, but is not limited to, people, memories and material objects. How we are orientated towards (or away from) these objects depends upon our own histories and human meaning-making practices, which bind together objects (in this case Gurkhas) and affects of happiness and hope. The object Gurkha is made meaningful in its association with the underdevelopment and poverty that mark a great deal of everyday life in Nepal. Juxtaposed to this, becoming a Gurkha, or being immediately associated with one, is a lifeline out of extreme forms of poverty. In this context, then, Gurkhas come to accumulate and are saturated with affects of security and stability. Marrying a Gurkha enables these women to have a life where they have time and space to plan a future for themselves and their children. Becoming a Gurkha wife matters not only because of the material consequences, but also because marriage 'hold[s] promise in the present moment . . . and a whole cluster of affects [including hope, joy and pain] magnetised to the [promise of marriage]' (Stewart 2007, 2). For both Neha and Sunika, marrying a Gurkha was also an affective promise of happiness through the accumulation of affects of security and safety that bind to the object of Gurkha. Happiness can be considered a future-orientated affect as much as a practice in the moment. As Songika put it, 'I will be happy when my children are all at home together' (Interview with Songika, Pokhara, Nepal, August 2016).

Happiness becomes a question of following the right pathway, rather than finding it 'out there'. It is, as Wetherell (2015) describes, a practice. So long as we do this or that, and continue this process, we will be happy. Therefore, happiness obscures other ways of feeling about the choice to become a Gurkha spouse – if that choice is, indeed, granted. For the Gurkha women I interviewed, becoming a Gurkha wife was about following the pathway to happiness. It meant lifting themselves out of poverty and having a future that was not bound with the same reproductive struggles of securing food and a roof over their heads.

Happiness – and how one becomes happy – is thus context-specific, and indeed, as cultural feminists like Ahmed (2010), Berlant (2011) and Halberstam (2011) remind us, it is not open to everyone. Not everyone is meant to be happy, or entitled to experience happiness. In this sense, happiness tells us a great deal about structural power within broader practices of life making. Nepal is a patriarchal state where gendered divisions of labour are determined and sustained through naturalising 'women's work' as the care work done both in and outside of the home. Even women who are socially and financially affluent, and who work outside the home in business, politics or development, for example, experience an enormous amount of pressure to marry, to have children and to care for their ageing parents, parents-in-law and husbands. This sort of labour and the constrained choices available to women are further dependent on one's caste. So, overall, women do most of the social reproductive work across the country, but women of lower castes have fewer opportunities to negotiate a life outside of this division of labour.

Conclusion

Raising the visibility of the concrete social reproductive work wives do to support Gurkhas working the private security industry is an important first step in understanding the role of the Gurkha family. This chapter has demonstrated the role that affect plays in sustaining these women within a particular life pattern of familial duties, which also include the affective work involved in keeping Gurkhas resilient as they work 'over there'. Such resilience comes through making the women a part of the social fabric by bringing them into the everyday banal activities of child and adult care work and community engagement, as well as investment planning for the future.

In many ways, the testimonies of Sunika and Rabindra, and Neha and Jitendra are novel, but their stories also fit with how other Gurkha families articulate their experiences. These experiences also align in many ways with other security and military households written about globally. But reproductive and care work does not just happen in the home; nor does it entail only the work of women. We now travel away from Nepal, back to Kabul, to illuminate other emotional and care work being produced in the intimate everyday encounters between security clients and Gurkha security providers.

In all of this, happiness, as an affective relation to military service and to being a Gurkha wife, has to be placed within the broader patriarchal and capital structures into which these women are born and raised. Despite the trauma and violence detailed specifically by Sunika and Neha, but also by other Gurkha wives, becoming a Gurkha wife is, indeed, a game changer. It pulls many of these women out of a lifetime of extreme poverty, where having an everyday life filled with routine and habit is aspirational. Still, this kind of happiness continues to come at a significant cost.

These women's value as wives comes through their ability to endure without complaint and to do all the care work, to keep life going in the home and to plan for their own and their children's futures. Their work and its contribution to the global security markets are often unacknowledged by broader global security actors and theoretical framings around security markets. But, just as scholars who look at military households and household labour have found, the kinds of reproductive work that Gurkha wives do to keep life going are indispensable to how global security markets function. I now turn to a different kind of security reproductive and affective labour, that of Gurkha men. In the next chapter, I examine the kinds of affective work these men do, and how this work is valued within both broader global security framing and the intimate security encounters between Gurkhas and the Western clients they are contracted to protect.

Notes

1. The exception here is the work myself and Maya Eichler have done on UK female spouses of British-national security contractors (Chisholm and Eichler 2018).
2. To consult, for example, the feminist writing on the military household, see the works of Parashar (2013), Enloe (2000), Hedström (2017), Basham and Catignani (2018), Chisholm and Eichler (2018), Chisholm and Stachowitsch (2016) and Spanner (2020).
3. See the growing feminist political economy work on wives to illustrate the gendered politics that continue to position women and families on the periphery of economies (Mies 1986) and in peace studies (Lyytikainen, Yadav and Wibben 2020), even while they continue to be coercively brought into market relations (LeBaron 2010).
4. I am heavily influenced here by the cultural feminist writings of Stewart (2007), Ahmed (2004, 2010), Halberstam (2011) and Berlant (2011), who have rigorously demonstrated the ways affect is foundational to how we live and feel our way through the world.
5. Nepupane was a Brahmin-born girl who grew up in the eastern hills of Nepal in 1860–8. She was married at the age of nine (possibly younger). After her first husband died, faced with the social exclusion common for Nepali widows, she left her married home to go back to her family, where she fell in love and married another man from her local village – despite the cultural practice forbidding widows to remarry. Nepupane spent a lifetime committed to non-violent peace activism (Lyytikainen, Yadav and Wibben 2020, 11–12). Nepupane's life history of defying gender, caste and local cultural expectations for a woman of her standing remains an aspirational story for Nepali women, but it is also a reflection of how Nepali women's lives and how they negotiate them are conditioned by intersections of gender, caste, class and geography, amongst other social markers.

6. For a great in-depth sociological inquiry into spouses of retired British Gurkhas now settled in the UK, see Neha Choudhary's 2015 MA thesis, entitled 'The Gurkha Wives of United Kingdom: Challenges to Social Integration', from the London School of Economics. See also the work of Low (2016) on the Gurkha migrant diaspora in Asia and Southeast Asia and how military service, over sentiments of nationhood, continues to influence feelings of belonging within these communities. Ware (2012) also explores how caste-based social organising forms an important part of integration and bonding amongst Nepali Gurkha communities in the UK, impacting women's integration.

7. See the work of Nepal (2020) for an illustration of the significant social and financial influence and wealth that Gurkhas and Gurkha families bring to Nepal through remittances and broader development projects.

8. Connecting to Mies's (1986) theory of housewification, feminisation remains an important concept for feminists to account for the gendered politics that underpin the organisation of work. The concept was introduced by Guy Standing (1989), who revisited it (in 1999) to highlight the global shift of workforces from men to women, alongside a broader move towards deregulation and flexibilisation of work. Feminisation as a concept continues to find purchase in illuminating the concrete discursive and structural politics that render work taken up largely by women as devalued (Enloe 2014; Peterson 2005). See the exemplary empirical use of this concept and how it relates to global structures of coloniality and race in the works of Encarnación Gutiérrez-Rodríguez (2014).

9. For an exemplary account of how the military continues to control the everyday lives of families and appropriate reproductive labour for military ends, see the works of Basham and Catignani (2018) on the role of military reserve families in support of British military operations and Gray (2019) on domestic violence support in the British military.

10. MacLeish's (2013) chapter 'Being Stuck and the Other Problems in the Reproduction of Life' is exceptional in its detailed accounts, through the experiences of soldiers and their spouses, of the heaviness of the everyday life a military family leads.

11. I am indebted to the rich cultural feminist research on affect here, particularly on how happiness runs alongside failure, and how both affects tell us a great deal about how world making is also about structural privilege. As Sara Ahmed (2010) reflects, happiness is also very much about who gets to be happy and who is entitled to happiness.

CHAPTER 5

Race, Gender and the Political Economy of Feeling Secure

In previous chapters, I drew upon postcolonial and cultural feminist scholarship to examine how affect sticks to certain security bodies, and how Gurkhas and their families become saturated with colonial histories of martial race. I explored how these affects then materialise in how these individuals are understood as subaltern military subjects and the ways in which they come to understand their own positionalities. I also looked at how friendship and expressions of a colonial military familial love materialise from these imperial histories in ways that further reinforce the unequal relationship between Gurkhas and British Gurkha officers. The book then moved to a discussion of the politics of happiness. As a future-orientated affect, happiness was examined in Chapter 4 to illuminate how this affect draws Gurkha wives and husbands into military life and militarised pathways in the hopes of being happy in the future. I traced how repeated phrases like 'we will be happy' co-exist with stories of pain and trauma from the past, rendered meaningful within the broader context of extreme poverty, and how all of this works to explain away and obscure the visceral pain and trauma that run parallel to the celebratory joyful experiences that being a Gurkha, and being married to one, can bring. Overall, Chapters 2–4 focused on how affect sustains us in particular life patterns and practices – even when they prove toxic and traumatic, and our dreams are impossible to achieve.

This chapter explores the feminist political economy and postcolonial scholarship on how affect is taken up in the everyday within these gendered and raced market relations, and how it has shaped and is shaping global racial and gendered logics. I extend the emotional and reproductive labour analysis from Chapter 4 by focusing on the political economy of affect that goes into reproducing a secure life for security company clients in Kabul. This includes the affective labour that works to 'induce or suppress feeling in order to sustain the outward countenance that produces the proper state of mind in others' (Hochschild 1985, 7), and the metabolising of unwanted affects and affective byproducts, including how we absorb and stuff down affects of shame and anger in managing a collective atmosphere as well as other people's emotions (Whitney 2017, 643).

I proceed by first revisiting the important feminist affective labour research that has exposed the racialised global structures that underpin how emotions and affect are brought into market relations. I then move on to discuss how emotional work in private security becomes naturalised on to the bodies of racialised security practitioners and more concretely illuminate the kinds of emotional and affective labour that feature in global commercial security in making clients feel safe. Here, I make clear that the racialised and gendered bodies of Gurkhas and the histories that stick to them as martial bodies invariably shape the affective work they are expected to do. These men take on the bulk of the devalued and thankless care work involved in making clients (and other contractors) feel secure, which, as discussed in Chapter 4, is also reflective of the experiences of Gurkha wives. I then shift to explore how value in security labour is articulated through the everyday and intimate settings in which this labour is actually performed and practised. This section largely focuses on the perceptions of security and security value from the standpoint of white Western clients being protected in Kabul.

The final section examines the commodification and circulation of affect within security and talks about which racialised and gendered bodies are allowed to offload and to have surplus affect and those who are supposed to swallow the negative affects of others, or, in the words of Whitney (2017), be the affective waste disposals in security. What I focus on in this section is how racialised men tend to be positioned in such a way that makes them receptacles for other people's outbursts, be it in anger or frustration. While these outbursts might make the person expressing them feel better, lending a sense of release, they deplete and wear out those who are intended to absorb these surplus feelings. This final section is attuned to the psyche and physical harms that run through this kind of labour.

Raced Markets and the Global Political Economy of Emotions

The security industry that this book explores is part of the global raced markets that are structured around the exploitation and extraction of labour from Global South brown and black bodies for the material and affective benefit of Global North populations (Chisholm 2014a; Barker 2015). Indeed, the security industry is underpinned by the global 'colour line' (Du Bois 1903; Fanon 1967; Razack 2004; Roy 2001; Anievas, Manchanda and Shilliam 2015) that mediates whose labour is taken up and the nature and conditions of that labour. Black feminists have long sought to demonstrate how women of colour continue to navigate structures of classism, racism, and sexism in domestic political economies (Davis 1981; Crenshaw 1993). This scholarship and insights from black feminists have also gone global in critiques of international labour markets, as well as in research on everyday lives and gendered and racialised divisions of labour (Federici 2011; Nevins and Peluso 2008; Agathangelou 2004; Henry 2012; Chisholm 2014a; Tilley and Shilliam 2018; Rai, Hoskyns and Thomas 2013; Gutiérrez-Rodríguez 2014; Whitney 2017; Elias, Rethel and Tilley 2019). Overall, the research illuminates the ways in which imperial histories, colonial geographies, sexism and racism continue to shape domestic and global markets, and how people from domestic black and brown communities and from the Global South come to participate in them. Once we take into account how economic structures shape experiences, we begin to see how concepts such as race (and racism) impact more than just ideology or identity. As Tilley and Shilliam remind us:

> race must be apprehended as a mode of classifying, ordering, creating, and destroying people, labour power, land, environment and capital; race precedes scientific racism by some centuries. (2018, 537)

As the previous chapters have shown, race and gender profoundly structure access to these markets, the experiences and material realities of Gurkhas and other Global South labourers working in global private security, and the families' support of these markets. Understanding private security markets as underpinned by racism, then, alerts us to how race underlies the movement of people in and out of security markets, to security labour conditions, to how divisions of security labour are organised and to whose lives matter and are worth making safe. This chapter begins with a structural understanding of the market, to better attend to how race and racism play out in everyday security practices between Gurkhas and the predominantly white Western clients they protect. Its particular focus is on how security contractors are perceived as valuable and what kinds of labour they are expected to perform.

Affective work, or attending to the emotional wellbeing of clients, colleagues and other contractors, is the central labour that this chapter explores. Feminist scholars have been at the forefront of showing how this labour gets taken up, the broader feminisation of it as it is made into women's work, and the raced, classed and gendered structures that underpin the broader organising of this kind of work (Davis 1981; Schultz 2006; Oksala 2016; Whitney 2017). An accumulation of decades of feminist research shows that while affective work continues to be largely taken on by women, not all women do the same kinds of work. Indeed, black feminist scholars have been keen to remind us of the race divide in emotional and care work, enabling white middle-class women to maintain a purity around the self and the home, while black domestic workers have undertaken the 'dirty work' (Oksala 2016; Davis 1981). As this kind of work continues to be brought into market relations and to go global, racialised men, just as much as women, are also taking on this affective work. Consequently, it is important not only to name what affective labour is, but also to account for the ways in which this kind of labour is structured around class, race and gender at the international level (Whitney 2017; Schultz 2006; Oksala 2016). In other words, we need to track the nature of this affective work within global security, and also who is performing it. Accounting for this kind of labour shows how certain racialised bodies come to be seen as naturally suitable for this work, and also reveals the material and emotional costs for the contractors taking up this labour.

The Everyday of Doing Security Work

I am interested in the affect labour that underpinned the reproduction of securing lives for clients living and working in Kabul at the time of my research, and how Gurkhas and other TCN contractors come to be seen as naturally suitable for this work. Echoing the observations of other feminist International Political Economy (IPE) scholars exploring affect, I propose that this kind of labour is heavily racialised and that it generally falls to the feminised and racialised security bodies to manifest pleasant and friendly dispositions and to absorb negative affect, often in the form of abusive outbursts, without responding. To explore the nature of this affective labour, who does it and how it gets (de)valued in everyday security encounters between clients and Gurkha contractors, we will now move geographically from the homes and experiences of Gurkha wives in Nepal back to Kabul, Afghanistan, to show the reproductive work that is done to keep PMSCs clients' lives going.

The everyday life of doing security in Kabul is underpinned by broader colonial histories that shape divisions of labour and how global workers access certain markets. Such geographies shape the movement of people globally, including where they go, what work they seek and how they become understandable as global security workers (Condos 2017; Metcalf 2007). Feminists remind us that these raced markets are reinforced through states acting as brokers for their citizens (Magalit-Rodriguez 2010), and that, as a consequence, they reproduce and further entrench racialised and gendered forms of global domestic and care labour (Agathangelou 2004). The work of both Magalit-Rodriguez and Agathangelou focuses on the kind of world-building and life-making activities that are central to Global North families' everyday lives, and how it all fundamentally depends upon the physical and emotional exploitation of women from the Global South. While neither scholar specifically engages in affective labour, they both demonstrate how extractive this kind of market-based relationship is and how it is predicated on broader colonial and raced global market logics that normalise this kind of exploitative practice and use of brown and black bodies.

Feminist IPE scholars have also paid attention to how these affects become commodified and the racialised and gendered nature of this kind of work. As detailed in Chapter 1, key feminist scholars include Hochschild (1985), McDowell (2009) and Wolkowitz (2006). Hochschild's seminal book *The Managed Heart* accounts for the ways the airline industry takes up and draws upon affects to make their customers feel special, safe and happy. She calls attention to how feelings and affects considered private, such as the emotions and work done by unpaid wives and other women, come to take on market value and how private emotions become commoditised. Hochschild (1985) is quick to note the gendered nature of this kind of market value, and how some gendered bodies are seen as more naturally suitable for this work. Her work is further developed by Schultz (2006), who highlights how this kind of gendered 'women's' work is not universal; rather, racial and racist structures ensure that predominantly brown and black women are taking on the 'dirty' emotional and care work to free up time for white Global North women and households.[1]

The various feminist political economy engagements with affect show us how global markets and states are complicit in the exploitation and extraction of Global South labour. They also illuminate the ways in which affect circulates in market relations and how embodiments of race and gender impact where affect sticks – who is allowed to release affect, who must swallow negative affects and the harm that doing this affective work does to individual bodies. But what affective labour is done to produce affects of safety and security? To answer this, I pay attention to how affects circulate and what affects are expected to be conjured, as well as who conjures them and who uses them. What I want to explore now is how racialised male security bodies come to be seen as suitable for producing affects and, in the words of Whitney (2017), absorbing negative affects.

The Racialised Performances in Security Work

The concept of security does not carry with it an ontological truth. It is not an object we hold; nor is it one we can possess. Rather, security and being secure are often produced through a series of narratives, practices and performances involving a multitude of actors. The security environment in which this analysis is situated is a security performed in such a way that it brings the security provider into immediate contact with the client. It is a service economy insomuch as it involves 'serving the needs of the [client] or caring directly for their bodily needs . . . [in ways] that cannot be stored for later use' (McDowell 2009, 30). Inside the security economies, measurable performativities by the contractors, such as intelligence briefings, perimeter checks and training drills, are all productive in that they demonstrate security is being done (Krahmann 2017). Performativity refers to the way one acts and 'performs' one's work through regular and ritualised patterns. How a security contractor performs is, just as much as one's credentials and skill sets, fundamental in shaping how security is valued (McDowell 2009, 32). Consequently, security becomes embodied. It is also underpinned by the racialised and gendered histories that saturate security bodies. Therefore, as this chapter will illuminate, both colonial and gendered histories condition which bodies perform which security functions.

Doing security work also involves feelings. Knowing that one is secure occurs in part because one feels secure. Knowing and feeling security come through an evaluation of how security is being performed (Higate and Henry 2009). These practices of security, and security bodies, evoke feelings in the client. They are designed to make the client feel secure. But these performances can also make that same client feel very much unsafe. For example, as will be detailed later, hypermasculine and militarised performances by Western contractors sometimes materialise into unwanted flirtatious advances during their female clients' off time. This was a shared common experience for both myself and the women I interviewed who were working in Kabul. In such moments, we were made to feel uncomfortable in how we managed the situation, in that, while rejecting these advances, we needed to be aware of not emasculating the men at the same time.

The clients, depending upon their own cultural cues and common sense, understand some performances of security as more appropriate than others, but also understand some bodies as more appropriate to do security work than others. Security, then, as this chapter shows, is relational, contextual and history-specific. Higate and Henry's (2009) work on UN peacekeepers is exemplary in demonstrating this point. In their ethnography-based book focusing on peacekeepers in Liberia and Haiti, the authors illustrate how perceptions of security and insecurity were based upon how different actors understood particular security practices as credible. Consequently, evaluating security involved evaluating how security was being performed.

Higate and Henry's (2009) assessment certainly resonates with my own experiences of being protected by the very security contractors I was researching during my fieldwork visits to Kabul, Afghanistan, between 2008 and 2010. Within the setting of Kabul, knowing I was secure also meant building a relationship with the men tasked to make me feel safe. Regular conversations, polite morning and evening greetings and shared laughter gave me the confidence that these security contractors were invested in me and thus would, if the time ever came, protect me. These everyday security encounters between the client and the contractors that I write about are underpinned by affect and emotions, even if they are not broadly acknowledged. It is how affects are mobilised and how they are made to make others feel safe (and by whom) that I am curious about. To understand better how security is valued and the divisions of labour in terms of who does what, I focus on how perceptions of security influence the broader racial and gendered nature of this security work. In particular, what is the nature of the affective labour involved in making clients feel safe, and who is tasked to do this labour?

Intimate Settings of Security Work

The security labour I have spoken about in this book can very much be constituted through what McDowell (2009) refers to as a service industry. Security is practised and produced through an immediate exchange and often in personal and intimate settings, in which the security provider/contractor and the end user/client are bought into immediate physical proximity. The client observes the performances of security that are being done and implicitly also evaluates this labour. In making sense of how this happens, I am alerted to the diverse and multitudinous feminist works dedicated to looking at how geographies and encounters between service providers and end users produce value (see the works of Ehrenreich and Hochschild (2003), Weeks (2011), McDowell (2009), Hochschild (1985), Agathangelou (2004) and Skeggs (2004)). In many ways, the domestic and intimate settings in which care and cleaning work are done are replicated in security. I found this to be the case particularly in Afghanistan, where I often observed clients and security contractors living and working (and spending leisure time) in the same spaces. This kind of security work involves intimate knowledge of clients' private and work lives as they encounter and interact with contractors in the same shared living, working and leisure spaces.

I have written elsewhere about how security materialises between the client and the contractors (see Chisholm 2017).[2] To demonstrate this, I drew upon my own experiences and encounters with those who protected me as a researcher while I was conducting fieldwork in Afghanistan. This chapter brings those experiences together with the conversations I have had over the years with other individuals working in Afghanistan who were also protected by Gurkhas and other security professionals. These security clients included people working for the United Nations as well as other international commercial companies between 2008 and 2015, at a time when many international staff were not in gated compounds, but resided in various villas throughout districts of the city. Keeping them – keeping us – safe very much involved a 'service' that seeped into our personal spaces and lives. The interviews took place between October and November 2014, four years after my own experiences, ranged from one to two hours and were facilitated by Skype.

The security contractors who lived and worked with us, the clients, did not share these spaces in the same way, though; nor were they all understood as suitable for doing the same security labour. Gurkhas and other racialised security bodies often wore uniforms to signpost their role as contractors. Their work positioned them largely as perimeter static security and gate guards. They did not move within the compounds or throughout the city with the same ease and mobility as white Westerners and Eastern European security contractors. They did not share the same dining facilities with us; nor did I ever see them in the gym. In contrast, I and the other clients I spoke with were constantly sharing these more intimate spaces with Western as well as Eastern European security contractors. We ate together, travelled throughout the city together, spent leisure time together and worked out together.

I have written elsewhere about how white security contractors take on a flawed professionalism, whereas Gurkhas are maintained as a mythical martial race from the perspective of the Western clients who are being protected (Chisholm 2017). This professionalism comes through the assumption that, by virtue of being white and coming from a Western military or policing background, these men know what they are doing. The flawed aspect comes through in their everyday encounters, particularly with women clients, at whom flirtatious advances and unwanted sexual propositions are aimed, as mentioned earlier. In such moments, both myself and the women I talked to felt that our security was in peril unless we managed the situation well. Would they still protect us when required if we rejected them? How should we protect ourselves from them in those moments when we experienced the advances? The fact that we got to see the 'flawed' side of these contractors – their misogyny and subtle (or not so subtle) racism – was because of our shared whiteness. It was due to this shared whiteness that we were able to navigate the city and share the same spaces, notably in ways we never would with Gurkhas and other TCN security contractors.

This colonial geography that structured mobility and the use of space meant that Gurkhas did not eat with us clients or share the same gym and leisure facilities. If Gurkhas got drunk or if they acted out in misogynistic ways, neither I nor the clients I interviewed ever witnessed it. Our interactions were always coded in a colonial reserved and cordial friendship/relationship. In most cases, I rarely got beyond the 'Hello, ma'am', 'Are you well, ma'am?' and 'How is your family, ma'am?' dialogue with the Gurkhas who were protecting me. Other women clients such as Beth (detailed below) drew feelings of warmth and gratitude from the more affective caring duties Gurkhas provided – by bringing her cups of tea and asking her how her day was.

This type of caring role was certainly never spoken about as expected or was even deemed appropriate for Western contractors. What, then, does this say about how clients, as those who are being protected, shape colonial cartographies of security labour? For me, it immediately makes visible the kind of affect labour involved in this type of security protection. On the one hand, white female clients are in charge of securing Western men's masculinities, specifically in how they rebut unwanted sexual advances. On the other hand, Gurkhas become valuable as safe security contractors through their friendly, but distant, and caring disposition. Both encounters make clear how gendered and colonial histories shape how (white) clients feel safe and through whom, as well as what kinds of security work are being done.

Logics of race and racialisation also immediately presented themselves when I asked how clients evaluated the quality of the security Gurkhas provided for them. In Chapters 2 and 3, I detailed how broader global security markets are assured of Gurkhas' security value through the men's established years of colonial military service on behalf of the British empire. The clients I spoke with came to know about Gurkhas and be assured of their value in different ways. Beth, a female working with a commercial construction company in Kabul, found out about their reputations through online research and talking to managers of Gurkhas. Her comfort with Gurkha security labour came through what I have labelled the Gurkha security package – a package involving Gurkha security protection under the supervision of white Western contractors. Beth stated: 'I did not have any issues with this security. Ian [the white director] was very good. Steve [the white country manager] was also very good.'

For Beth, the assurance of value was in the fact that white Western security contractors managed Gurkhas. The white contractors' military training was familiar to her. She felt she could trust their experiences and military drills to keep her safe. Like Beth, the others I conversed with also felt that the value of security came through what one knew and what was familiar. For both Linda and Mike (two US nationals), the US Special Forces contractors were the most desired security contractors because they both knew the training they had undergone and were familiar with the men's cultural behaviour as soldiers and as contractors. Linda, for example, detailed,

> I knew there were a lot of Americans, ex Special Forces, who were on the Green Village who were coming from a military training that I was familiar and comfortable with.

Mike felt Gurkhas could be trusted when he realised their training was closely affiliated with British military training.

> I never knew the name Gurkha. I actually Wikipedia them to find out what they are all about. I got the understanding that they were highly trained, hand-picked, British trained, [and that] there was a rigorous process in selecting Gurkhas. That made me feel secure.

Leeann had only become interested in Gurkhas when she found out she was going to be protected by them when she deployed to Kabul. She stated,

I heard about Gurkhas, I was familiar with the thought process that goes behind them and their reputation. That they don't run away from bullets, that they run into bullets, which from my own experience I found to be true.

In all three of the cases above, these clients had initially preferred the security of white contractors. They were reassured of the value of Gurkhas' security labour because of the men's colonial relations with the British (or other Western forces). Such reassurance is made intelligible in the larger industry narrative that values and projects white masculine security contractors and performativities as the most professional and ideal (Joachim and Schneiker 2012; Chisholm 2014b). Yet, for some I conversed with, the association of Gurkhas with white contractors was not enough to assure clients of their own safety. Linda in particular expressed concern:

In talking with my husband and deciding where to live, because I had a choice at that point, one of the driving forces was actually the fact that there were more international security people at the Green Village. I wasn't comforted by the fact that I was going to be guarded by Gurkhas. Mine was more of an idea that I really wanted to know that we would have as many weapons around as possible should anything happen.

The deciding factor for Linda, when she was picking a place to live in Kabul, was based not upon Gurkhas, but on the number of US contractors who lived and worked there. Whereas myself, Mike, Linda, Leeann and Beth had come to know about Gurkhas first through popular books and vignettes about them (they never run from bullets, they are fierce and brave), we remained sceptical about their security potential. I personally felt that security came through fortified spaces, armoured equipment, and personal military competency around weapons handling and hostile environment training. Linda shared my feelings about security through equipment and professional (read Western) military training. Here, Linda explained it through race and Gurkhas' (and other Global South labourers') inability to obtain the same equipment and achieve the same training standards as white Westerners:

Of course, race matters. It is what I'm familiar with and what I feel comfortable with. When I think of developing nations' militaries, I'm not necessarily thinking of the most capable individuals. It's through no fault of their own. Maybe they don't have the funding, the equipment. It has nothing to do with them as individuals.

For Linda, racial embodiments of contractors and their relational value in the security market were mapped on to geopolitical and military inequalities. White security (observed in Western military training) was seen as the ideal because it was the best funded and could spend money on training. Other races/nationalities were held to be suspect due to her unfamiliarity with their training – and assumptions that it was of a poorer standard because of the Global South state's lower socioeconomic international indicators. Gurkhas thus had to prove their worth to clients as men who were able to protect them. This largely occurred through everyday encounters with clients, and the disposition they displayed as polite yet distant contractors, as opposed to through popular cultural writings about their martial worth.

Security contractors oversaw the protection and safety of clients throughout the day and the night. This required contractors to be available for both official and personal trips the clients made outside the compound, as well as ensuring perimeter security for the compound, a task that Western contractors and clients often shared. In this case, the separation of work and personal life was blurred. During official work hours, in spaces that required protection, in vehicles and in risk assessments and mitigation strategies, white Westerners were valued for their professional military backgrounds – ones familiar to myself and those I interviewed. However, this was not necessarily the case during personal hours or in spaces involved in shopping, going to the gym and socialising. Throughout my conversations with women in particular, Western contractors were often viewed as a source of insecurity, as their flirty, misogynistic jokes and male gaze made women feel uncomfortable. Alternatively, many women appeared to prefer the caring and distant security the Gurkhas provided. Beth commented:

> Beth: We all live together in the same house, and we get to know them personally whereas the Gurkhas you don't get to know them in the same way. The circumstances are different. The access I have to these 'risk managers' is different. They live in the house; they control a lot of the things we do. We eat with them; we travel with them, but they refer to us as [the] client. So, I guess we see them as people like us. Maybe there is something more exotic about the Gurkhas surrounding them that we want to keep them – you see this sort of aura this person has and don't want to put a chink in that armour. You want that illusion or aura to be strong. You don't want to know that they are just as human as we are. I quite liked that differentiation between the Gurkha and myself because it allowed me to have this presentation in my mind of who was providing my security. Whereas now, the guys who

are providing my security are just ordinary people. They make mistakes, they get scared, they get angry. But there was an aura about the Gurkhas and there is just a magic about them and maybe that's why I felt safe. They knew nothing about me but that they were contracted to protect me. It was quite special really, but I don't know how much of that was in my mind . . . I put my faith in these guys and hope that it never gets tested.

Amanda: Yes, security is based upon a lot of faith.

Beth: The other thing is, too, you can tell who is [doing the] protecting [from how they behave] . . . the Americans and British and . . . just from how they acted, what they were wearing . . . whether it is the tight t-shirts, the muscles showing. You know I never saw a Gurkha go to the gym. You know there is this thing about the younger ones.

Amanda: Vanity?

Beth: Vanity and arrogance, and if you are not their client, they don't want anything to do with you. You don't exist. We have two projects here, and one time I was in the car with the security contractor for another project, and from a security point of view it was as if I didn't exist because I wasn't his client. I'm sure if something would have happened, they would look after both of us, but it was subtle that I didn't really matter. It's like two extremes. During off duty [hours] they are very friendly and on duty there is a lack of compassion. That would be a worry for me to have someone who could be two extremes. In the case of an emergency, what are you going to get?

Beth's experiences resonated with me. There was something about intimacy being articulated differently, depending on whom you were encountering. In encountering these white Western contractors in my everyday living – eating with them, drinking with them, going to the gym with them and then being protected by them – I saw them as more than just security contractors. They were more than just men who were contractually obligated to keep me safe – they were men who cheated on their wives, who drank too much and who obsessed over their own body image. These were men who flirted with me in their 'off time', who made misogynistic comments about the UN and NGO women in the city, who lamented the security jobs they had to do and who expressed frustration over clients not taking their expert advice seriously. Seeing these security contractors as flawed men who made mistakes, who contradicted themselves and who expressed their feelings openly created feelings of insecurity and opened up questions as to whether they would protect us when and if needed.

The dialogue between Beth and me highlights how familiarity, intimacy and security collate differently in Western contractors' versus

Gurkhas' encounters with white female clients. There is a geography that is important here. For Beth, Gurkhas' security value was reassured because she never had the opportunity to see the men as anything other than security providers. As white women, both Beth and I were unable to overcome the colonial decorum that mediated our relations with Gurkhas. With the exception of a few Gurkhas, we encountered them only in their roles as security providers and our roles as clients. Gurkhas were spatially segregated from our social lives. They ate and slept and socialised amongst themselves. The times we encountered them in more intimate ways were when they drove us to various appointments and waited patiently for us to finish so they could drive us home. There was a constant polite professionalism about them. They brought Beth cups of tea in the morning. They said goodnight and wished me happy dreams before I went to bed at night. These different geographies and uses of space allowed the perpetuation of a Gurkha myth – the idea that this is how these men always act/interact. Such relations of intimacy mediated through reimagined colonial encounters are also documented in feminist political economy literature – for example, on global nannies and sex workers, whose labour we understand to be more valuable than that of others – and these relations rest upon particular mythologies of race and gender (Agathangelou 2004). This type of relationship also says a lot about how we as clients defined our own security.

This everyday security encounter was counterposed with our inter-actions with Western contractors, who fostered a paternal relationship, whereby they used discourses of security to control our everyday. Beth's and my experiences also highlight how mythologies of race and gender – of which some bodies are more valuable than others – matter. Western security contractors' abilities to provide us with a safe and secure environment were immediately a given. We knew we could trust them because broader industry practices had told us this. These men were understood as professional. In everyday situations in Kabul, they acted confidently. This confidence, they told us in various conversations, came from military and police training in their respective Western countries. However, it was through these same everyday encounters with them that their professionalism was brought into question.

For Gurkhas, the assurance of their security value was quite the oppo-site. I and the other clients I conversed with did not initially know about their abilities. It was through our encounters with them that our belief in their ability to keep us safe was solidified. For Mike, Gurkhas' security value was seen in everyday, ritualised security performances:

Just watching the way in which [Gurkhas] handle themselves, I could tell they were doing their job in making sure the car was checked thoroughly before [being] granted access into the parking lot. So, knowing about their background but also having that interaction with them and observing their shift change . . . I could tell they were in sync with each other so that if something went down, they were well trained enough to have a coordinated response.

Beth's feelings of security with Gurkha contractors came through what she observed in their ability to be respectful to the client, keep a friendly distance from the client and blend into immediate environments. She explained:

Beth: I went on this trip around the country where we looked at UN programmes. Travelling up with them, I just found [Gurkhas] extremely respectful. They fitted in with Afghans. They didn't stand out and, somehow, they just seemed to meld in, so I never felt we were conspicuous. They could have been taken for Tajiks or Uzbeks. It was just another layer of protection that was positive.

Amanda: Like, layer of protection because they blend in?

Beth: Yes, they always carried weapons with them, but they did blend in. We had these two, Tiger and Puna. They looked after Linda and I, and when we came up to this trip, they ended up providing hot water bottles for us. They would deliver a cup of tea in the morning. Those are the things I remember, and it just made it so much personable. They were very real people and I felt they really cared. I never felt uncomfortable. I felt very well looked after.

In Mike's case, the Gurkhas' value was proven in their everyday security rituals of checking vehicles and performing various security drills. Beth saw their value in their racialised bodies. For her, Gurkhas' value was not necessarily in their professional skill sets, or at least not entirely. Their worth came from their physical bodies, which allowed them to blend in more easily with local populations. Such a logic was also highlighted by security directors I spoke to about the merits of Gurkhas' labour – that these men, given their bodies and their ability to speak similar languages, could integrate easier than white people and gather more immediate intelligence about the local area.

In these two cases, contractors were gendered and racialised through different mechanisms. Western men were seen as professional during work hours, but they were a source of potential insecurity during social times. Their male gaze upon female clients and their flirtations with clients during off hours, alongside their expressed attitude towards women in general, tore away at their professionalism. Where the Western contractor's worth was immediately there, and then perhaps diluted through everyday social encounters, the Gurkha's worth came through biology (naturally blending in) and caring abilities (bringing cups of tea). Such valuations of Gurkhas (re)produce an oriental imagining of these men that naturally separates them from their Western contractor counterparts. As in the case of Global South maids and nannies (Huang and Yeoh 1998; Agathangelou 2004), Gurkhas' worth is understood only through broader cultural reproductions and myths about Gurkhas and other Global South security labourers – myths that reinforce the labour divide between the perceived Global South, feminised, natural security abilities of Gurkhas and the competencies of Western security contractors, whose worth is measured through professional acquired skill sets. As mentioned in Chapters 2 and 3, Gurkhas' martial raced histories continue to stick to them, and they are knowable as security contractors through these colonial histories.

Leeann commented that she immediately trusted US contractors in particular because she knew their training through her own experience of having family members in the US military. Alternatively, her belief in the value of Gurkha labour came only through an actual violent encounter in Kabul, where her vehicle was just metres away from a detonated improvised explosive device (IED). She explained:

> I was in a vehicle one hundred feet from another vehicle that [the] Taliban exploded. What I saw during that time was just incredible. There is debris and falling body parts falling all over the place but there wasn't a moment where I saw anyone turn away and run. The Gurkhas were running right to the incident. Our vehicle was used as a shield during that time. I saw Gurkhas dragging other Gurkhas into the compound. They took care of their people and not only that they ran toward everything that happened. There wasn't a moment that they shied away.

In Leeann's account, Gurkhas' value was acquired only in their response to a violent encounter. They proved their worth when they ran towards the IED attack and not away from it. She went on to explain how Gurkhas rescued her colleagues from a direct attack.

> These little, tiny Gurkhas came and tackled [my very large and injured colleague] and dragged him inside for safety. These little guys stood in front of us and ran with us from the vehicle to the compound. I'll never ever forget that, and I'll never question again the role that they play. And when shit hits the fan, the guys are there, and they are not going to run away from it.

The racialisation of Gurkhas' bodies in Leeann's case, then, was also rooted in the long-standing cultural reproduction of them as martial raced men. The comment 'little, tiny' here works to infantilise Gurkhas as much as it is meant to produce a curious juxtaposition of the concepts of harmless and childlike, on the one hand, and fierce warrior on the other. This racial logic is also the very foundation that culturally reproduces Gurkhas as beloved warrior gentlemen (Caplan 1995; Streets 2004) – as men who, as I have articulated in previous chapters, are almost but not white contractors and whose value comes through their association with white security or actual demonstrations of security (Chisholm 2014a). The aforementioned cases demonstrate how none of the clients I interviewed was immediately convinced of Gurkhas' merits and their ability to provide good security. This confidence came through personal interactions, where Gurkhas' consistency, friendliness, diligence and, in extreme cases, ability to react quickly and efficiently shone through. Gurkhas, unlike their Western counterparts, had to prove their value to these Western clients, and yet their value continued to be understood through broader racial logics – logics reproduced through popular cultural representations of them that perpetuate an almost but not white imagining.

For Beth and myself, Gurkhas' close association with the white men who managed them gave us reassurance of our own security. This was then reinforced through the kindness and hospitality we received in our everyday interactions with them. For Mike, Gurkhas' worth was observed through regular and ritualised security performances. In Leeann's case, Gurkha masculine labour was proved through an actual violent encounter. Where Gurkhas initially obtain their value through the martial myth about their military prowess, Western men's value is already a given – their position already secure as professional and valued contractors in an industry that rests upon the assumption that whiteness is the ideal (Chisholm 2015b). Their privileged status is a product of the broader market that sustains Western whiteness and Western security training as the necessary 'skills' one must have to perform security (Chisholm 2015b; Joachim and Schneiker 2015).

Yet it is through everyday encounters of intimacy that such assumptions about ideal white security are called into question. The men's security reputations were understood only in relation to one another. As clients, we could trust Gurkhas because their natural martial masculinities had been refined and professionalised through years of service with the British military. For some, however, this was not enough to feel safe. Gurkhas had to prove themselves initially through demonstrations of security performances and through regular and ritualised perimeter/ vehicle checks and various other drills. Western men were almost immediately trusted, but then trust was lost if they were seen to be acting in contradiction to the professional security image they were known for. Gurkha and Western contractors' value was also articulated through temporal and spatial constitutions. No one I interviewed had ever socialised with Gurkhas the same way they did with Western contractors.

With the exception of a few Gurkhas I was in touch with through my own fieldwork, Gurkha men were known only through their contractual obligations to protect their clients. Consequently, the professional security relationship was never challenged by clients seeing these men in any way other than as security protection. Therefore, the myth of their unfettered loyalty and professionalism was never challenged.

These types of security contractor are not, of course, universalised and this is all heavily dependent on context. However, in my own experience and as was discussed by clients in interviews, the hypermasculine contractor was the one who relied upon overt security props, tight tops, dark wraparound sunglasses and an overt showing of weaponry. Such performativities of security have been detailed by Scahill (2007) as embodied in the Blackwater US contractor, who is concerned more with how he looks than with the security he is tasked to perform. Higate (2012) also mentions the hypermasculine US contractor, who is referred to as a 'Billy Big Bollocks' in security training programmes. However, for the US national clients I spoke with, they felt reassurance in these same props. As James commented,

> The Americans were contractors who were PSD [personal security detail] guys for people around. Those were the same guys that would be in my same social circle and there was a difference between the Special Forces guys who were intelligent and more interesting than the nineteen-year-old American soldier. These guys were much more worldly. If something went down, I would totally trust these American Special Forces guys. I saw them as intelligent competent people – not guys getting drunk at the bar.

For both James and Linda, the US contractor was not inherently dangerous. They saw these contractors as continuing with the ethics and professionalism they had learned in the military and taking those qualities with them into the market. Their understandings of these men, and, in turn, their ability to provide security, work to highlight the ambiguities in these tensions between state and market. This also demonstrates how racial logics about security value and who embodies the 'right' security contractor also inform perceptions of insecurity. The idea of implicitly trusting US contractors and at the same time having to have Gurkhas prove their worth as security providers demonstrates this point. Linda's and James's understanding of US Special Forces contactors as 'intelligent competent people' also offers an alternative to Higate's (2012) empirical work on hypermasculine depictions of US contractors in training programmes. Such contradictions highlight how the nationality of the security contractor, and therefore familiarity with particular military practices and appropriate masculine performativities, matter in how the individual sees and reinforces gender hierarchies.

Because of Linda's and James's personal knowledge of US military training, for them the US Special Forces individual, now security contractor, represented the highest level of feeling secure because of his former training and intelligence, which they viewed as originating from the professional military training he had received. Alternatively, whereas assurance of Western value was embedded in broader understandings of the political economies of Western militaries, which afford them a high level of military training, the value of Gurkhas was rooted in their racialised bodies and the naturalising myths of who they were as men. As with Agathangelou's (2004) research on the global sex industry, my own work found that it was the broader mythologies of race and gender that mapped on to the bodies of Western men as highly skilled and professional and on to Gurkhas as natural warriors that provided a rationale as to why one labour force was to be instantly trusted over the other. Gurkhas' racialised bodies were rendered exotic through popular culture and vignettes that sought to naturalise them as mythical warriors. The reimagined colonial relationship that informed the everyday interactions between clients and Gurkha men only reinforced the exotic polite gentlemen and fierce warrior mythology recounted in numerous oral and written stories about Gurkhas (Caplan 1995; Streets 2004). While their ability to keep us safe in our professional capacity – travelling to and from work, for example – had to be demonstrated, for myself, Linda and Beth, Gurkhas were less likely to be a source of insecurity through flirting and male gazes within our personal and everyday spaces of eating, working out and socialising.

This section of the chapter has demonstrated how gendered and colonial histories continue, in the words of Ahmed (2004), to 'stick' to Gurkha bodies. These histories inform how clients understand their various encounters with these security contractors, as well as who they feel safe around and what kinds of security work they value. These histories also structure how space is used, where clients encounter Gurkhas and other security contractors, and how clients determine their value as men assigned to keep them safe. These histories continue to make sensible the racial divide between the Westerner as the professional – albeit flawed – contractor and the Gurkha as the exceptional – under the right management – security contractor.

Consequently, the more affective and emotional labour, the kind that is designed to foster feelings of safety and security in clients, is largely placed upon Gurkhas and other TCN contractors, while at the same time it is rendered an invisible labour. It is their regular positive disposition and their polite but distant demeanour, which Beth in particular spoke about, that make clients feel these men are harmless to them, but also protective of them. But this kind of labour comes at a cost. It can lead to a slow death (Berlant 2011), a wearing out, and a psychic and physical depletion of these bodies (Rai, Hoskyns and Thomas 2013). This, I argue, is not an accident, as the kinds of thankless emotional work placed upon these bodies and the emotional and mental damage it does to them are a part of the larger security market regimes that position them as subordinate, undervalued and, moreover, disposable. The final section of this chapter moves to account for this kind of 'affective dumping' (Whitney 2017) labour, and the potential harms and costs to the security community that takes this labour on. Accounting for this labour matters in making visible the same colonial histories that divide Westerners from Gurkhas and other third country nationals. For myself and those I interviewed, these histories impacted on who we saw as naturally suitable for offloading surplus negative affects of anger and/ or frustration on, or for comforting us when we needed to release our own pent-up emotions, and the affect that comes with living in a city understood as being in conflict.

Affective Waste and Surplus Management Labour

I was sitting in the living room of a security compound waiting for my first one-on-one interview with a Gurkha for the day. I was looking through my notes and re-examining my interview questions when Rabindra, a young Indian army Gurkha, came into the room. We exchanged pleasantries, shook hands and he sat across from me on a chair whilst I sat on the sofa. I was about to ask my first question when I heard a lot of shouting coming from the hallway. We both looked up and moved to the door to take a closer look at what was happening. One man was yelling at another man. He had tears in his eyes and his voice was shaky. He repeatedly shouted at the man to give his passport back and that he wanted to go home. He then yelled in a language I later found out to be Gurkhali. I asked the young Indian Gurkha what the yelling was about, and he shook and lowered his head. He replied that the yelling man wanted his passport because he wanted to go home and said it was not fair to keep him here against his will. I assume the young Gurkha saw the surprised expression on my face, as he quietly added, 'This is not how Gurkhas should act. He is not right.' (Fieldnote observation, Kabul, Afghanistan, February 2010)

This observation indicates, on the surface, that the man was expressing frustration and anxiety about his current employment situation in Afghanistan. Such a frustrated outburst would normally be justified; in fact, one would expect someone to be upset when they realised their passport was being withheld from them. But, within the security market, who actually gets to have an outburst? Who gets to let off steam? I witnessed semi-public dressing-downs of Gurkhas from Gurkha security company directors for conduct the director had decided was unbecoming. These outbursts were seen as a necessary part of the broader management of Gurkhas – to ensure everyone was witness to the high standards expected of these men and the cost of an infraction. I also observed numerous situations where white security contractors expressed anger or had frustrated outbursts over fairly banal experiences such as a dropped call, a delayed driver, or a sudden loss of electricity that resulted in them losing work they had been doing on the computer. Alongside this there were regular outbursts, particularly directed at Afghan security guards, where white security contractors would openly berate the men for various things such as not closing the compound gate fast enough, for not signing someone in at the gate or, indeed, for signing someone in at the gate. During these various outbursts, both Gurkhas and Afghan guards would come to attention, absorb this yelling without physically responding, and then retreat to do what they were being told to do or just physically remove themselves from the immediate space once the yelling was over.

For me, my observation around who is allowed to have such affective encounters also reveals who gets to offload negative affects and who must, in the words of Whitney (2017), be the waste managers. Returning to the original observation, I find it striking how the young Gurkha attempted to regulate the reputation of Gurkhas with his voiced disapproval of his colleague's outburst. To be a Gurkha, for this young Indian, meant that one is unable to be anything other than disciplined and polite. Gurkhas could experience anger – and, indeed, many expressed these feelings during my interviews with them – but they could never show it. This inability to show emotion, to reset and to recharge through emotional release, renders these racialised contractors vulnerable to what Berlant (2011) calls a slow death. These regular affective management practices of swallowing, of stuffing down individual emotions that arise in the process of, for example, being yelled at, wear the men out emotionally and psychologically.

This kind of affective labour, in reference to the labour involved in making others' lives better by smoothing over emotions, playing the peacekeeper or just absorbing verbal and emotional abuse, underpins everyday security practices and encounters between security contractors and clients. According to Whitney (2017, 637) this kind of labour, that of stuffing down and not reacting to others' emotional outbursts, is byproductive. That is, the affect does not just disappear but circulates within the space – it creates an atmosphere. The affective labour involved in managing these affects materialises in the 'metabolising [of] affective surplus and containing [of] affective waste' (Whitney 2017, 637). So, it is not just about conjuring up a friendly disposition or bringing cups of tea, tasks for which Gurkhas are seen as the natural labourers. It is also about physically absorbing negative affects such as anger – by continuing to stand still while being yelled at by one's security manager, for example – and even quietly disapproving of any outbursts of anger from other Gurkhas.

The expelling of frustration might uplift the manager, enabling them to let out the surplus affects of frustration that build up when living in an environment where luxury amenities are difficult to come by and where things do not come easily. However, on the part of the racialised contractor, the absorbing of this frustration in bearing the brunt of these outbursts can lead to a further emotional and physical wearing out. Whitney (2017) argues that it is precisely through this type of very affective exchange and the divisions of labour that racialised communities feel their lives being depleted in order to sustain and regenerate the lives of others. This kind of labour, the labour that goes into managing other people's emotions and affect, is even less visible than the 'he brings me cups of tea' labour that Beth acknowledged. And yet, as my research indicates, this all has a significant impact on security contractors' ability to regenerate their own emotional lives.

The aforementioned discussions highlight how clients in Kabul, myself included, valued Western professionals for their intelligence, particularly in providing briefings and managing teams. As clients, we saw them as already professional because their military experience was knowable. We also valued Gurkhas through the tales of mythical martial races we had read and were informed about. Gurkhas remained mythical to us as clients because we never actually were able to spend time with them the way we did with Westerners. We also valued them for making us feel safe, for their seemingly genuine investment in our lives, and for their lack of typical military behaviour such as unwanted public acts of aggression or sexual advances, as Beth mentioned. What clients value in Gurkhas is the affective labour they perform in security markets in helping to maintain a calm, friendly and safe atmosphere. The kind of affective labour I am thinking about is that which makes clients feel safe – but that also goes into regenerating those same clients. Affect is produced by being in tense and often frustrating environments. As other feminist scholars[3] have explored, to examine these processes I ask: who actually gets to be angry? Who gets to let off steam, on to whom and at which bodies? Who is made to swallow others' negative affects, not to respond? What does that do to their bodies? These questions begin to get at the important affect work that is done in allowing some to recharge whilst depleting others. It is these concerns that I want to turn to.

While Gurkhas always appeared as outwardly friendly, during their interviews, they also expressed a great deal of frustration and anxiety around the structural inequalities they experienced because of their race, and the lack of agency afforded to them to do anything about it. In particular, Bishal stated:

I don't know why there is such a big difference in pay and living [conditions]. Sometimes, yes, I know the British are well educated [more] than us and are more professional than us and in that case the salary could be different, but in some cases, Nepalese are talented and educated, but even they are not getting that salary. Some Nepalese are working in Britain or have the passport and are not getting [the] same as ex-pats. (Interview, 2 May 2010)

Here, it is clear that Bishal understood the racialised hierarchy amongst security contractors (and other global workers) as unfair and unjustified. Whereas most of the Gurkhas I spoke with understood why divisions of security labour might take place, the differences in living conditions between the expat Westerners and the Gurkhas were harder for them to accept. Roshan commented on this difference:

The living [arrangements] and clothing are different. Like, the ex-pats used to stay in, [it was] one person one room, and we are staying in one room for five to six people. There is different dining and different food and different drinks. Whatever food is in the kitchen they [the Westerners] can take [some] whenever they want but we cannot. We have specific times [to eat]. Always one food, same meal every day, [and it] will not change. (Interview, 2 May 2010)

Roshan's statement demonstrates how some Gurkhas I interviewed did not buy into the colonial logic of difference when it came to living and working conditions. These men were also frustrated over their inability to do anything about their immediate situation. For Roshan, this came through a highly regulated private life, such as eating the same food every day, at the same time. Alongside this frustration was a sense of disempowerment. Specifically, Roshan commented, 'I feel bad, but what to do? If you do anything you will be kicked out.'

Being a Gurkha, for some of the men, was seen as a barrier to achieving what they felt they ought to be able to, given that they had acquired the same skills and were thus entitled to equal opportunities and treatment. Men like Roshan saw their relations with the British and other Westerners as immovable and beyond their immediate control. This lack of control frustrated them, and yet they continued to be required to stuff these feelings down and maintain a 'professional' and positive outward appearance.

Hochschild (1985) and Whitney (2017) both illuminate the physical and emotional costs for those who are forced to do the affective labour in making others feel safe, happy or other desired affects. Hochschild describes this labour as inducing or suppressing feelings 'in order to sustain the outward countenance that produces the proper state of mind in others' (1985, 7). Within the context of daily security encounters in Kabul, such emotional labour included Gurkhas maintaining an outwardly pleasant disposition, by smiling and offering a seemingly genuine warmth in how they greeted clients. For Western contractors, this emotional work might involve expressing an outward confidence and calm disposition in more harrowing moments. For female clients such as myself, Beth and Leeann, this might mean maintaining a friendly disposition and politely excusing ourselves from the unwanted sexual advances of male colleagues. All of this is emotional work we do, that we take on, in order to make others feel a particular way. Of course, there is nothing particularly novel about this. We all do some sort of emotional labour and management in our private and public lives. What I want to do here is account for how this work remains central – if never acknowledged – to producing security and making people feel safe. Consequently, I am concerned with how PMSCs draw upon this labour to achieve these security goals – what it looks like, who does it and at what cost – all the while rendering this labour largely invisible.

Different kinds of emotional labour were accounted for in Chapter 4, particularly the unacknowledged labour that goes into the life-building activities done by Gurkha wives. While not directly produced for the security industry, the industry certainly benefits from these activities. What I have explored in this chapter is the emotional labour done inside security market environments, those activities that involve making the client feel a particular way. Not all security contractors are expected to conduct this type of work. Rather, race and gender underpin who takes it on and what the work actually entails. If we return to Beth's valuation of Gurkha labour, for her, Gurkhas' value came through their more pastoral care work, through them bringing her cups of tea.

These men, then, become bodies that are structurally designed to make (white) bodies feel good and feel safe. These are racial structures as much as they are gendered. Both race and gender work in tandem to position the men as disposable, rendering their bodies as the ones at risk of wearing out. Exploring affective labour management – the ways in which we make people feel secure through emotional management – highlights the unevenness of experiences in everyday life, in keeping life going, in the security environment in Kabul. Gurkhas are structurally positioned not only to work on keeping their own lives going and on being resilient for their families back home, but also to do the affective labour involved in maintaining a particular kind of life for those they protect and for those who manage them.

The material implications and consequences of doing this work can result in the actual wearing out of bodies, families and communities. Rai, Hoskyns and Thomas (2013) draw upon the concept of depletion to account for what happens when there are fewer hands in the household, and for how women in the household take on the reproductive and productive tasks, which leads to a spiritual, mental and physical wearing out of bodies. My research connects to this in the sense that Gurkhas are taking on such enormous affective and life-building work in managing other people's feelings and the broader atmosphere in security environments that they are exhausted and emotionally drained. While this came across most acutely in my interviews with unarmed Nepali security contractors in Qatar, a shared frustration across all interviews was the feeling of being treated unfairly, including having to absorb verbal abuse and not being able to do anything about it.

Gurkhas, like other TCN workers, are the men that do the dirty work in the security industry. Beyond being put into more physically demanding and dangerous positions, as well as taking on devalued security work, they also assume a great deal of the emotional labour. Gurkhas bring their clients cups of tea, they ask about their day and they take a seemingly genuine interest in them as clients and their back stories. They are always smiling. It was not until I was able to talk to more Gurkha security contractors that I became attuned to the high degree of affective waste disposal they also do, and the frustrations they hold on to in understanding the unevenness of security markets and not being able to do anything about it.

Conclusion

This chapter has explored the ways in which affect is commodified and brought into the market as a transactional exchange. It has looked at how histories of race and racism mediate encounters between clients/ end users and service providers/contractors. Race and colonial structures within the industry also mediate how space is used, who gets to travel and who gets to take up space. The chapter showed how it is important to move beyond exploring how race shapes security labour and value to highlight the degree to which affect and emotions underpin the production of 'feeling safe'. It is predominately Gurkhas and other racialised security contractors who do this affective work. It is demanding and devalued work. It is also central to regenerating the (white) bodies who extract this emotional labour and who use Gurkhas and other men as 'punching bags' to expel their own feelings of frustration and anger. At the same time, such expelling of emotions and extracting of emotional and affective labour lead to the wearing out and wearing down of the brown and black bodies that perform this security work.

Overall, this book accounts for the nuanced and overt ways in which colonial histories, race/racism and gender continue to structure the life pathways for Gurkhas and their families in how they negotiate access to and work within the security industry. It has also highlighted how affects of hope, love and happiness sustain these men and women in their current lives and underpin how they make sense of their pasts, their contemporary lives and what their futures may hold. This chapter moved discussions of affect from the realm of an atmosphere, a tension and a future-orientated feeling that holds us to a particular life pathway to examine how these same affects are taken up and commodified, with profit being extracted from them. This research is about the life-building, everyday practices these men and women do to support the security industry. But it is also about how they and their experiences are always so much more than the capitalist, patriarchal and imperial structures within which they are situated.

I want to turn now to the concluding chapter of this book to return to the key contributions this research makes to the field, and to examine where we might move forward conceptually and empirically. The chapter begins with Lauren Berlant's (2011) concept of slow death to begin to answer an enduring question: why do these men and women continue to participate in a global market where they are expected to sacrifice so much, and for so little in return? This question and the resulting affective discussion beg us to rethink agency in an environment that is saturated with a crisis that is quite ordinary. This crisis is about an ordinary life that is marked with such a high degree of uncertainty and precarity, observed in the (in)ability to reproduce life, that even having an everyday marked with routine, rhythms and banality becomes aspirational.

The concluding chapter ends with a story of failure to account for all the men (along with their families) who were unable to become Gurkhas. Ending this book with a discussion of failure shows the continued political and economic pressures that make the security industry so desirable – despite the documented racism, colonial histories and gendered structures that wear out and wear down security bodies. It also begins to show the other kinds of life-building and world-making activities that run parallel to the Gurkha security story – and the continued hope for another way of living and community building, albeit with its own insecurities. It is within the context of slow death and the ordinary crisis of a large population of potential recruits and Gurkha communities that I now turn to investigate Sameer's story of failing to become a Gurkha, and the stories of all those other young men who were unsuccessful in becoming Gurkhas.

Notes

1. The feminist political economy scholarship on global care work is vibrant and diverse in its theoretical and empirical mapping of who takes up care work and under what conditions, and the nature of this work. Key scholarship that has informed this research includes Ehrenreich and Hochschild's (2003) *Global Women: Nannies, Maids and Sex Workers in the New Economy*, Agathangelou's (2004) *The Global Political Economy of Sex: Desire, Violence and Insecurity in Mediterranean Nation States*, Bakan and Stasiulis's (1997) *Not One of the Family: Foreign Domestic Workers in Canada*, Benoit and Hallgrimsdottir's (2011) *Valuing Care Work: Comparative Perspectives*, Boris and Salazar Parreñas's (2010) *Intimate Labors: Technologies, and the Politics of Care*, Brown's (2016) 'Re-examining the Transnational Nanny: Migrant Care Work Beyond the Chain' and Federici's (2011) 'On Affective Labour'.

2. Many of the interview transcripts and much of the discussion that follows in this section of the chapter are drawn from my previously published *Critical Military Studies* article, 'Clients, Contractors and Everyday Masculinities'. The security clients I talked to all worked in Kabul for extended periods of time with the United Nations or commercial construction companies. I was introduced to these people through personal contacts I had made during my time in Kabul and who remained in the city. These people were all white, Western nationals. In total, three men and five women were interviewed. Their names have been changed to protect their anonymity.

3. See the works of Whitney (2017), Hochschild (1985) and Oksala (2016).

Slow Death and Failure in the Life Building of Gurkha Communities

This book has focused so far on the everyday lives and experiences of Gurkhas and Gurkha wives who come to participate in global security markets. I have explored the martial histories that continue to shape the experiences of these men and women. These histories inform us of how Western clients interpret and value Gurkha security practices in Afghanistan, and how white British nationals, who were formerly Gurkha officers and are now security company directors, draw upon these martial histories in their management of Gurkhas. The book has shown how affects of love and happiness sustain these men and women in colonial and gendered relations within security markets. It has also examined the gendered and racialised affective labour that is taken up by Gurkhas in their everyday practices of making security clients feel safe. All of this has illuminated how affective relations to militarism, structurally conditioned through colonial geographies, bind these communities to global security markets in the hope of a good life.

Failure and the (Un)making of the Gurkha Good Life

I want to dedicate some space to the other side of the Gurkha story – those young men who failed to secure the position of Gurkha and their families. As the opening chapter showed, failure to become a Gurkha carries much more certainty than success does. To be sure, failure comes with a whole host of affective attachments, including shame, despair and disillusionment. But it also, as Halberstam reminds us, provides us with an opportunity to 'poke holes in the toxic positivity' (2011, 3) that ideas of success and of following the Gurkha life pathway to happiness often bring. Failure opens conceptual space to think through how acts of 'losing, forgetting, not knowing, undoing and unbecoming might indeed offer more creative, cooperative, and surprising ways of living and being' in the world (Halberstam 2011, 2–3). Failure also alerts us to the heterogeneity of life stories of failure – that even when notions of failure are institutionally embraced, not everyone is allowed to fail and/or experience failure in the same way (Lisle 2018). While some may indeed *fail up*, for others who are not afforded the same structural and social privileges, failing can result in significant trauma, material loss, shame and disappointment (Halberstam 2011; Lisle 2018). With reference to Gurkhas, failure can further disrupt the dominant Gurkha celebration story and illuminate the colonial structures that underpin the martial race Gurkha (Chisholm and Ketola 2020). Contrary to the martial race myth, birthright alone cannot secure this position. In this section of the concluding chapter, I focus on the story of Sameer – a young man coming from three generations of Gurkha men on both sides of his family, who failed to become a Gurkha himself. Focusing on life after such a failure, I ask: what other futures are presented as possibilities? What affects materialise out of this failure? And finally, is the pull towards militarism sustained when the prospect of being a Gurkha is no longer possible?

The pathway to success in becoming a Gurkha is gruelling and, for most, impossible. Despite this, young men aged 17–19 throughout Nepal apply to become a British Gurkha through an annual selection process. The process sees roughly 4,000 candidates competing for 250–400 positions each year. These men have two chances at success, and then they become too old to apply. In various interviews with Gurkhas and recruiters, I was informed that the Indian Gurkha recruitment success rate is not as stark as the British one, but it is not easy to succeed in either. Given this, failure is almost certain. And yet it is the significant financial and social rewards that can literally uplift communities out of poverty that drive these young men and their families to continue to invest in this life pathway emotionally, financially and intellectually.

A focus on failure immediately alerts us to the colonial, gendered and racialised structures of what it means to participate in global security markets successfully. These structures work in in tandem in shaping the lives and life potential for many young men and women from the Global South. Colonial geographies, urban/rural divides, race/caste and gender underpin the heterodox life stories of failure just as much as they affect the potential to create a life outside of military service. Attempting, and failing, in this context is still exclusive to men. At the time of my research, women could not apply to become Gurkhas, and even now the policy on female recruits continues to remain unclear. How failure is articulated, felt and experienced very much speaks to the precarity of reproducing everyday life that these people deal with, and points to how they become drawn into military pathways as an important lifeline out of this precarity. I turn now to the story of Sameer and his family to illuminate how failure operates in the everyday life making of this one Gurkha family.

Sameer's Story

I met Sameer in a small meeting room in one of the university buildings at the Qatar Foundation in Doha, Qatar. The Qatar Foundation is a government-run organisation that houses and supports the running of various foreign countries' satellite campuses, including Georgetown University, Texas A&M University and Carnegie Mellon University. The running of these facilities, inclusive of the cooking, cleaning and door and gate security, is all done by foreign nationals originating from the Global South. Sameer was a security contractor from Nepal, and came from a long line of Gurkha men on both sides of his family. At the time I first met him, he had been working as an unarmed security guard for the Qatar Foundation for just over a year.

> Amanda: What drew you into security? This sort of work?
> Sameer: Mostly because my grandfather is also a Gurkha, and my father is also a Gurkha, so it's security . . .
> Amanda: It's always been in the family.
> Sameer: It's always been in the family, so I find it suitable for me.
> Amanda: Did you try the military?
> Sameer: Yes . . . I could not pass the education and some other critical . . .

At this point, Sameer paused and shifted in his chair across from me. My throat tightened, too. After a decade of research on Gurkhas, I was very much aware of the social and economic stakes involved in becoming a Gurkha. In that moment, I searched for some comforting words.

> Amanda: It's a fierce competition.
> Sameer: Yeah . . . and I could not pass so I looked for security [work] elsewhere.

Sameer's story illuminates the other side of this Gurkha story, one parallel to the celebratory martial history around Gurkhas. The failure to become a Gurkha carries with it a whole host of affects that include shame, regret and guilt.

Figure C.1 Unsuccessful Nepali men leaving the British Gurkha camp in Pokhara, Nepal, during the annual recruitment drive, in August 2017. Photo credit to Amanda Chisholm.

Amanda: Do you think your father is proud of you?
Sameer: I hope he is, but I'm not sure.

I want to focus in here on the fact that failure is also about – or begins with – thinking through and imagining one's life otherwise (Halberstam 2011). Conceptually, failure makes clear the structural and cultural inequalities that exist and the privileges that some have over others (Lisle 2018), as well as the ingenuity and expression that those outside of the success story cultivate just to keep life going (Halberstam 2011; Ahmed 2004). As Lisle (2018), Halberstam (2011) and Ahmed (2004) all argue, the associated affects of failure do not, then, stick to all bodies in the same way. For Sameer, failing to become a Gurkha was shameful, and he certainly had anxiety over how his parents would perceive him, but it did not rupture the intergenerational affective relationships he and his family had with foreign military service. He still understood security work as the primary life pathway for him. Failure to become a Gurkha had brought Sameer to Doha as an unarmed security contractor working at one of the US satellite university campuses. This kind of security work continued to make sense to him, but also to his family. In a later conversation I had with Sameer's mother, she explained that it was still foreign security work, and it still supported him and his family through remittances, but it did not carry the same dangers that armed security work did.

The rhythms of Sameer's foreign security work became a part of his life making and life building in a similar way to that of the Gurkha men I spoke with who worked as armed contractors in Kabul. These men have regular communications with their wives and families, actively co-plan for futures involving land investments and decisions on boarding schools for their children, and are involved in daily family decisions. All of this was a part of their life-making activities while on the job as security contractors. As we sat in the small room in Doha, Sameer continued to tell me about his family and his wife, a migrant working in Portugal.

> Sameer: My wife is now in Portugal.
> Amanda: Oh, so you are a global family.
> Sameer laughed: Yeah, kind of. She is working there as a cleaner in a restaurant, ma'am.

Sameer told me about how they talked every day, how her life was very hard there, and how she sent the small amount of money left over after paying her rent and living costs back home to their family. Sameer's life was also hard and structured around work. His workday was 14–16 hours long, including a 12-hour shift along with a 1–2-hour transit ride to and from his labour camp, depending on traffic. When Sameer was not working, he ate, did laundry, showered, called his family, and slept before beginning his next workday. Similar to his own work, Sameer described the regimented nature of his wife's work and the continual feeling of exhaustion. Amid these long and difficult working lives, both Sameer and his wife made future life plans. At the time of my interview with Sameer, he had a longer-term plan eventually to join his wife in Portugal. He shared:

> We plan to both be in Portugal together and then I [will] bring my mother and sister over. I [will] work there for some years or so and maybe my children will also get educated there.

Over the course of our hour-long conversation, Sameer not only shared his disappointment over failing to become a Gurkha, but also told me of his and his wife's plan to have children and how all the difficulties they faced in keeping life going would be worth it in the future. Anchoring them in the moment-to-moment pressures involved in keeping life going, in holding a marriage together across time and space, was the happiness their future would bring. As for so many of the Gurkha wives I spoke with, happiness remained 'somewhere other' (Ahmed 2010, 161) than where Sameer and his wife were in the present. Happiness was once rooted in the past dream of becoming a Gurkha and the secure future that life as a Gurkha would bring, and now it was anchored to a different 'somewhere else', some distance away, in a different kind of future. Happiness as a future-orientated affect enabled Sameer (and, indeed, enabled Gurkha wives) to endure, to make sense of and to imagine alternative possibilities that would come out of his present life.

I met up with Sameer and his family back in Pokhara, Nepal, only six months after this interview. During that time, Sameer had left his work in Doha and had made a plan to become an undocumented worker in Portugal, so he could join his wife. There was an anxious atmosphere in his family home as I asked for more details of this change in his career path. The entire family was faced with the certainty that, yet again, they would have to take out loans to afford the visa and associated travel to get Sameer to Portugal. Sameer's mother expressed to me a great ambivalence about this new pathway for Sameer, all the while detailing how she continued to save to help him.

> I am happy if he goes to stay with his wife. Officially, you must be happy . . . Of course, I have many wishes, but [Sameer and his wife] don't have an education. But I have a great dream for my son and daughter to have a luxurious life. But they must work, [and] we cannot afford [to help much], because my husband and I are only on pensions. So, they must earn themselves and live themselves happily. That's my wish.

For his mother, the anxiety about the enormous expenses necessary to facilitate Sameer's migration to Portugal, alongside the precarity of this life path for Sameer and his wife, was also matched with excitement over what possible futures this precarious beginning could bring to them as a family. Over an afternoon, Sameer's family shared their plans to all end up together eventually in Portugal, where Sameer's mother and sister would take care of the future children he and his wife have yet to have. Sameer's mother shared:

> Then we will have a nice life. When my son will go there, then only we will have a nice life after five years or so, [when] he can get his residency and bring

us over . . . now we will always try to sit together, we will not separate, we will
sit together.

Like Sameer, Sameer's mother was expressing a happiness that would
materialise in the future. This future-orientated happiness affectively
helped her navigate her current situation, with her only son about to
embark on another precarious journey for work and for his marriage,
this time to become an undocumented worker in Portugal. It reassured
her that everything would be okay in the future. Failing at becoming
a Gurkha had sent Sameer down a different life-building path – one
where he and his wife would be together. Yet because of, or despite, this
new opening for a different kind of future, he and his family carried a
hope for different opportunities that enabled them to endure a present
marked by such a high degree of uncertainty.

Failure did not detach Sameer or his wife from the broader colonial geographies that also condition what it means to be a Gurkha or
a Gurkha wife. They faced new challenges. But they also faced new
and different future opportunities that might have not been thought of
otherwise. For example, in the version of Sameer's future he shared, he
could imagine the possibility of being physically present in the raising

Figure C.2 Amanda Chisholm talking with Sameer as she shows him photos on
his phone, in Pokhara, Nepal, November 2018. Photo credit to Robic Upadhayay.

of his children – an activity that was denied to Rabindra and so many other Gurkhas. Sameer's story tells us that failure can certainly open up new possible futures outside of military service, but also that it does not overcome the extraordinary structural barriers and broader precarities around securing a kind of life that lies outside of what Berlant (2011) articulates as slow death. This slow death references the regular and systematic wearing out of certain communities as they try to reproduce life, particularly in conditions where their living environment is marked by an enduring crisis of social reproduction.

To return to Lisle's (2018) work, failure is an affect that has heterodox stories. Since only a fraction of the journeys of those young men and their families who invest so much time, emotion and energy in becoming a Gurkha will end in success, failure is an affect that circulates throughout the Gurkha communities. It is very much the other side of the same Gurkha coin. Failure also attaches to the life stories of men and women who succeed in becoming Gurkhas and Gurkha wives. This can be observed when we reflect upon the story of Rabindra and Sunika. Failure to provide educational opportunities for their children had placed Sunika and Rabindra in an impossible position, whereby Rabindra felt compelled to take up military service as a Gurkha with the Indian army. As a result, Rabindra continued to harbour regrets about not being physically present to see his children grow up and to help with the day-to-day running of the household. For Sunika, she had stuffed down so much pain from over twenty-six years ago, when she felt that she had to force Rabindra into this military life. As a woman in Nepal, there were few options and opportunities open to her that would enable her to help take care of the family financially – this responsibility fell upon Rabindra, but still profoundly impacted her life as well. The structures of patriarchy, of poverty and of underdevelopment in Nepal made securing a life for Rabindra and Sunika feel impossible – so much so that the pull towards military life as a path to a secure life was significant. But it, too, came at a cost.

Taking the stories of Rabindra and Sunika and of Sameer and his family, and, indeed, taking all the rich experiences that Gurkhas and their families shared with me over a decade into account, we can see that failure is not the end story of affective relations to militarism or to being or becoming a Gurkha. It does not always open up creative life-producing paths outside of militarism, colonial histories and global capital. Rather, failure connects to the broader conflicting affects of joy, happiness, regret, shame and pain that circulate alongside and within the global movement of security workforces and security knowledge.

It speaks to how the security industry is just one lifeline for Nepali families as they navigate global raced markets in their pursuit of a good life – where even having an everyday life, with its rhythms, routines and banality, remains, for many, aspirational. It is within and through the structures of colonial geographies and martial histories that we can see the diverse ways in which these communities feel their way through the world and affectively relate to ideas of militarism as they continue to keep life going.

The Pushes and Pulls of Militarism

Throughout this book I have woven in stories of Gurkhas and Gurkha wives who participate in global private security. I have shown the everyday experiences of these people, and how they encounter the global security industry and make sense of their own positions within this global market, all the while keeping their own lives going. These stories have illuminated the ways in which joy and pain can run parallel, and how affective relations shape and are shaped by histories, inform the present and condition what possible futures might unfold. The book has demonstrated the strong pull that militarism and military service exert on the Gurkha communities – communities where everyday lives are so saturated with over 200 years of foreign military service that entertaining another possible life path becomes unthinkable.

What is compelling in these various accounts of entanglements with foreign security work and life-building and small world-making activities is how Gurkhas and Gurkha wives continue to hold on to this kind of militarised life-making pathway, even when it proves toxic or harmful. This was certainly the case for Neha, whose life as a Gurkha wife began with the trauma of her marriage, planned without her knowledge or consent. Feelings of pain and loss were also expressed in Rabindra's story of being forced to seek foreign military service to provide a financial lifeline for his young family, and by Sunika, a mother and young wife who felt compelled to force her husband into foreign military service.

To understand their affective relations to militarism and military service – a service that perpetually positions this community at the margins of global security – is also to account for Gurkhas' relations to colonial histories and geographies and to structures of patriarchy and militarism, which all condition their motivations and pulls into military service. For example, Sunika, as a Nepali woman, did not have the choice to pursue foreign military work. As a young and uneducated wife and mother displaced by the Maoist revolution in Nepal, Sunika was caught in significant structural restraints. To secure a chance at a different future for their children, she had to convince Rabindra to become a Gurkha, and then make concrete decisions along the way to stay that course, all the while keeping life going. These smaller decisions, often made in the moment, included not responding to Rabindra's emotionally charged letter to her, saying that he hated the military and that they treated him like a dog. Stuffing the pain of her husband down and not responding to his letter, for Sunika, meant that Rabindra would stay in the military. This was essential for them as a family unit, to ensure a sense of security and stability for their children, even while it caused both a great deal of individual pain. Yet for many others, such as Kiran and Neta, becoming a Gurkha and a Gurkha wife was the game changer they had wanted. Military service enabled life building that brought investment opportunities, wealth, social status and the ability to invest financially in a future that might otherwise feel impossible. Often in interviews, expressions of happiness and gratitude sat comfortably alongside expressions of pain and frustration.

With this research, I originally sought to understand the motivations for Gurkhas and their families that caused them to sign on for or be pulled into foreign security work through the concept of a neoliberal bargain (Sa'ar 2005; Chisholm 2014a). This is a bargain that is understood as a conscious decision and as self-actualising agency that individuals choose after weighing up options within constrained structures. But this bargain does not account for the weight and rhythms of everyday life making for Gurkhas and their families; nor does it acknowledge that, for many of our decisions, we feel our way through – with feelings that are embedded in colonial histories as much as in unreflected moments and routines within a community. Indeed, Wool's (2015) description of James, a US military veteran, presents a similar reflection on how subjects of war and militarism understand their own encounters and agency. Experiences of war, like pulls towards military life, are not retold or understood through a grand narrative form of nationalism. More often, as in the case of James, they are 'weird shit he recollects' within the labours of life in the moment (Wool 2015, 37).

It is within the context of life-building and life-practising activities in an environment of broader insecurity and precarity of everyday life that motivations, ambivalent relations to military service, individual agency and pulls to militarism are located. Like Wool's (2015) observations on how subjects understand their encounters with war and their own agency in micro moments, Gurkhas and their families do not articulate their motivations and engagement with military life in a broader narrative form of colonialism, capitalism or a bargain they made. There is no grand strategy of personal self-actualisation. Conversely, many of the decisions in life for those I interviewed were based in the everyday, where the challenges, the exhaustions and the habitual nature of reproducing life amid impoverishment make such a task exhausting (Berlant 2011; Davies 2016).

The stories detailed throughout the book attest to how the practice of keeping life going 'exhausts practical sovereignty' and how 'at the same time that one builds a life the pressures of its reproduction can be exhausting' (Berlant 2011, 116). Stories like Sunika and Rabindra's make us rethink how we conceive of agency and choice beyond the self-actualising agency of either resistance or adaptation to these constraints. For this couple, military service addressed the more immediate concern of reproducing life, of taking care of their young family and of carving out a different future for their children. Life decisions are made in smaller micro moments to address immediate needs. Indeed, Sunika and Rabindra's story reminds us of what Berlant argues: 'most of what we do, after all, involves not being purposeful, but inhabiting agency differently, in small vacations from the will itself' (2011, 116). Agency, then, can be observed in smaller life-building activities – activities that at times provide a reprieve from the painful recounting of military service and the difficult decisions individuals have made to keep life going. This could be in planning homecomings for Gurkhas, when so much energy goes into making such moments filled with joy.

We do a huge disservice to these rich accounts of all the Gurkhas and Gurkha wives I have interviewed and spent time with over these past fourteen years if we locate their agency to participate in global security only in a wilful choice. The '"will" is often depleted from "coordinating one's pacing"' (Berlant 2011, 116), in work and in the reproduction of life and recovery from it. It is also inappropriate to explain the affective pulls towards militarism in a way that plucks the everyday experiences and knowledge of Gurkhas and their wives upwards to a higher truth of universal notions of colonialism, neoliberalism or capitalism, and then analytically moves back down to 'solve' these local problems (Tuhiwai Smith 1999; Page 2017). To articulate better how agency is expressed and what motivates these communities to partake in a global security industry from the periphery and look to militarism as a key in reproducing their lives, we need to displace the Western ontologies and sensibilities that continue to frame our understandings of global politics.

As I write this book and continue to think about the multitude of rich and nuanced stories shared with me, the various encounters I have had and the observations I have made, I recognise how much I have learned and how grateful I am for the generosity of this community in opening their homes and life worlds to me. I am also aware that there is still so much I am not seeing, so much I am not fully understanding and so much that is withheld (Lather 2016). This raises two important questions for me when thinking about this book and what concluding remarks I can possibly write. First, how can we account for what pulls these communities into a militarised pathway beyond thinking that they are duped, or that the global constraints are too much and that they do not have a choice? And second, how can we write about what motivates these communities to continue to invest in militarism as a pathway to, as Berlant calls it, the good life, and in such a way that does not smooth over the ambivalence or override the moments when our own knowledge of politics and understanding in these encounters fall short (Gunaratnam and Hamilton 2017)? These are important ontological, epistemological and temporal questions, specifically as we move away from familiar existing knowledge of militarism and militarisation that is largely based upon Global North militaries and militarised communities. They are the foundational questions that have guided me through writing each chapter in this book, inspired by Haraway's call to 'stay with the trouble' (2016).

These questions have informed my research methods and the ways I went about vulnerably writing (Page 2017) about Gurkhas and Gurkha wives – paying attention to the long histories and particular contexts that inform these communities' everyday lives and how they understand their roles within local and global spaces. I return to these epistemological and ontological questions again here to guide me in thinking through agency and affective pulls into militarised life pathways I have not personally experienced. To write about the motivations of Gurkhas and Gurkha wives, then, I turn to Berlant's (2007, 2011) concept of slow death.

Slow Death and Life Building

In 2007 and 2011, Lauren Berlant introduced the concept of slow death to capture the 'wearing out of a population in a way that points to its deterioration as a defining condition of its experience and historical existence' (2007, 754). The concept is situated in contemporary historical experiences of communities throughout the United States in a time of hypercapitalism and neoliberalism. Slow death is a low theory concept that begins analysis with the people who experience extreme precarity and crisis as part of and alongside their ordinary everyday lives. It illuminates how these communities live, where 'life building and life attrition are indistinguishable and where separating incoherence, distraction and habituation from deliberate activity becomes impossible' (Berlant 2011, 96). Berlant focuses here on people whose ordinary life is governed through the logic of crisis, where structural constraints that become associated with keeping life going, such as poverty, holding down multiple jobs and poor housing facilities, are slowly wearing out those communities.

Berlant's slow death concept was designed to illuminate the racialised, gendered, disability-related and classed structures that cause the condition of 'being worn out by the activity of reproducing life' (2007, 758), and to show how crisis is not an acute time-bound event, but rather something that perpetually informs ordinary and everyday lives. The concept helps us get at how people make decisions, choose pathways and life-build/life-practise within broader structures of precarity and crisis that render having an everyday life aspirational. Within my work, slow death helps me think through how Gurkhas and their families continue to invest in militarism, and why there continues to be such a surplus of new recruits willing to sign up for foreign military service as a pathway to the good life.

Slow death speaks against a broader self-actualising subjectivity and/ or agency founded upon a notion of active resistance, the act of being oppressed or the bargain the individual consciously makes. Slow death also rejects the more structural explanation of being so disenfranchised that any other option becomes mute – or a self-actualising activity where the individual invests in knowledge and politics with a linearly focused temporality. Such understandings of agency treat it as something that is practised for a future political goal, by a fully formed subject who is aware of what is at stake and the structural constraints around them, and whose decisions are based upon navigating those constraints. The concept speaks against the 'moral science' of biopolitics that associates administration of life with the 'melodrama of the care of the monadic self', instead focusing upon 'activity exercised within the spaces of ordinariness' that does not always follow a logic of 'visible effectuality, bourgeois dramatics, and lifelong accumulation or self-fashioning' (2011, 99).

Conversely, then, slow death points us to rethinking agency as an activity located within the everyday, banal and micro practices of keeping life going. It does not carry a particular lineal temporality that we can understand in advance. Slow death enables us to observe agency through 'activity of maintenance, not making; fantasy, without gran-diosity; sentience without full intentionality; inconsistency, without shattering; and embodying, alongside embodiment' (2011, 100). To be sure, agency requires struggle, action and exertion, often occurring at the same time (Mahmood 2011). Consequently, in reconceptualising agency in these everyday and often unreflected spaces of reproducing life, we focus our attention on how our bodies affectively move through the world in ordinary life-building activities. This remains central to understanding the affective relations of militarism and military life for Gurkhas and their families.

Slow death is very much embedded in broader queer concerns of temporality and epistemological and ontological claims around what propels us forward and pulls us back. Tiffany Page (2017) uses slow death as a methodological tool to write about communities we are unfamiliar with in a way that does not reproduce epistemic violence to smooth over stories of trauma. For Page, slow death attunes us, as feminists from Global North institutions, not to be quick to find famil-iar categorisations and vernaculars that smooth over in a way that, in the process of translation, '"tames" what we observe as unintelligible into a Eurocentric temporality, where timing becomes synonymous with intention, and knowledge is produced in advance of time' (2017, 16). We need to displace and become comfortable with the disquieted moments in everyday encounters with communities who do not share our ontological commitments to time, to space, to agency, and to what we think politics is and where we locate it. Slow death becomes a meth-odological guide, the analytical context, for feminists to ask openly: 'what might it mean not to fully comprehend the lives upon which we make epistemic claims' (Page 2017, 16). It moves us away from seeing a subject as constantly trying to better themselves and to improve their position in life, to refocus our analytical attention on how we all 'endure life, which while preventing our immediate death, is also wearing us out' (Page 2017, 23). As such, we are less invested in telling a linear, narrative arc story of resisting or adapting to structural forces – and moving to one that explores the nuances, the ambivalences and the everyday activities of keeping life going.

This book has illuminated the everyday lives of Gurkhas and their families. It has sought to explore the creative possibilities of living and building communities otherwise than and outside of the existing global capitalist security regimes. Indeed, Halberstam (2011) reminds us that creativity and ingenuity in community and life building always run parallel for those people that systems were not designed for. Slow death, then, is a concept that is at the nexus of queer, feminist, postcolonial and disability thinking. It shows us the structural constraints that result in a systematic and slow deterioration and ultimate death of certain communities under existing structures of power – but also spaces of hope and alternatives to life outside of these power relations.

For me, slow death is important in describing the harms associated with Gurkhas and other racialised bodies working in the security indus- try, but it also addresses the question of why these men and women continue to participate in a global market that asks so much of them and yet gives so little in return. Hanna Ketola and I (2020) have written elsewhere about how Gurkhas and Gurkha wives navigate their own affective relations to militarism under a crisis ordinary, where the ability to reproduce life and keep life going is structurally organised around so much uncertainty that is not bound by acute moments or episodes, but that very much is drawn out to frame their everyday environments. Slow death complements this work. Where crisis ordinary is the struc- tures and conditions in which Gurkhas and Gurkha communities are located, slow death marks the life-building and life-practising activities of Gurkhas and their spouses – activities that are about keeping life going rather than the desire to improve one's lot in life. Slow death attunes us to how Gurkhas and their wives are bound into daily routines of keeping life going amid racial and gendered structures designed to wear them out and wear them down. In these moments, the acts of living and reproducing life are an act of agency. Slow death in a crisis ordinary brings into focus the interrelated nature of affect, militarism and colonial histories in reproducing life for Gurkhas and their families.

Chapter Summaries

The intersections of affect, militarism and colonial histories have informed this entire book project. I have been mindful of analysing these intersections, and how they come to derive meaning, by privileg- ing the everyday as my analytical grounding. The Introduction set the context and introduced key actors involved in PMSC security operations, including the clients, the contactors and the spouses of contractors. It began to foreground how racial histories construct a hierarchy of secu- rity contractors and how the value of security is assigned. This chapter introduced who Gurkhas are and how they have come to derive value as racialised contractors due to their over 200 years of military history with the British. Such a history gives them preferred access to security mar- kets when compared with other communities from the Global South, and at the same time conditions their experiences as racialised men in global security environments. The chapter then moved to consider feminist political economy questions on the global security industry that included how labour hierarchies are formed and sustained, the role of social reproduction in reproducing this global industry, how affective economies materialise, and the affective labour involved in making people feel safe.

Chapter 1 moved to explore the theoretical framework I apply to understand how Gurkhas and their families come to invest affectively in militarism, and the central role of affect in shaping security encounters and experiences. Here, I made the case that security bodies are always affective bodies. Centring questions of affect changes what questions we ask about PMSCs and how we come to understand Gurkhas and their communities' motivations and experiences within global security markets. As I stated in this chapter, affect describes 'the messy dynamics of attachment, self-continuity and the reproductions of life that are the material scenes of living' (Berlant 2011, 15). It illuminates not only how affect shapes experiences of war, but also how Gurkha men and their spouses attach to militarised life patterns as a means of building their own worlds and futures for their children. The chapter then conceptually explored how practices and logics of militarism, capitalism and colonial histories entangle in producing these affective security bodies and shaping how experiences are felt. The Introduction and Chapter 1 made the case for why we need to concern ourselves with these three interrelated operating concepts, how they materialise within global security markets and what paying attention to them enables us to ask politically.

Chapter 2 focused on the histories that stick to Gurkha bodies in such a way that produce them as almost but not fully complete security professionals. The chapter showed how militarism and martial race saturate these communities and are within the fabric of their life-building activities. It is intergenerational. The chapter then further explored how these sticky histories underpin how Gurkhas are, and are perceived, in various encounters and interactions with white British serving soldiers, as well as the public. In this chapter we heard from Roshan, a retired British Gurkha working in management for a security recruitment company. His own account of his martial history is one that brings pride and joy as much as it illuminates the structural racism experienced by Commonwealth soldiers within the British military, a topic that is also widely documented in Vron Ware's research on migrant workforces in the British military (2010, 2012).

These histories, as Chapter 3 noted, have shaped perceptions of Gurkhas' capabilities as security contractors and naturalise a management structure I have called the Gurkha security package (Chisholm 2014b). In this chapter, I explored the politics of love that sustains this security package. Love here is the affect that binds Gurkhas to their white British officers in an uneven way, producing what I understand as a protective father and dutiful son metaphorical hierarchy. Love also insulates this 'father/son family' from the outside security work, positioning Gurkha British officers as champions of Gurkhas and Gurkhas as dutiful and loyal to these officers for finding them work in private security. Overall, Chapter 3 showed how love obscures at the same time as it naturalises the colonial politics that divide these men, the labour they perform, and how they are valued within the Gurkha family as well as outside of it, in the broader security industry.

In Chapter 4, I looked at the politics of happiness in producing the (un)grateful wife/benefactor of the global security industry. Largely focusing on the stories of Neha and Sunika, the chapter first showed the concrete ways in which reproductive labour is central to the global security industry. It also illuminated how this labour is obscured through broader narratives that position these women's labour as household activities disconnected from global markets, and the women as benefactors of, not participants in, global security. The chapter then moved to explore the affect of happiness that binds these women into these military market relations. Happiness, as a future-orientated affect, binds Gurkha wives to labour conditions as reproducers of life and life-building activities that continue to support the broader global security industry. Happiness is mediated through structures of patriarchy and of caste, as well as poverty. Pathways to happiness, then, are observed through marriage and through marrying a husband who can secure a financial future in which reproducing life is not marked by extreme forms of poverty. Happiness is also the common sense that underpins how these women can experience and feel about their roles of wives and mothers. The words 'I am happy' or 'I will be happy' were often declared to me in interviews, alongside stories of pain and frustration that had come from reproducing life in a family where the main earner is physically absent.

Chapter 5 brought us back to Kabul, Afghanistan, to explore the everyday encounters between Gurkha security contractors and the Western clients they protect. Here, I examined the affective labour of doing security work, the nature of this labour, and how it gets valued and placed upon racialised bodies to perform. The chapter largely focused on how the underpinning racial logics naturalise the divisions of labour amongst the professional Western contactors and the Gurkhas. Gurkhas are understood as naturally suitable to perform the devalued caring work of making people feel secure, and there are concrete material and emotional costs to them in performing this kind of work.

This final chapter has explored questions around agency and how we come to think about the pulls into militarism and military service as a pathway to the good life. To do this, I have drawn upon queer feminist concepts of failure and slow death. The concept of failure enabled me to explore life pathways of those young men who never actually succeed at becoming Gurkhas, along with those of their families. I illuminated how failure is not just about shame and disappointment. Failure also enables thinking through different kinds of futures and pathways to achieving them. These futures, at least in the case of Sameer and his family, did not necessary lead them to pull away from militarism and a kind of life building outside of colonial, gendered and racial global structures. But it did open a different possibility for them for building a happy future. I then moved to the concept of slow death to write about agency in these communities, in that it offers conceptual space for ambivalence and for locating decisions and choices in the life-building activities of everyday life – particularly when these activities that are supposed to build the kind of life we desire are also the very activities that exhaust us. Agency, then, is not something that carries a grand narrative with a self-actualising subject. Rather, agency is located within the reproduction of our own lives, with the banality of everyday life and the quest for a secure future. All of these affective relations of happiness, failure, love and pain to militarism and military pathways to a good life that is located 'somewhere else' are embedded in broader everyday life building. Life building located in small world-making activities amid communities whose very lives continue to be marked through a crisis of social reproduction.

Conclusion

This book has explored the different experiences of Gurkhas, Gurkha wives and British Gurkha officers who are now security company owners, and their roles in working and supporting the global security industry. It has also documented how Western women and men come to encounter and interpret these encounters with Gurkhas in Afghanistan. Paying attention to the experiences of these different actors that make up global security markets, I have engaged with the various affects that bind people on to militarised life patterns, and with how affect is taken up as a particular kind of labour within private security in making people feel safe.

I have also sought to show how these affects are taken up by PMSCs in the broader provision of security. Affect, as it connects to militarism and global markets of security, has been the primary operating concept used here to link the different experiences, divisions of labour and market relations. Affect in this book has been brought to the fore to illuminate all those feelings, impulses and atmospheres that pull Gurkhas and their families into military life patterns – including the life-sustaining and life-building patterns. Importantly, these affects of martial race that 'stick', along with the affects of love and of happiness, all keep Gurkhas and their families in militarised relations with the British and in private security, even when these very relations prove to be toxic or impossible. Finally, and specifically referencing Chapter 5, I highlighted from the position of the client/the protected, how everyday security in Afghanistan is embodied. These embodiments naturalise the divisions of labour for the professional white soldier and the martial raced Gurkha.

Overall, this book has grappled with what binds communities who are structurally located on the periphery of global capitalism and the security market to logics of militarism and military pathways. It asked what keeps these communities actively engaged in global structures that condition them to sacrifice the most and gain the least. To answer this, I turned to the concept of affect and how we feel our way through global politics. I have used affect to show how we find ourselves on life pathways that prove toxic and impossible, and yet we continue to derive pleasure from being inside them. Affect can be immediate or orientated to the future, or can frame our past, and it can make our position in life meaningful. Affect is also about labour. In this book, I have discussed how labour becomes commoditised in such a way that, even when it is not constituted as productive, it continues to enable global security markets to garner profits and to extract labour.

I finished with a brief discussion about slow death, referring to the slow wearing out of communities positioned in a structural crisis ordinary. Here, I examined how crisis and the ability to sustain life are enduring features of Gurkha communities. They underpin their geo-political and social environments, and profoundly shape how these people relate affectively to militarism and to military work as a pathway to a good, secure life. This slow death of Gurkha communities shows how agency is practised within an everyday where, as Berlant (2011) notes, the will to self-actualise, to improve one's life, is exhausted from the reproductive tasks of keeping life going. Here, we can see agency manifesting more in the habitual, the unreflected and the immediacy of keeping life going in the now.

I remain indebted to the Gurkhas, their families and the British Gurkha officers who have opened their homes, their histories and their hopes for their futures to me. These diverse and entangled relations illuminate not only the structural aspects of racism, sexism and colonialism that continue to condition the movement (and profits) of the global security industry, but also, as Pedwell puts it, 'the intersections, borderlands and in-between spaces of both geo-political domains and disciplinary bodies of knowledge' (2012, 2). Love, for example, is perpetually conditioned and materialised through colonial histories and structures of power that sustain uneven friendships between Gurkhas and British Gurkha officers. Happiness, for Gurkha wives, is manifested through intersections of patriarchy, imperialism, caste and rural/urban divides. Failure to become a Gurkha opens critical opportunities to live otherwise and away from militarised pathways, but it does not overcome the geopolitical inequalities of poverty and underdevelopment that also compel the foreign migration industry in Nepal. It is within these ambiguous spaces that we see affective relations that hold people in place, as well as critical ways for them to imagine and live otherwise. I am inspired by the ways in which these individuals and families keep life going, and how they hold communities together, despite the great sacrifices that doing foreign military work entails. These accounts have shown just how much affect drives the global security industry, and how colonial histories and gender relations continue to shape Gurkhas' and Gurkha wives' experiences as global security contractors.

REFERENCES

Abrahamsen, Rita, and Anna Leander. 2016. *Routledge Handbook of Private Security Studies*. London: Routledge.

Abrahamsen, Rita, and Michael C. Williams. 2009. 'Security Beyond the State: Global Security Assemblages in International Politics'. *International Political Sociology* 3, no. 1: 1–17.

Acharya, Meena. 2008. 'Global Integration of Subsistence Economies and Women's Empowerment: An Experience from Nepal'. In *Beyond States and Markets: The Challenges of Social Reproduction*, edited by Isabella Bakker and Rachel Silvey, 55–71. Abingdon: Routledge.

Agathangelou, Anna. 2004. *The Global Political Economy of Sex: Desire, Violence and Insecurity in Mediterranean Nation States*. New York: Palgrave Macmillan.

Åhäll, Linda. 2016. 'The Dance of Militarisation: A Feminist Security Studies Take on "the Political"'. *Critical Studies on Security* 4: 154–68.

Åhäll, Linda. 2018. 'Affect as Methodology: Feminism and the Politics of Emotions'. *International Political Sociology* 12: 36–52.

Åhäll, Linda, and Thomas Gregory, eds. 2015. *Emotions, Politics and War*. London: Routledge.

Ahmed, Sara. 2004. 'Affective Economies'. *Social Text* 22: 117–39.

Ahmed, Sara. 2010. *The Promise of Happiness*. Durham, NC: Duke University Press.

Ahmed, Sara. 2014. *The Cultural Politics of Emotions*. Edinburgh: Edinburgh University Press.

Anderson, Ben. 2016. 'Becoming and Being Hopeful: Towards a Theory of Affect'. *Environment and Planning: Society and Space* 24: 733–52.

Anderson, Bridget. 2000. *Doing the Dirty Work? Global Politics of Domestic Labour*. London: Zed Books.

Anderson, Clare. 2007. *The Indian Uprising of 1857–58: Prisons, Prisoners, and Rebellion*. London: Anthem Press.

Anievas, Alexander, Nivi Manchanda and Robbie Shilliam. 2015. *Race and Racism in International Relations: Confronting the Colour Line*. London: Routledge.

Avant, Deborah. 2005. 'Private Security Companies'. *New Political Economy* 10: 121–9.

Avant, Deborah, and Renee de Nevers. 2011. 'Military Contractors and the American Way of War'. *Daedalus* 140, no. 3: 88–99. <https://www.researchgate.net/pub lication/241890739_Military_Contractors_the_American_Way_of_War> (last accessed 24 May 2022).

Bakan, Abigail B., and Daiva Stasiulis. 1997. *Not One of the Family: Foreign Domestic Workers in Canada*. Toronto: University of Toronto Press.

Baker, Catherine. 2016. 'The "Gay Olympics"? The Eurovision Song Contest and the Politics of LGBT/European Belonging'. *European Journal of International Relations* 23, no. 1: 97–121.

Baker, Catherine, ed. 2020. *Making War on Bodies: Militarism, Aesthetics and Embodiment in International Politics*. Edinburgh: Edinburgh University Press.

Bakker, Isabella, and Stephen Gill. 2003. *Power, Production and Social Reproduction: Human In/security in the Global Political Economy*. London: Palgrave Macmillan.

Ball, Rochelle. 2004. 'Divergent Development, Racialised Rights: Globalised Labour Markets and the Trade of Nurses – The Case of the Philippines'. *Women's Studies International Forum* 27: 119–33.

Barkawi, Tarak. 2017. *Soldiers of Empire: Indian and British Armies in World War II*. Cambridge: Cambridge University Press.

Barker, Isabelle V. 2009. '(Re)Producing American Soldiers in an Age of Empire'. *Politics and Gender* 5, no. 2: 211–35.

Barker, Isabelle V. 2015. '(Re)Producing American Soldiers in an Age of Empire'. In *Gender and Private Security in Global Politics*, edited by Maya Eichler, 75–94. Oxford: Oxford University Press.

Barua, Pradeep. 1995. 'Inventing Race: The British and Indian's Martial Races'. *The Historian* 58: 107–16.

Basham, Victoria. 2013. *War, Identity and the Liberal State: Everyday Experiences of the Geopolitical in the Armed Forces*. New York: Routledge.

Basham, Victoria. 2015. 'Waiting for War: Soldiering, Temporality, and the Gender Politics of Boredom and Joy in Military Spaces'. In *Emotions, Politics and War*, edited by Linda Åhäll and Thomas Gregory, 128–40. London: Routledge.

Basham, Victoria. 2018. 'Liberal Militarism as Insecurity, Desire and Ambivalence: Gender, Race and the Everyday Geopolitics of War'. *Security Dialogue* 49: 32–43.

Basham, Victoria, and Sergio Catignani. 2018. 'War Is Where the Hearth Is: Gendered Labor and the Everyday Reproduction of the Geopolitical in the Army Reserves'. *International Feminist Journal of Politics* 20: 153–71.

BBC News. 2004. 'Nepalese Hostages Killed in Iraq'. 31 August. <http://news.bbc. co.uk/1/hi/world/south_asia/3614866.stm> (last accessed 24 May 2022).

BBC News. 2010. 'Nepal Government Lifts Iraq Working Ban'. 28 July. <https:// www.bbc.co.uk/news/world-south-asia-10795646> (last accessed 24 May 2022).

Belkin, Aaron. 2012. *Bring Me Men: Military Masculinity and the Benign Facade of American Empire*. London: Hurst.

Bellamy, Christopher. 2011. *The Gurkhas: Special Force*. St Ives: John Murray.

Ben-Asher, Smadar, and Ya'arit Bokek-Cohen. 2020. 'Commemoration Labour as Emotional Labour: The Emotional Costs of Being an Israeli Militarized National Widow'. *Gender, Place and Culture* 28, no. 8: 455–75.

Benoit, Cecilia, and Helga Hallgrimsdottir. 2011. *Valuing Care Work: Comparative Perspectives*. Toronto: University of Toronto Press.

Berlant, Lauren. 2007. 'Slow Death (Sovereignty, Obesity, Lateral Agency)'. *Critical Inquiry* 33, no. 4: 754–80.

Berlant, Lauren. 2011. *Cruel Optimism*. Durham, NC: Duke University Press.

Berndtsson, Joakim, and Christopher Kinsey. 2016. *The Routledge Research Companion to Security Outsourcing*. Abingdon: Routledge.

Bleiker, Ronald, and Emma Hutchison. 2008. 'Fear No More: Emotions and World Politics'. *Review of International Studies* 34: 115–35.

Blumberg, Rae Lesser. 1978. *Stratification: Socioeconomic and Sexual Inequality*. Dubuque, IA: William C. Brown.

Boris, Eileen, and Rhacel Salazar Parreñas. 2010. *Intimate Labors: Cultures, Technologies, and the Politics of Care*. Stanford: Stanford University Press.

Bourke, Joanna. 1996. 'War and Violence'. *Thesis Eleven* 86, no. 1: 23–38.

Brennan, Teresa. 2000. *Exhausting Modernity: Grounds for a New Economy*. New York: Routledge.

Brown, Rachel. 2016. 'Re-examining the Transnational Nanny: Migrant Care work Beyond the Chain'. *International Feminist Journal of Politics* 12: 210–29.

Bruff, Ian, and Stefanie Wohl. 2016. 'Constitutionalizing Austerity, Disciplining the Household: Masculine Norms of Competitiveness and the Crisis of Social Reproduction in the Eurozone'. In *Scandalous Economics: Gender and the Politics of Financial Crisis*, edited by Aida A. Hozic and Jacqui True, 92–108. Oxford: Oxford University Press.

Bullock, Christopher. 2009. *Britain's Gurkhas*. London: Third Millennium.

Candler, Edmund. 1919. *The Sepoy*. New Delhi: Lancer.

Caplan, Lionel. 1995. *Warrior Gentlemen: 'Gurkhas' in the Western Imagination*. Oxford: Berghahn.

Caso, Federica. 2020. 'The Political Aesthetics of the Body of the Soldier in Pain'. In *Making War on Bodies: Militarism, Aesthetics and Embodiment in International Politics*, edited by Catherine Baker, 54–73. Edinburgh: Edinburgh University Press.

Chisholm, Amanda. 2014a. 'Marketing the Gurkha Security Package: Colonial Histories and Neoliberal Economies of Private Security'. *Security Dialogue* 45: 349–72.

Chisholm, Amanda. 2014b. 'The Silenced and Indispensible: Gurkhas in Private Military Security Companies'. *International Feminist Journal of Politics* 16: 26–47.

Chisholm, Amanda. 2015a. 'From Warriors of Empire to Martial Contractors: Reimagining Gurkhas in Private Security'. In *Gender and Private Security in Global Politics*, edited by Maya Eichler, 95–113. Oxford: Oxford University Press.

Chisholm, Amanda. 2015b. 'Postcoloniality and Race and Global Private Security Markets'. In *The Routledge Handbook of Private Security Studies*, edited by Anna Leander and Rita Abrahamsen, 177–86. London: Routledge.

Chisholm, Amanda. 2017. 'Clients, Contractors and Everyday Masculinities in Global Private Security'. *Critical Military Studies* 3: 120–41.

Chisholm, Amanda, and Maya Eichler. 2018. 'Reproductions of Global Security: Accounting for the Private Security Household'. *International Feminist Journal of Politics* 20: 563–28.

Chisholm, Amanda, and Hanna Ketola. 2020. 'The Cruel Optimism of Militarism: Feminist Curiosity, Affect and Global Security'. *International Political Sociology* 14: 270–85.

Chisholm, Amanda, and Saskia Stachowitsch. 2016. 'Everyday Matters in Global Private Security Supply Chains: A Feminist Global Political Economy Perspective on Gurkhas in Private Security'. *Globalizations* 13: 815–29.

Choudhary, Neha. 2015. 'The Gurkha Wives of United Kingdom: Challenges to Social Integration'. MA thesis, London School of Economics.

Chowdhry, Geeta, and Sheila Nair, eds. 2004. *Power, Postcolonialism and International Relations: Reading Race, Gender and Class*. Abingdon: Routledge.

Coleman, A. P. 1999. *A Special Peace Corps. The Beginnings of Gorkha Service with the British*. Edinburgh: Pentland Press.

Condos, Mark. 2017. *The Insecurity State: Punjab and the Making of Colonial Power in British India*. Cambridge: Cambridge University Press.

Crane-Seeber, Jesse Paul. 2016. 'Sexy Warriors: The Politics and Pleasure of Submission to the State'. *Critical Military Studies* 2: 41–55.

Cree, Alice. 2020. '"People Want to See Tears": Military Heroes and the "Constant Penelope" of the UK's Military Wives Choir'. *Gender, Place and Culture* 27: 218–38.

Crenshaw, Kimberly. 1993. 'Mapping the Margins: Intersectionality, Identity Politics and Violence Against Women of Colour'. *Stanford Law Review* 43: 1241–99.

Cross, J. P., and John Chapple. 2007. *Gurkhas at War: Eyewitness Accounts from World War II to Iraq*. London: Greenhill.

Daigle, Megan. 2015. *From Cuba with Love: Sex and Money in the Twenty-First Century*. Berkeley: University of California Press.

Das, Santanu. 2006. *Touch and Intimacy in First World War Literature*. Cambridge: Cambridge University Press.

Das, Santanu. 2018. *Indian Empire and the First World War Culture*. Cambridge: Cambridge University Press.

Davies, Matt. 2016. 'Everyday Life as a Critique: Revisiting the Everyday in IPE with Henri Lefebvre and Postcolonialism'. *International Political Sociology* 10, no. 1: 22–38.

Davis, Angela Y. 1981. *Gender, Race, Class*. New York: Penguin Press.

Des Chene, Maria. 1991. *Relics of Empire: A Cultural History of Gurkhas, 1815–1987*. PhD Dissertation, Stanford University.

Des Chene, Maria. 1999. 'Military Ethnology in British India'. *South Asia Research* 19: 121–35.

Du Bois, W. E. B. 1903. *The Souls of Black Folk: Essays and Sketches*. Chicago: A. C. McClurg.

Dyvik, Synne. 2016. 'Valhalla Rising: Gender Embodiment and Experience in Military Memoirs'. *Security Dialogue* 47: 133–50.

Ehrenreich, Barbara, and Arlie Russell Hochschild. 2003. *Global Women: Nannies, Maids and Sex Workers in the New Economy*. London: Granta.

Eichler, Maya. 2014. 'Citizenship and the Contracting out of Military Work: From National Conscription to Globalized Recruitment'. *Citizenship Studies* 18: 600–14.

Eichler, Maya. 2015. *Gender and Private Security in Global Politics*. Oxford: Oxford University Press.

Elias, Juanita. 2005. 'Stitching-up the Labour Market: Recruitment, Gender and Ethnicity in the Multinational Firm'. *International Feminist Journal of Politics* 7: 90–111.

Elias, Juanita, and Samanthi J. Gunawardana. 2013. *The Global Political Economy of the Household in Asia*. London: Palgrave Macmillan.

Elias, Juanita, and Shirin M. Rai. 2019. 'Feminist Everyday Political Economy: Space, Time and Violence'. *Review of International Studies* 45: 201–20.

Elias, Juanita, Lena Rethel and Lisa Tilley. 2019. 'International Political Economy and International Political Sociology Meet in Jakarta: Feminist Research Agendas Seen through Everyday Life'. *International Relations* 33, no. 4: 599–604.

Elshtain, Jean Bethke. 1982. 'On Beautiful Souls, Just Warriors and Feminist Consciousness'. *Women Studies International Forum* 5, nos. 3–4: 341–48.

Elson, Diane, and Ruth Pearson. 1981. 'The Subordination of Women and the Internationalization of Factory Production'. In *Of Marriage and the Market*, edited by Kate Wolkowitz, Carol Young and Roslyn McCullagh, 212–24. New York: Routledge.

English, Richard. 1985. 'Himalayan State Formation and the Impact of British Rule in the Nineteenth Century'. *Mountain Research and Development* 5: 61–78.

Enloe, Cynthia. 1982. *Ethnic Soldiers: State Security in a Divided Society*. Middlesex: Penguin.

Enloe, Cynthia. 1993. *The Morning After: Sexual Politics at the End of the Cold War*. Berkeley: University of California Press.

Enloe, Cynthia. 2000. *Maneuvers: The International Politics of Militarizing Women's Lives*. Berkeley: University of California Press.

Enloe, Cynthia. 2013. *Seriously! Investigating Crashes and Crisis as if Women Mattered*. Berkeley: University of California Press.

Enloe, Cynthia. 2014. 'Women's Labor Is Never Cheap: Gendering Global Blue Jeans and Bankers'. In *Bananas, Beaches and Bases: Making Feminist Sense of International Politics*, 2nd ed. Berkeley: University of California Press.

Fanon, Franz. 1967. *The Wretched of the Earth*. London: Penguin.

Federici, Sylvia. 2011. 'On Affective Labor'. In *Cognitive Capitalism, Education, and Digital Labor*, edited by Michael A. Peters and Ergin Bulut. New York: Peter Lang.

FSI WorldWide. n.d. 'Our History'. <http://fsi-worldwide.com/about-us/history/our-history/> (last accessed 7 May 2021).

G4S Ltd. 2021. 'G4S – Who We Are'. <https://www.g4s.com/who-we-are> (last accessed 24 May 2022).

Gandhi, Leela. 2006. *Affective Communities: Anticolonial Thought: Fin-de-Siecle Radicalism, and the Politics of Friendship*. Durham, NC: Duke University Press.

Gill, Peter, and Janakraj Sapkota. 2020. 'Nepali Afghanistan and Iraq Victims Seek Compensation, Justice'. *The Kathmandu Post*, 1 September. <https://kathmandu post.com/national/2020/09/01/nepali-afghanistan-and-iraq-victims-seek-com pensation-justice> (last accessed 24 May 2022).

González, Roberto J., Hugh Gusterson and Gustaaf Houtman, eds. 2019. *Militarization: A Reader*. Croydon: Duke University Press.

Gould, Tony. 1999. *Imperial Warriors: Britain and the Gurkhas*. London: Granta.

Gray, Harriet. 2019. 'The "War"/"Not-War" Divide: Domestic Violence in the Preventing Sexual Violence Initiative'. *British Journal of Politics and International Relations* 21, no. 1: 189–206.

Gregory, Thomas. 2019. 'Dangerous Feelings: Checkpoints and the Perception of Hostile Intent'. *Security Dialogue* 50: 131–47.

Grossman-Thompson, Barbara. 2016. 'Protection and Paternalism: Narratives of Nepali Women Migrants and the Gender Politics of Discriminatory Labour Migration Policy'. *Refuge* 32: 40–48.

Gunaratnam, Yasmin, and Carrie Hamilton. 2017. 'Introduction: The Wherewithal of Feminist Methods'. *Feminist Review* 115, no. 1: 1–12.

Gutiérrez-Rodríguez, Encarnación. 2010. *Migration, Domestic Work and Affect: A Decolonial Approach on Value and the Feminization of Labor*. New York: Routledge.

Gutiérrez-Rodríguez, Encarnación. 2014. 'The Precarity of Feminisation: On Domestic Work, Heteronormativity and the Coloniality of Power'. *International Journal of Politics, Culture and Society* 27: 191–202.

Halberstam, Judith. 2011. *The Queer Art of Failure*. Durham, NC: Duke University Press.

Haraway, Donna. 2016. *Staying with the Trouble: Making Kin in the Chthulucene*. Durham, NC: Duke University Press.

Hardman, Robert. 2010. 'As a Gurkha is Disciplined for Beheading a Taliban: Thank God They Are on Our Side!' *Daily Mail*, 10 July. <www.dailymail.co.uk/debate/article-1296136/As-Gurkhas-disciplined-beheading-Taliban-Thank-God-side.html> (last accessed 24 May 2022).

Hardt, Michael, and Antonia Negri. 2001. *Empire*. Harvard: Harvard University Press.

Hedström, Jenny. 2017. 'The Political Economy of the Kachin Revolutionary Household'. *The Pacific Review* 30: 581–95.

Hedström, Jenny, and Elisabeth Olivius. 2020. 'Insecurity, Dispossession, Depletion: Women's Experiences of Post-War Development in Myanmar'. *European Journal of Development Research* 32: 379–403.

Hemmings, Clare. 2005. 'Invoking Affect: Cultural Theory and the Ontological Turn'. *Cultural Studies* 19: 548–67.

Hemmings, Clare. 2012. 'Affective Solidarity: Feminist Reflexivity and Political Transformation'. *Feminist Theory* 13: 147–61.

Henry, Marsha. 2003. 'Where Are You Really From?: Representation, Identity and Power in Fieldwork Experiences of a South Asian Diasporic'. *Qualitative Research* 3: 229–42.

Henry, Marsha. 2012. 'Peacexploitation? Interrogating Labor Hierarchies and Global Sisterhood Amongst Indian and Uruguayan Female Peacekeepers'. *Globalizations* 9, no. 1: 15–33.

Henry, Marsha. 2015. 'Parades, Parties and Pests: Contradictions of Everyday Life in Peacekeeping Economies'. *Journal of Intervention and State Building* 9, no. 3: 372–90.

Henry, Marsha. 2017. 'Problematizing Military Masculinity, Intersectionality and Male Vulnerability in Critical Military Studies'. *Critical Military Studies* 3: 182–99.

Hickey, Sam, and Andries du Toit. 2007. *Adverse Incorporation, Social Exclusion and Chronic Poverty.* Manchester: Institute for Development Policy and Management of Environment and Development.

Higate, Paul. 2012. 'Drinking Vodka from the "Butt-Crack": Men, Masculinities and Fratriarchy in the Private Militarized Security Company'. *International Feminist Journal of Politics* 14, no. 4: 450–69.

Higate, Paul. 2015. 'Aversions to Masculine Excess in the Private Military and Security Company and Their Effects: Don't Be a "Billy Big Bollocks" and Beware the "Ninja!"' In *Gender and Private Security in Global Politics*, edited by Maya Eichler, 131–45. Oxford: Oxford University Press.

Higate, Paul, and Marsha Henry. 2009. *Insecure Spaces: Peacekeeping, Power and Performance in Haiti, Kosovo and Liberia.* London: Zed Books.

Hochschild, Arlie Russell. 1985. *The Managed Heart: Commercialization of Human Feelings.* Berkeley: University of California Press.

Holm, Timothy. 1996. *Strong Hearts, Wounded Souls: Native American Veterans of the Vietnam War.* Austin: University of Texas Press.

Horn, Denise. 2010. 'Boots and Bed Sheets: Constructing the Military Support System in a Time of War'. In *Gender, War, and Militarism: Feminist Perspectives*, edited by Laura Sjoberg and Sandra Via, 57–68. Oxford: Praeger Security International.

Hoskyns, Catherine, and Shirin Rai. 2007. 'Recasting the Global Political Economy: Counting Women's Unpaid Work'. *New Political Economy* 12: 297–317.

Howell, Alison. 2015. 'Making War Work: Resilience, Emotional Fitness, and Affective Economies in Western Militaries'. In *Emotions, Politics and War*, edited by Linda Åhäll and Gregory Thomas, 141–53. Abingdon: Routledge.

Howell, Alison. 2018. 'Forget "Militarization": Race, Disability and the "Martial Politics" of the Police and of the University'. *International Feminist Journal of Politics* 20: 117–36.

Huang, Shirlena, and Brenda S. A. Yeoh. 1998. 'Maids and Ma'ams in Singapore: Constructing Gender and Nationality in the Trans-nationalization of Paid Domestic Work'. *Geography Research Forum* 18: 21–48.

Human Rights Watch. 2016. *Our Time to Sing and Play: Child Marriage in Nepal.* New York: Human Rights Watch.

Hutchings, Kim. 2008. 'Making Sense of Masculinities and War'. *Men and Masculinities* 10, no. 4: 389–404.

Hutchison, Emma. 2017. *Affective Communities in World Politics: Collective Emotions After Trauma*. Cambridge: Cambridge University Press.

Hyde, Alex. 2013. *Inhabiting No-Man's-Land: The Military Mobilities of Army Wives*. London: London School of Economics and Political Science (LSE).

IDG Security. 'About Us'. <https://idg-security.com/about-us/> (last accessed 13 September 2021).

International Labour Organisation (ILO). 2014. *Nepal Labour Market Update*. Patan: ILO Country Office for Nepal.

Joachim, Jutta, and Andrea Schneiker. 2012. 'New Humanitarians? Frame Appropriation Through Private Military and Security Companies'. *Millennium: Journal of International Studies* 40: 365–88.

Joachim, Jutta, and Andrea Schneiker. 2015. 'The Licence to Exploit: PMSCs, Masculinities and Third Country Nationals'. In *Gender and Private Security in Global Politics*, edited by Maya Eichler, 114–28. New York: Oxford University Press.

Joras, Ulrike, and Adrian Schuster, eds. 2008. 'Private Security Companies and Local Populations: An Exploratory Study of Afghanistan and Angola'. Working Paper. Basle: Swiss Peace.

Khalidi, Omar. 2001–2. 'Ethnic Group Recruitment in the Indian Army: The Contrasting Cases of Sikhs, Muslims, Gurkhas and Others'. *Pacific Affairs* 74: 529–52.

Killingray, David, and David Omissi. 1999. *Guardians of Empire: The Armed Forces of Colonial Powers, c. 1700–1964*. Manchester: Manchester University Press.

Kinsey, Christopher. 2006. *Corporate Soldiers and International Security: The Rise of Private Military Companies*. London: Routledge.

Kirk-Greene, Anthony H. M. 1980. '"Damnosa Hereditas" Ethnic Ranking and the Martial Races Imperative in Africa'. *Ethnic and Racial Studies* 3: 393–414.

Kochhar-George, Ché Singh. 2010. 'Nepalese Gurkhas and Their Battle for Equal Rights'. *Race and Class* 52: 43–61.

Krahmann, Elke. 2008. 'Security: Collective Good or Commodity?' *European Journal of International Relations* 14: 379–404.

Krahmann, Elke. 2017. 'From Performance to Performativity: The Legitimization of US Security Contracting and its Consequence'. *Security Dialogue* 48: 541–59.

Krahmann, Elke, and Anna Leander. 2019. 'Contracting Security: Markets in the Making of MONUSCO Peacekeeping'. *International Peacekeeping* 26, no. 2: 165–89. <https://www.tandfonline.com/doi/full/10.1080/13533312.2018.1557051> (last accessed 24 May 2022).

Kunz, Rahel. 2017. 'Beyond the "Helpless Nepal Woman" versus the "Fierce Maoist Fighter": Challenging the Artificial Security/Economy Divide'. *Politics & Gender* 13: 733–9.

Kurowska, Xymena. 2020. 'Interpreting the Uninterpretable: The Ethics of Opaqueness as an Approach to Moments of Inscrutability in Fieldwork'. *International Political Sociology* 14, no. 4: 431–46.

Lakamper, Judith. 2017. 'Affective Dissonance, Neoliberal Postfeminism and the Foreclosure of Solidarity'. *Feminist Theory* 18: 119–35.

Lather, Patti. 2016. 'Top Ten+ List: (Re)Thinking Ontology in (Post)Qualitative Research'. *Cultural Studies. Critical Methodologies* 16, no. 2: 125–31.

Leander, Anna. 2005. 'The Power to Construct International Security: On the Significance of Private Military Companies'. *Millennium: Journal of International Studies* 33: 803–25.

Leander, Anna. 2012. 'What Do Codes of Conduct Do? Hybrid Constitutionalization and Militarization in Military Markets'. *Global Constitutionalism* 1, no. 1: 91–119. <https://doi.org/10.1017/S2045381711000074> (last accessed 24 May 2022).

Leander, Anna. 2013. *Commercialising Security in Europe: Political Consequences for Peace Operations.* London: Routledge.

Leander, Anna, and Rens van Munster. 2007. 'Private Security Contractors in the Debate about Darfur: Reflecting and Reinforcing Neo-liberal Governmentality'. *International Relations* 21: 201–16.

LeBaron, Genevieve. 2010. 'The Political Economy of the Household: Neoliberal Restructuring, Enclosures, and Daily Life'. *International Political Economy* 17: 889–912.

Lisle, Debbie. 2018. 'Failing Worse? Science, Security and the Birth of a Border Technology'. *European Journal of International Relations* 24, no. 4: 887–910.

Loader, Ian, and Adam White 2015. 'How can we better align private security with the public interest? Towards a civilizing model of regulation'. *Regulation and Governance* 11, no. 2: 166–84.

Low, Kelvin E. Y. 2016. 'Migrant Warriors and Transnational Lives: Constructing a Gurkha Diaspora'. *Ethnic and Racial Studies* 39: 840–57.

Lugones, Maria. 2010. 'Toward a Decolonial Feminism'. *Hypatia* 25: 742–59.

Lunn, Joe. 1999. 'Les Races guerrières: Racial Preconceptions in the French Military about West African Soldiers During the First World War'. *Journal of Contemporary History* 34: 517–36.

Lutz, Catherine. 2019. 'The Emotional Life of Militarism'. In *Militarization: A Reader*, edited by Roberto J. González, Hugh Gusterson and Gustaaf Houtman, 109–10. Croydon: Duke University Press.

Luxton, Meg. 2018. 'The Production of Life Itself: Gender, Social Reproduction and IPE'. In *Handbook of International Political Economy of Gender*, edited by Juanita Elias and Adrienne Roberts, 37–49. Cheltenham: Edward Elgar.

Lyon-Callo, Vincent, and Susan Brin Hyatt. 2003. 'The Neoliberal State and the Depoliticization of Poverty: Activist Anthropology and "Ethnography from Below"'. *Urban Anthropology and Studies of Cultural Systems and World Economic Development* 32: 175–204.

Lyytikainen, Minna, Punam Yadav and Annick Wibben. 2020. 'Unruly Wives in the Household: Toward Feminist Genealogies for Peace Research'. *Cooperation and Conflict* 56: 3–25.

McDowell, Linda. 2009. *Working Bodies: Interactive Service Employment and Workplace Identities.* Chichester: Wiley-Blackwell.

Mackenzie, Megan. 2015. *Beyond the Band of Brothers: The US Military and the Myth that Women Can't Fight*. Cambridge: Cambridge University Press.

MacLeish, Kenneth T. 2013. *Making War at Fort Hood: Life and Uncertainty in a Military Community*. Princeton: Princeton University Press.

Macleod, Sorcha, and Rebecca Dewinter-Schmitt. 2019. 'Certifying Private Security Companies: Effectively Ensuring the Corporate Responsibility to Respect Human Rights?' *Business and Human Rights Journal* 4, no. 1: 55–77.

Magalit-Rodriguez, Robyn. 2010. *Migrants for Export: How the Philippine State Brokers Labor to the World*. Minnesota: Minnesota University Press.

Mahmood, Saba. 2011. *Politics of Piety: The Islamic Revival and the Feminist Subject*. Princeton: Princeton University Press.

Marjomaa, Risto. 2003. 'The Martial Spirit: Yao Soldiers in British Services in Nyasaland (Malawi), 1895–1939'. *The Journal of African History* 44: 413–32.

Metcalf, Thomas R. 2007. *Imperial Connections: India in the Indian Ocean Arena, 1860–1920*. Berkeley: University of California Press.

Mies, Maria. 1986. *Patriarchy and Accumulation on a World Scale: Women in the International Divisions of Labour*. London: Zed.

Miles, Robert. 1982. *Racism and Migrant Labour*. London: George Allen and Unwin.

Montgomerie, Johnna, and Daniela Tepe-Belfrage. 2017. 'Caring for Debts: How the Household Economy Exposes the Limits of Financialisation'. *Critical Sociology* 43: 653–68.

Mynster Christensen, Maya. 2015. 'The Underbelly of Global Security: Sierra Leonean Ex-Militias in Iraq'. *African Affairs* 115: 23–43.

Myrttinen, Henri. 2020. 'Death Becomes Him: The Hypervisibility of Martyrdom and Invisibility of the Wounded in the Iconography of Lebanese Militarised Masculinities'. In *Making War on Bodies: Militarism, Aesthetics and Embodiment in International Politics*, edited by Catherine Baker, 121–47. Edinburgh: Edinburgh University Press.

Nepal, Ratna Mani. 2020. 'The Gurkha Recruitment, Remittances and Development'. *International Journal of English Literature and Social Science* 5: 1526–36.

Nepali Times. 2020. 'Canada Settlement with Families of Nepali Guards'. 4 October. <https://www.nepalitimes.com/latest/canada-settlement-with-families-of-nepali-guards/> (last accessed 24 May 2022).

Nevins, Joseph, and Nancy Lee Peluso, eds. 2008. *Taking Southeast Asia to Market: Commodities, Nature and People in the Neoliberal Age*. Ithaca, NY: Cornell University Press.

Nightingale, Andrea. 2011. 'Bounding Difference: Intersectionality and the Material Production of Gender, Caste, Class and Environment in Nepal'. *Geoforum* 42, no. 2: 153–62.

Oksala, Johanna. 2016. 'Affective Labour and Feminist Politics'. *Signs: Journal of Women in Culture and Society* 41, no. 2: 281–303.

Page, Tiffany. 2017. 'Vulnerable Writing as a Feminist Methodological Practice'. *Feminist Review* 115: 13–29.

Parashar, Swati. 2013. 'Armed Resistance, Economic (In)Security and the Household: A Case Study of the Maoist Insurgency in India'. In *The Global Political Economy of the Household in Asia*, edited by Juanita Elias and Samanthi J. Gunawardana, 43–58. London: Palgrave Macmillan.

Pariyar, Mitra, Bal Gopal Shrestha and David N. Gellner. 2014. 'Rights and a Sense of Belonging: Two Contrasting Nepali Diaspora Communities'. In *Facing Globalization in the Himalayas: Belonging and the Politics of the Self*, edited by Gerard Toffin and Joanna Pfaff-Czarnecka, 133–60. New Delhi: Sage Publishing India.

Parker, John. 1999. *The Gurkhas: The Insider Story of the World's Most Feared Soldiers*. London: Headline.

Parsons, Timothy. 1999. 'Wakamba Warriors Are Soldiers of the Queen: The Evolution of the Kamba as a Martial Race, 1890–1970'. *Ethnohistory* 46: 671–701.

Pedwell, Carolyn. 2012. 'Affective (Self-)Transformations: Empathy, Neoliberalism and International Development'. *Feminist Theory* 13: 163–79.

Pedwell, Carolyn, and Anne Whitehead. 2012. 'Affecting Feminism: Questions of Feeling in Feminist Theory'. *Feminist Theory* 13: 115–29.

Peers, Douglas M. 1991. 'The Habitual Nobility of Being: British Officers and the Social Construction of the Bengal Army in the Early Nineteenth Century'. *Modern Asian Studies* 25: 545–69.

Penttinen, Elina. 2013. *Joy and International Relations: A New Methodology*. London: Routledge.

Peterson, V. Spike. 2004. 'Feminist Theories Within, Invisible to, and Beyond IR'. *The Brown Journal of World Affairs* 10: 35–46.

Peterson, V. Spike. 2005. 'How (the Meaning of) Gender Matters in Political Economy'. *New Political Economy* 10: 499–521.

Peterson, V. Spike. 2008. '"New Wars" and Gendered Economies'. *Feminist Review* 88: 7–20.

Peterson, V. Spike. 2010. 'Gender Identities, Ideologies and Practices in the Context of War and Militarism'. In *Gender, War and Militarism: Feminist Perspectives*, edited by Laura Sjoberg and Sandra Via, 17–29. Santa Barbara: Praeger.

Peterson, V. Spike. 2014. 'Family Matters: How Queering the Intimate Queers the International'. *International Studies Review* 16, no. 4: 604–8.

Phillips, Nicola. 2011. 'Informality, Global Production Networks and the Dynamics of "Adverse Incorporation"'. *Global Networks* 11: 380–97.

Phoenix, Ann. 1994. 'Practicing Feminist Research: The Intersections of Gender and "Race" in the Research Process'. In *Researching Women's Lives from a Feminist Perspective*, edited by Mary Maynard and June Purvis, 49–71. London: Taylor and Francis.

Pin-Fat, Véronique. 2019. '"What's Love Got to Do With It?" Ethics, Emotions, and Encounter in International Relations'. *Review of International Studies* 45: 181–200.

Rai, Shirin, Catherine Hoskyns and Dania Thomas. 2013. 'Depletion: The Cost of Social Reproduction'. *International Feminist Journal of Politics* 16: 86–105.

Rand, Gavin, and Kim A. Wagner. 2012. 'Recruiting the "Martial Races": Identities and Military Service in Colonial India'. *Patterns of Prejudice* 46: 232–54.

Rashid, Maria. 2020. *Dying to Serve: Militarism, Affect, and the Politics of Sacrifice in the Pakistan Army*. Stanford: Stanford University Press.

Rashid, Maria. 2021. 'Precarious attachments: soldiers and erasures of the feminine in the Pakistan military'. *International Feminist Journal of Politics*, available at: <https://www.tandfonline.com/doi/full/10.1080/14616742.2021.1995460> (last accessed 27 May 2022).

Razack, Sherene. 2004. *Dark Threats, White Knights: The Somalia Affair, Peacekeeping, and the New Imperialism*. Toronto: University of Toronto Press.

Razack, Sherene. 2007. 'Stealing the Pain of Others: Reflections on Canadian Humanitarian Responses'. *Review of Education, Pedagogy and Cultural Studies* 29: 375–94.

Regmi, Mahesh C. 1976. *Land Ownership in Nepal*. Berkeley: University of California Press.

Ritcher-Montpetit, Melanie. 2014. 'Beyond the Erotics of Orientalism: Lawfare, Torture and the Racial-Sexual Grammars of Legitimate Suffering'. *Security Dialogue* 45, no. 1: 43–62.

Ritcher-Montpetit, Melanie. 2017. 'Everything You Always Wanted to Know about Sex (in IR) But Were Afraid to Ask: The Queer Turn in International Relations'. *Millennium Journal of International Studies* 46, no. 2: 220–40.

Robinson, Nick. 2016. 'Militarism and Opposition in the Livingroom: The Case of Military Videogames'. *Critical Studies on Security* 4: 255–75.

Rossdale, Chris. 2021. *Resisting Militarism: Direct Action and the Politics of Subversion*. Edinburgh: Edinburgh University Press.

Roy, Kaushik. 2001. 'The Construction of Regiments in the Indian Army: 1859–1913'. *War in History* 8: 127–48.

Ruwanpura, Kanchana N. 2007. 'Shifting Theories: Partial Perspectives on the Household'. *Cambridge Journal of Economics* 31: 525–38.

Ryan, Louise. 2015. '"Inside" and "Outside" of What or Where? Researching Migration Through Multi-Positionalities'. *Forum: Qualitative Social Research* 16, no. 2. <https://doi.org/10.17169/fqs-16.2.2333> (last accessed 24 May 2022).

Sa'ar, Amalia. 2005. 'Postcolonial Feminism, The Politics of Identification, and the Liberal Bargain'. *Gender and Society* 19, no. 5: 680–700.

Safa, Helen. 1981. 'Runaway Shops and Female Employment: The Search for Cheap Labor'. *Signs: Journal of Women in Culture and Society* 7, no. 2: 418–33.

Safri, Maliha, and Julie Graham. 2010. 'The Global Household: Towards a Feminist Postcapital International Political Economy'. *Signs: Journal of Women in Culture and Society* 36: 99–125.

Salazar Parreñas, Rhacel. 2008. *The Force of Domesticity: Filipina Migrants and Globalization*. New York: New York University Press.

Scahill, Jeremy. 2007. *Blackwater: The Rise of the World's Most Powerful Mercenary Army*. London: Serpent's Tail.

Schultz, Susanne. 2006. 'Dissolved Boundaries and "Affective Labour": On the Disappearance of Reproductive Labour and Feminist Critique in Empire'. *Capitalism Nature Socialism* 17, no. 1: 77–82.

Seddon, David. 2005. 'Nepal's Dependency on Exporting Labour'. *Migration Information Source*. Washington, D.C.: Migration Policy Institute.

Sharma, Gopal. 2016. 'Nepali Migrants Banned from Working in Afghanistan, Iraq, Libya and Syria'. *Reuters*, 24 June. <https://www.reuters.com/article/us-nepal-migrants-ban-idUSKCN0ZA2UG> (last accessed 24 May 2022).

Sharma, Sanjay. 2020. 'The Migration of the Gurkhas with Sanjay Sharma'. *The Gladden Podcast*. Podcast hosted by D. Garmonduy Whorway. Kathmandu, Nepal.

Shrestha, Maheshwar. 2017. 'Push and Pull: A Study of International Migration from Nepal'. Policy Research Working Paper Series. World Bank Group, 1–38.

Sijapati, Bandita, Amrita Limbu and Manisha Khadka. 2011. *Trafficking and Forced Labour in Nepal: A Review of the Literature*. Kathmandu: Himal Books.

Singer, Peter W. 2003. *Corporate Warriors. The Rise of Privatized Military Industry*. Ithaca, NY: Cornell University Press.

Singh, Gajendra. 2015. *The Testimonies of Indian Soldiers and the Two World Wars: Between Self and Sepoy*. London: Bloomsbury.

Sinha, Mrinalini. 1995. *Colonial Masculinity: The 'Manly Englishman' and the 'Effeminate Bengali' in the Late Nineteenth Century*. Manchester: Manchester University Press.

Skeggs, Beverley. 2004. *Class, Self, Culture*. London: Routledge.

Spanner, Leigh. 2020. '"The Strength Behind the Uniform": Acknowledging the Contributions of Military Families or Co-Opting Women's Labour?' *Atlantis: Critical Studies in Gender, Culture and Social Justice* 41: 57–71.

Sramek, Joseph. 2011. *Gender, Morality and Race in Company India, 1765–1858*. New York: Palgrave Macmillan.

Stachowitsch, Saskia. 2015. 'The Reconstruction of Masculinities in Global Politics: Gendering Strategies in the Field of Private Security'. *Men and Masculinities Studies* 18: 363–86.

Standing, Guy. 1989. 'Global Feminization through Flexible Labor'. *World Development* 17, no. 7: 1077–95.

Standing, Guy. 1999. 'Global Feminization through Flexible Labor: A Theme Revisited'. *World Development* 27, no. 3: 583–602.

Stasiulis, Daiva, and Abigail B. Bakan. 1997. 'Negotiating Citizenship: The Case of Foreign Domestic Workers in Canada'. *Feminist Review* 57: 112–39.

Stewart, Kathleen. 2007. *Ordinary Affects*. Durham, NC: Duke University Press.

Streets, Heather. 2004. *Martial Races: The Military, Race and Masculinity in British Imperial Culture, 1857–1914*. Manchester: Manchester University Press.

Sylvester, Christine. 2012. *War as Experience: Contributions from International Relations and Feminist Analysis*. Abingdon: Routledge.

Tamang, Seira. 2009. 'The Politics of Conflict and Difference or the Difference of Conflict in Politics: The Women's Movement in Nepal'. *Feminist Review* 91: 61–80.

Tamang, Seira. 2011. 'Exclusionary Processes and Constitution Building in Nepal'. *International Journal on Minority and Group Rights* 18: 293–308.

Tavernise, Sabrina. 2004. '12 Hostages from Nepal Are Executed in Iraq, a Militant Group Claims'. *New York Times*, 1 September. <https://www.nytimes.

com/2004/09/01/world/middleeast/12-hostages-from-nepal-are-executed-in-iraq-a-militant.html> (last accessed 24 May 2022).

Teaiwa, Teresia K. 2005. 'Articulated Cultures: Militarism and Masculinities in Fiji During the Mid 1990s'. *Fijian Studies: A Journal of Contemporary Fiji* 3: 201–22.

Teaiwa, Teresia K. 2011. 'Bleeding Boundaries: Gendered Analysis of Militarism in the Western Pacific'. *Asian Pacific Viewpoint* 52: 1–4.

Thieme, Susan, and Simone Wyss. 2005. 'Migration Patterns and Remittance Transfer in Nepal: A Case Study of Sainik Basti in Western Nepal'. *International Migration* 43: 59–98.

Tidy, Joanna. 2019. 'War Craft: The Embodied Politics of Making War'. *Security Dialogue* 50: 220–38.

Tilley, Lisa, and Robbie Shilliam. 2018. 'Raced Markets: An Introduction'. *New Political Economy* 23: 534–43.

True, Jacqui. 2020. 'Introduction to Special Section of *Social Politics*: Postconflict Care Economies'. *Social Politics* 26: 535–37.

Tuhiwai Smith, Linda. 1999. *Decolonizing Methodologies: Research and Indigenous Peoples*. London: Zed.

Tuker, Francis. 1957. *Gorkha: The Story of the Gurkhas of Nepal*. London: Constable.

UN Human Rights (OHCHR). 2018. *Report on the Gendered Human Rights Impacts of Private Military and Security Companies*. Working Group on the Use of Mercenaries. 29 July. <https://www.ohchr.org/EN/Issues/Mercenaries/WGMercenaries/Pages/GenderPrivateMilitarySecurityCompanies.aspx> (last accessed 24 May 2022).

UNICEF. 2017. *Ending Child Marriage in Nepal*. Kathmandu: UNICEF Regional Office of Southeast Asia.

Väyrynen, Tarja. 2019. 'Mundane Peace and the Politics of Vulnerability: A Nonsolid Feminist Research Agenda'. *Peacebuilding* 7: 146–59.

Väyrynen, Tarja, and Eeva Puumala. 2015. 'Bodies of War, the Past Continuous, and (Ar)rhythmic Experiences'. *Alternatives: Global, Local, Political* 40: 237–50.

Ware, Vron. 2010. 'Whiteness in the Glare of War. Soldiers, Migrants and Citizenship'. *Ethnicities* 10: 313–30.

Ware, Vron. 2012. *Military Migrants. Fighting for YOUR Country*. New York: Palgrave Macmillan.

Waring, Marilyn. 1989. *If Women Counted: A New Feminist Economics*. London: Macmillan.

Weeks, Kathi. 2011. *The Problem with Work: Feminism, Marxism, Antiwork Politics, and Postwork Imaginaries*. Durham, NC: Duke University Press.

Wegner, Nicole. 2021. 'Rituals, Rhythms, and the Discomforting Endurance of Militarism: Affective Methodologies and Ethico-Political Challenges'. *Global Studies Quarterly* 1, no. 3. <https://doi.org/10.1093/isagsq/ksab008> (last accessed 24 May 2022).

Welland, Julia. 2017. 'Violence and the Contemporary Soldiering Body'. *Security Dialogue* 48, no. 6: 524–40.

Welland, Julia. 2018. 'Joy and War: Reading Pleasure in Wartime Experience'. *Review of International Studies* 44: 438–55.

Welland, Julia. 2021. 'Feeling and Militarism at Ms Veteran America'. *International Journal of Feminist Politics* 23, no. 1: 58–79. <https://www.tandfonline.com/doi/abs/10.1080/14616742.2020.1858719> https://doi.org/10.1093/isagsq/ksab008.

Wetherell, Margaret. 2015. 'Trends in the Turn to Affect: A Social Psychological Critique'. *Body and Society* 21: 139–66.

Whelpton, John. 2005. *A History of Nepal*. Cambridge: Cambridge University Press.

Whitney, Shiloh. 2017. 'Byproductive Labour: A Feminist Theory of Affective Labour Beyond the Productive-Reproductive Distinction'. *Philosophy and Social Criticism* 44: 637–60.

Wibben, Annick. 2018. 'Why We Need to Study (US) Militarism: A Critical Feminist Lens'. *Security Dialogue* 49: 136–48.

Wilson, H. F. 2017. 'On Geographies and Encounter: Bodies, Borders and Difference'. *Progress in Human Geography* 41, no. 4: 451–71.

Wolkowitz, Carol. 2006. *Bodies at Work*. London: Sage.

Wool, Zoe H. 2015. *After War: The Weight of Life After Walter Reed*. Durham, NC: Duke University Press.

INDEX

Abrahamsen, Rita, 3, 22
absorption of negative affect, 150,
  164–70
Acharya, Meena, 8, 121, 124
affect
  affect circulation, 30–2, 38, 44–5,
    140–1, 149, 150, 166
  affective and intellectual investments,
    9
  affective attachments, 30–2, 38
  affective economies, 39–44
  affective economies and global
    security, 39–44
  affective waste, 44–8, 164–70
  collective affect, 29, 35
  commoditisation of affect, 39–44,
    145–72, 191
  and danger, 73
  and emotions, 28, 83
  future-orientated affect, 178
  and global security, 26–53
  happiness, 110, 118, 139, 140–2,
    173, 178, 180, 182, 189, 191, 192
  love, 81–114, 189
  pain, 83, 90, 109–10, 118, 127–30,
    135, 180–2
  politics of, 83–7
  as practice, 140
  racialisation of, 148–50
affective labour
  in global security households,
    115–44
  Gurkha wives', 130, 134–5, 189
  Gurkhas in private security, 145–72,
    189–90

militarism, 29, 39–44
  see also emotional labour
Afghanistan
  bans on migration to, 130
  estimated numbers of Gurkhas in, 68
  lack of Nepalese embassy, 70
  security work in, 6, 26, 68, 69–70,
    72, 74, 87, 104–11, 148–70
  as site of fieldwork, 10–12, 14, 82,
    106
Agathangelou, Anna, 5, 23n, 149, 152,
  158, 160, 163
agency, 21, 102, 167, 171, 182–7, 190,
  191
agents, 76–7
Åhäll, Linda, 27, 28, 29, 30, 31, 37, 83
Ahmed, Sara, 19, 20, 28, 30, 31, 32,
  35, 37, 52n, 55, 90, 103, 118, 140,
  141, 163, 176, 178
airline attendants, 42, 45, 149
alcoholism, 120, 130
allowances, 120
ancestral links, 72; *see also*
  intergenerational attachments
Anderson, Clare, 30, 42
anger, who gets to show, 165–6, 167,
  170
Anglo-Nepalese War, 58–65
Anievas, Alexander, 86, 147
anthropology, 57, 61, 95
anti-racism scholarship, 16
appropriation of women's labour by
  militaries, 137–8
archetypical contractors, 5
arranged marriage, 119, 121–2, 181

EU representative:
Easy Access System Europe
Mustamäe tee 50, 10621 Tallinn, Estonia
Gpsr.requests@easproject.com

www.ingramcontent.com/pod-product-compliance
Lightning Source LLC
Chambersburg PA
CBHW070322270326
41926CB00017B/3727